Religion in the
Contemporary World

THE UN
T

For Meryl Aldridge

Religion in the Contemporary World

A Sociological Introduction

Second Edition

ALAN ALDRIDGE

polity

Contents

Preface to the Second Edition

The first edition of this book, written at the close of the twentieth century, began by justifying religion as an object worthy of serious sociological study. A few years later, no such justification is required. The idea that religion has lost social significance – the secularization thesis – is itself losing credibility. Far from being a matter of indifference, religion is emphatically on the agenda of public debate. Sadly, instead of being informed by knowledge and understanding, discussions of religion are all too often fuelled by ignorance and powered by fear.

If those who are ideologically opposed to religion cannot have a world free from it, they often argue that, as a second-best solution, religion should be confined to the private sphere as a matter of individual choice with no impact on anyone else – a kind of harmless hobby. None of the world's great religions could possibly accept being relegated to the status of a private consumer choice. The secularist objective of privatizing religion is achievable only in authoritarian societies, and even there, as the example of the former Communist regimes demonstrates, when the repression is lifted, religion typically surfaces as a significant power in the new social order.

Instead of repressing religion, most societies seek an accommodation with it. This typically entails granting special status to some favoured religious institutions while denying it to others – a distinction that is seldom easy to justify. It also throws up conflicts over human rights. At the time of writing, a controversy is building in the UK over proposed legislation to ban discrimination against lesbians and gay men in the provision of goods and services. Under such legislation, adoption agencies would no longer be able lawfully to refuse to place a child with a gay couple. The head of the Roman Catholic Church in England and Wales has said that Catholic adoption agencies would have to close, rather than implement a policy they regard as contrary to their faith. Should Catholic agencies be exempted from the legislation, or should it apply to all? Everyone agrees that the child's interests should be paramount, but that does not answer the question. And what of the perhaps inconvenient fact that Catholic agencies have had unrivalled success in finding homes for children who, because of disabilities, are difficult to place?

Modern societies are saturated with mass communications. To make informed decisions as citizens, we need to be media-literate. This does not mean that we have to be told what to think; rather, what we need are the conceptual tools to help us understand the conditions under which media communications are produced, transmitted and received. In the same way, we benefit by being literate in the field of religion.

Hotly debated issues are confronted throughout this book, whether in the guise of brainwashing in religious cults, or the rise of fundamentalism, or Islamophobia, or a supposed clash of civilizations, or a crisis of multiculturalism. If debates about religion are to rise above the level of phobias, stereotyping, scaremongering and mutual recriminations, we need evidence grounded in the social realities of religious cultures, religious movements, and the lives of the people involved in them. The aim of this book is to present such evidence to the reader.

Alan Aldridge
January 2007

Acknowledgements

I am delighted to have the opportunity to renew my gratitude to three eminent sociologists: Eileen Barker, Jim Beckford and the late Bryan Wilson. Bryan Wilson first excited my interest in the sociological study of religion; more recently, my colleague Christian Karner rekindled that enthusiasm at a very propitious time for me.

I should like to thank three anonymous referees for their generous and stimulating comments on the first edition of this book and on my first draft of this edition. I am also grateful to the staff at Polity, particularly my editor, Emma Longstaff, for her encouragement and sheer professionalism.

I repeat my gratitude to Ernest, Elsie and Marjorie Aldridge. Finally, and most importantly, I dedicate my book to Meryl Aldridge.

1

Religions and the Challenge of Diversity

The religious factor

Every society grants special status to religion.

The First Amendment to the American Constitution stipulates that 'Congress shall make no law respecting an establishment of religion, or prohibiting the free exercise thereof; or abridging the freedom of speech, or of the press; or the right of the people peaceably to assemble, and to petition the Government for a redress of grievances.' This placing of religion in the context of rights and freedoms shows that the Constitution's emphasis is on protecting religious beliefs and practices from interference by the state.

France, too, has a separation of church and state. Article 2 of the law of 9 December 1905 states that 'The Republic neither recognizes, nor funds, nor subsidizes any religion'. In contrast to the American case, the aim is not to protect religious beliefs and practices from state interference but to free the state from entanglement with religion. The immediate reaction from the Vatican to the 1905 law was Pope Pius X's encyclical *Vehementer Nos*, which roundly condemned 'the enemies of religion' who 'have succeeded at last in effecting by violence what they have long desired, in defiance of your rights as a Catholic nation and of the wishes of all who think rightly'. The law was a diplomatic affront to the Vatican, which had attempted to cultivate French political leaders in the hope that 'gratitude would have stayed those politicians in their downward path'. At stake was a fundamental principle:

That the State must be separated from the Church is a thesis absolutely false, a most pernicious error. Based, as it is, on the principle that the State must not recognize any religious cult, it is in the first place guilty of a great injustice to God; for the Creator of man is also the Founder of human societies, and preserves their existence as He preserves our own. We owe Him, therefore, not only a private cult, but a public and social worship to honour Him.

Superficially, maintaining what Thomas Jefferson famously called 'a wall of separation' between church and state, and what in France is known as the principle of *laïcité* (roughly translated as 'secularity'), might appear to be a straightforward matter. Survey evidence from the USA and France shows widespread public support for the principle of separation, which is deeply embedded in the political culture of those countries. Even so, the actual practice of church–state separation is contested, and the education system is a crucial arena in which such battles are fought – unsurprisingly, given the role of schools in the trans- mission of cultural values. Exclusive Brethren refuse to study computer science. Jehovah's Witnesses reject theories of evolution, and do not want them taught to their children. Many conservative Christian groups demand that creation science or intelligent design be taught as a genuinely scientific alternative to Darwinian evolution. Legislation developed in the West over the course of centuries, and designed to deal with the rights of mainstream Protestants, Catholics and Jews, now faces unenvisaged challenges.

In October 1989, three young Muslims were expelled from a state sec- ondary school at Creil in northern France for wearing *hijab* (the head- scarf or *foulard*). The *affaire des foulards* escalated to become the subject of an intense national debate, with charges of racist discrimi- nation countered by accusations of fundamentalist obscurantism (Kepel 1997: 184–9; Boyle and Sheen 1997: 298–300). Ironically, this took place in the year in which the nation was celebrating the bicenten- nial of the French Revolution.

In the wake of the headscarf affair, the Council of State, France's supreme court, ruled that schools could forbid the wearing of religious symbols only in order to prevent 'acts of pressure, provocation, prose- lytism, or propaganda'. Many people were not happy with this decision, which was seen on the one hand to give too much scope for arbitrary decisions by school authorities, and on the other hand to make it virtu- ally impossible for them to enforce a ban on religious symbols.

The furore that erupted in France was deeply revealing of the dilem- mas of church and state in multicultural societies. Islam was portrayed as the oriental Other: irrational, fundamentalist and fanatical, in contrast to Western rationality, individualism and civilized tolerance. Wearing *hijab* was taken to be a defiant act of Muslim fundamentalism, threatening to undermine the long-standing policy of cultural assimilation of ethnic minority groups from France's former colonies (Boyle and Sheen 1997: 296–7). French secular opinion, divided on the question of whether wearing *hijab* should be permitted or not, was united in defence of the values of the French education system. In French political culture the school is seen, idealistically, as an 'emancipatory space'. The leader of the anti-racist pressure group SOS-Racisme, Harlem Désir, was quoted as saying: 'Whether they wear a veil or not, these children will best learn how to resist obscurantism in the school of Rousseau, Voltaire and the Enlightenment' (Kepel 1997: 184).

The conflict was rekindled in 2004 when the National Assembly voted, by the crushing majority of 494 votes to 36, in favour of a law to prohibit the wearing in school of 'signs or dress by which students ostensibly express a religious belonging'. Symbols of religious allegiance are now to be removed at the school gates, so that all students may benefit equally from the intellectual enlightenment that the French educational system provides. Christian pupils cannot display crosses or crucifixes, Sikh boys cannot wear turbans, Jewish boys cannot wear yarmulkes, and Muslim girls cannot wear *hijab*.

After the law of 2004 was passed, opinion in France was even more bitterly divided than before (Thomas 2006). Although the law might have been interpreted as a disguised attack specifically on Islam, it was also opposed by leading figures in the Roman Catholic, Protestant and Orthodox Churches. Nor did it satisfy the National Front, whose leader, Jean-Marie Le Pen, argued that preoccupation with headscarves was a trivial diversion from the 'real problem' of massive immigration from North Africa. Who, then, supported the new law, and why?

To answer that question, as Thomas argues (2006: 246–9), we need to consider how non-Muslims interpret the symbolism of *hijab*. In many societies it is viewed favourably, as a voluntary statement by a young woman of her identity as a Muslim and her commitment to Islam as a faith guiding the whole of her life. It can be read as a refusal of enslavement to fashion, a rejection of degenerate consumer culture, and abhorrence of sexual display to envious women and lustful men. In France, however, such readings are rare. *Hijab* is seen as a symbol of women's subordination to patriarchy. Muslim girls have long been thought to be pressured into wearing *hijab* by parents and other close family members. Worse still, they are now feared to be the victims of radical clerics, community activists and gang leaders who promote fundamentalist Islam in opposition to the values of free Western democracies.

Such community pressures undoubtedly exist, particularly in the deprived suburbs of Paris and other cities with a concentration of migrants from North Africa.

The French Republic utterly rejects *communautarisme* – that is to say, a multiculturalist approach that legitimizes the formation of separate communities along regional, linguistic, ethnic or religious lines. Instead of granting special rights and privileges to cultural communities, the French state pursues a policy of assimilation and integration, using the education system as the instrument for transmitting shared cultural values to all citizens of the Republic. Unlike Britain, which confers different levels of citizenship depending on national origin, France grants either full citizenship or none at all. All citizens are formally equal under the law, but this does not guarantee social acceptance or equality of opportunity. Religion is a critical source of social division in France; as Willaime says (2004: 379), 'the tolerance of non-conformity weakens as soon as the religious dimension is present'.

From an Anglo-Saxon perspective, it may be tempting to see France's recent legislation as a reaction to the carnage of September 11 2001 and the threat of global terrorism. The evidence suggests otherwise (Thomas 2006: 249–51). If we are seeking an event that catalysed the change of policy in France, a stronger candidate would be the series of bombings in Paris in 1995 carried out by supporters of FIS (the Islamic Salvation Front), an Algerian Islamist movement. The response was a police crackdown aimed at Islamic extremists. It is this conflict, rather than the US-led 'war on terror', that set the context for France's renewed *affaire des foulards*.

In the United States, interpretations of the 'no establishment' and 'free exercise' clauses of the First Amendment have been deeply contested. The complexity of these debates shows that there is not a simple divide between religious activists who aim to destroy the wall of separation and committed secularists who want to keep the wall as high as possible. During the twentieth century, particularly from the 1940s onwards, the Supreme Court became increasingly active in enforcing First Amendment rights, striking down numerous state laws as unconstitutional. Underlying the complex legal debates are a number of crucial questions that reflect the challenge of social and cultural diversity.

Is the underlying reality that the United States is a Christian, or perhaps Judaeo-Christian, nation? When the law speaks of 'religion', is it giving, and should it give, pride of place to mainstream Christianity and also, arguably, Judaism? Should public institutions be permitted to display the Ten Commandments? If so, where does all this leave the other great Abrahamic religion, Islam? And what of the world's other major faiths such as Buddhism and Hinduism? What of the Mormon Church, which sees itself as the Christian Church restored to the fullness of faith? What, finally, of the host of minority religious movements, some of them imported, but the majority home-grown?

Even if the nation is thought not to give priority to any one religion, is there an assumption that religion in general takes precedence over unbelief? Is this what is implied by the motto 'In God We Trust' inscribed on the currency, or by the reference to 'one Nation under God' in the Pledge of Allegiance, or by the fact that Presidential addresses to the nation invariably end: 'God bless America'? Are these religious statements that breach the wall of separation between church and state, or are they, as the majority of Americans appear to believe, more a matter of political culture and tradition?

What counts as religion? Is desecrating the American flag a religious act, an irreligious act, or a legitimate form of political protest? Is reciting the Pledge of Allegiance a religious rite? Is intelligent design a scientific theory that should be taught in schools, or a matter of religious faith that should be kept out of them? Should school prayers be permitted, particularly if they are demanded and led by students? As in France, many of the contentious issues in church–state relations involve the place of religious beliefs and symbols in public (state) schools. This shows that although the First Amendment's 'free exercise' clause is designed to shield religion from state interference, the 'no establishment' clause carries some implication that, as in France, the state and its citizens need protection from religious coercion.

Whatever their philosophy of church–state relations, most modern societies operate on a 'rule-and-exemption' approach (Barry 2001: 32–62). Laws are passed that are binding on all citizens, except that certain specified categories of people are granted exemptions, mainly on the grounds of religion. Consider three such examples.

First, most societies have legislation on animal welfare that requires slaughter to be carried out humanely so that the animal suffers as little as possible. Humane slaughter implies that the animal will be stunned to render it unconscious before its throat is cut and it bleeds to death. Many societies grant an exemption from this provision to permit 'religious' slaughter by the Muslim *Dhabh* or Jewish *Shechita* methods, in which, traditionally, the animal is slaughtered without prior stunning.

Second, many societies have granted exemptions to Sikh men, permitting them to wear a turban instead of a safety helmet. In the UK, a law passed in 1976 exempted 'turban-wearing followers of the Sikh religion' from the requirement to wear a crash helmet when riding a motorcycle. Sikh men are the only people in the UK granted such an exemption.

Third, Amish communities in the USA and Canada benefit from various exemptions. A landmark United States Supreme Court decision of 1972 exempted the Amish from compulsory attendance at school beyond the eighth grade (after they are fourteen years old).

These cases, and others like them, are controversial. Why should any social group be exempt from the law? Barry (2001) maintains that it is almost invariably better either to impose a law on everyone or, alternatively, to abolish it. Abolishing unnecessary laws increases our freedom. If a law is necessary, members of a religious community still have choices. Jews and Muslims who object to a society's laws on humane slaughter have the choice of becoming vegetarians. As for Sikhs, nobody forces them to ride motorcycles; they could choose another means of transport.

Although it may be denied officially, the rule-and-exemption approach implies tacit assessments of the social value of different religious traditions; the state is never neutral. Judaism and Islam are recognized as two of the world's great salvation religions; their practices command widespread respect, and are therefore more likely to enjoy exemptions. The Amish fled Europe to escape persecution; this fact of history, and their peaceful presence in the USA and Canada for more than 200 years, is a powerful symbolic defence against apparent persecution in the New World. As for Sikhs, they have a strong military tradition; Sikh regiments fought with distinction in the British Army in two World Wars. Their war service was repeatedly cited as a reason for granting them an exemption from legal requirements on safety helmets. Military leaders argued that the British people owed a debt of honour to a faith community whose forebears went into battle wearing turbans. This may not have been a valid argument under British law, but it carried considerable weight as a social fact that helped the Sikhs to gain their exemption.

In all such debates the facts are disputed. Does religious slaughter inflict unnecessary suffering on an animal? Is high school education superior to education provided in Amish communities? And does a Sikh's turban offer effective protection? As well as factual arguments, there is the persistent question: are these practices required by the religion, or are they merely a matter of custom? A growing number of Muslims, and a far smaller number of Jews, accept that pre-stunning of animals does not render the meat ritually unclean. Some say that wearing a turban may be a long-standing custom among Sikhs, but is not formally required by the Sikh faith. And, if they were required to do so, presumably Amish would send their children to school without compromising their standing in the eyes of God? Is their wish not to do so really a matter of religion?

Such arguments presuppose a sharp distinction between religion and culture. If such a distinction is accepted, the conclusion is then drawn that only practices that are required on religious grounds are candidates for exemption. How, then, can a society distinguish between religion and culture? Can a predominantly Christian legislature correctly interpret the Hadith (the sayings of the Prophet) or the Qur'an? Could a secularist body adjudicate on Jewish ritual or the teachings of Jesus Christ? Renouncing such cultural imperialism, contemporary societies typically try to identify community leaders who will provide accurate information about the requirements of the faith community they claim to represent. This gives them an incentive to emphasize the religious elements of those communities. Because it is the path to recognition and respect, religion has become ever more important in the politics of community representation.

Secularists focus on the question: why should *religion* be exempt? Religion, they argue, should be treated as a matter for the individual, a personal preference confined to the voluntary sector and the private sphere. To grant religion a special status under the law is, they say, to pander to irrationality and bigotry. It gives too much power to community activists, who claim to speak for the whole of a community and who misleadingly define that community in terms of its religion. Many things that communities might like to do are rightly forbidden, even when a religious justification may be claimed for them, such as forced marriage, polygamy, child labour and genital mutilation of young girls. These practices have no place in a civilized society – and nor, by implication, in a civilized religion.

The fundamental problem with the secularist programme is its desire to force religion into the private sphere. That outcome would be acceptable only to those faith communities, such as the Amish, that seek to withdraw from the world. Provided they are allowed to practise their faith without undue interference, they are content. Withdrawal from society is one strand in Catholicism, Eastern Orthodoxy, Buddhism, Sufism, and the Hindu and Jain faiths, but it applies with full force only to religious virtuosi such as monks, nuns and hermits. For everyone else, the message of Judaism, Islam, and most of Protestant and Catholic Christianity is to call humanity to serve God through action in this world.

Religions are grounded in a source of *ultimate* meaning and authority; they command and demand respect. Any attempt to confine religion to a private sphere of individual belief and devotion is bound to be challenged. It is not possible, even in a society that aspires to be secular, to treat religion as a purely private affair to which the state can be indifferent.

The challenge of diversity

Affluent countries can afford to conduct regular censuses of their population, and have the bureaucratic and technical infrastructure that makes it possible to do so. A census is different from other forms of social survey, in that giving information is a legal requirement imposed on all citizens. A national census can therefore attain levels of coverage and accuracy that are unachievable by voluntary surveys. Census data are a crucial source of information for researchers and policy makers. It is therefore highly significant that countries such as the USA and France do not have questions about religion in their national censuses; to do so would breach the formal separation of church and state. Other countries such as the UK do include such questions, but they are almost invariably voluntary. This shows the extreme sensitivity of religion, in contrast to every other category by which we may be classified by others or by ourselves.

In their report on religion and cultural diversity in contemporary Australia, Cahill et al. (2004: 43) comment that Australia's minority Christian communities have been overtaken by other faiths. There are now more Scientologists than Quakers, more Muslims than Lutherans, more Buddhists than Baptists, and more Hindus than Salvationists. Turning to the country's mainstream Protestant denominations, there is clear evidence of decline. Between the 1947 and 2001 censuses, the proportion of the adult population identifying themselves as Anglican fell from 39 to 21 per cent, and the proportion identifying with the Methodist, Presbyterian, Congregational and Uniting Churches fell from 22 to 10 per cent. Roman Catholicism, in contrast, grew from 21 to 27 per cent – a rise caused in part by the abandonment in the 1970s of the 'white Australia' policy, resulting in increased migration from other Pacific Rim countries. Overall, whereas 88 per cent of Australians in 1947 identified themselves as Christian, by 2001 this figure had fallen to 68 per cent. Data such as these can cause a shock to a nation's self-image, showing as they do a shift away from the country's traditional religious heritage towards 'new' and 'other' faiths.

There is an inevitable time lag before cultural changes are recognized and confronted. Sociological textbooks can be slow to react. For example the portrait of the United States as a country with a white Protestant majority was true for more than two centuries, but is so no more; data from the National Opinion Research Center's General Social Surveys (GSS) show that by the mid-1990s the white Protestant category had fallen to 44 per cent of the population (Hamilton and Form 2003: 700).

The category 'white' is socially constructed. Clearly, white people are not literally white in colour. Whiteness is a social status. At the beginning of the twentieth century, Americans of Italian, Slavic, Greek and Jewish origin were not necessarily classified as 'white'; that status had to be achieved (Kivisto and Rundblad 2000: p. xxix).

It is not just that public perceptions are slow to catch up with social trends; equally problematic are the stereotypes that have never been true. More than thirty years ago, as Hamilton and Form remind us, the Catholic sociologist Andrew Greeley exposed the myth that Irish Americans are predominantly Catholic; surprisingly, the majority are Protestant – or perhaps not so surprisingly, given the volume of migration from the North as well as the South of Ireland. Similarly, it is easily overlooked that 14 per cent of Italian Americans and 19 per cent of Polish Americans identify themselves as Protestant.

New patterns of migration in a globalized world suggest that old strategies of 'multiculturalism', 'incorporation' or 'assimilation' may be inappropriate and ineffective. Addressing the situation in the UK, Vertovec (2005) diagnoses a new situation: 'super-diversity'. He emphasizes that more people are migrating from countries that lack a link to the British Commonwealth or the former British Empire; that they bring with them a greater linguistic diversity; that people migrate in smaller groups; that each group has its unique gender and age profile; that groups include a wide array of migration statuses; and that migrants have multiple links to their country of origin. Religious identities are one element in the complex mix of super-diverse societies.

Super-diversity means that migrants are less likely to find in their new society a well-established community sharing their religious and ethnic identity, a community which might, therefore, act on behalf of the wider society as 'proximal hosts' (Mittelberg and Waters 1992), who, it is hoped, will assist them in the process of integration. The proximal host community may not be wholly attractive to the migrants, as shown by Mittelberg and Waters's comparison of kibbutz-born Israelis and Haitians. Israeli migrants typically resist incorporation as 'American Jews'. The distinctive symbol of their cultural identity is less the Jewish faith than the Hebrew language. Haitians migrating to the United States, who are predominantly middle class, risk being categorized as 'black'. To avoid racial discrimination, many of them emphasize their identity as recent migrants. Given the significance of 'race' in assigning people to a social category, the Haitians experience more problems than do the Israelis in establishing their cultural identity.

Countries that have a policy commitment to multiculturalism are oriented to identifying and supporting 'communities'. It is therefore to the advantage of migrants to present as a community, even when such ties are relatively weak. In the UK, community groups have been formed to speak on behalf of refugees from Bosnia-Herzegovina, as a means of gaining financial and practical support from the British state. Such a strategy conceals the lack of grassroots community activity by the refugees, and the cultural diversity among them (Kelly 2003). Bosnians are routinely identified as Muslims, although many are not, and even those who are Muslim may not wish to be identified primarily by their religion.

In the USA, the passage of the 1965 Hart–Cellar Immigration Act opened up a debate about the 'new immigration' that followed (Warner and Wittner 1998; Ebaugh and Chafetz 2000). The Act abolished immigration quotas based on country of origin, which led to a rise in migration from East and South Asia, the Middle East, the Caribbean and Latin America. Although the 'new immigrants' brought with them 'new' religions, the majority of migrants were Christian. What they were not was European.

To analyse the social significance of the new immigration, many commentators have resuscitated a concept that had lost favour in the USA, and had always seemed problematic in other Western societies: the concept of 'assimilation'. Assimilation and multiculturalism are often presented as opposite ideologies, the latter rejoicing in diversity, the former seeking to obliterate it. To polarize opinion in this way is to oversimplify the debate. On the one side, research into processes of assimilation seeks 'to understand factors contributing to, as well as those inhibiting, the successful incorporation of newcomers into the economic mainstreams of the advanced industrial nations, the political institutions and civil societies of these liberal democratic regimes, and their cultural cores' (Kivisto 2005: 4). On the other side, theorists of multiculturalism regularly use near synonyms for assimilation: for example, incorporation, integration and inclusion. Unity in diversity is a concern that they share. They have focused primarily on ethnicity to the neglect of religion, although religious identities are increasingly debated as matters of public importance.

When the realities of diversity, super-diversity and new patterns of migration are recognized, the reaction is often alarmist. A recent example is Huntington's (2004: 221–56) thesis that Hispanic migration threatens to divide the United States into two languages, two cultures and two peoples. According to Huntington, Mexicans and other Latinos have failed, and even refused, to assimilate into the cultural mainstream, because they have rejected the American Dream and the Protestant values on which it is built. Huntington argues that the sheer volume of migration, much of it illegal, and the regional concentration of Hispanic migrants in political and linguistic enclaves, pose a grave threat to a coherent national identity. America needs to renounce the ideology of multiculturalism, he claims, and reaffirm 'its Anglo-Protestant culture and its religiosity' (Huntington 2004: 365).

Some fifty years ago, observers of social integration in America drew more comfortable conclusions about the consequences of migration. A classic exposition of the American experience is Will Herberg's *Protestant – Catholic – Jew*, first published in 1955. Herberg's aim is to address the paradox of the American religious scene, which he says is characterized by a unique combination of 'pervasive secularism amid mounting religiosity' (Herberg 1983: 2). Although American religion has been drained of its doctrinal content, this does not mean that people who participate in religious affairs are fools or hypocrites. Their religiosity is authentic, at least in the sense that it is serving a real function for them. Herberg's book is devoted to explaining the profound paradox of the 'secularism of a religious people', or 'religiousness in a secularist framework' (Herberg 1983: 3).

Herberg quotes what has come to be known as 'Hansen's law', named after the social historian Marcus Lee Hansen: 'What the son wishes to forget, the grandson wishes to remember.' On this analysis the immigrant experience undergoes three phases. First-generation migrants cling to their ethnic identity. They hark back nostalgically to the culture of the old country, and seek to transplant it to the new. They socialize within their ethnic group, speaking the language of their birth and keeping the faith of their childhood. The trauma of migration increases their sense of nationhood: status distinctions that would have been crucial in the old country lose their salience. The church is a haven in which ethnic identity can be reaffirmed; elsewhere – at school, in employment, in leisure pursuits – American folkways have to be adopted. Significantly, as Bruce (1996: 110) notes, ethnic groups from the same religious denomination – such as German, Swedish, Norwegian and Finnish Lutherans – each created their own language-group congregations. Even the Roman Catholic Church, with its principle of universalism, could not prevent the growth of churches with an ethnic flavour.

The majority among the second generation typically rebels against this inward-turned ethnicity and the symbols through which it is expressed. They seek thoroughgoing assimilation. The third generation, in contrast, tends to return to its origins in a search for heritage, identity and roots (Herberg 1983: 6–65). Since migration to the United

States was restricted from 1924 onwards, the world-view of the third generation came to be the dominant one.

With the passage of time and in the new social context, many aspects of the third-generation migrant's roots are beyond reach. Peasant life is irretrievable, the Jewish *shtetl* (the isolated rural villages of Russia, Poland and the Baltic states) cannot be re-created, and the mother tongue has fallen into disuse. Typically, however, religion is still available as a source of meaning, identity and belonging. Grandchildren can selectively retrieve elements of their grandparents' world, notably their religion.

For Herberg, a migrant's ethnic identity is submerged in his or her religious identity. The reason for this is that self-identification on an ethnic basis would imply incomplete integration into the American way of life. Not only is religious identity compatible with integration, Americans are expected to have a religious affiliation. Atheism and agnosticism are culturally deviant options espoused by a minority even among intellectuals. Religion is not socially divisive, since America conceives itself to be 'one great community divided into three big sub-communities religiously defined, all equally American in their identification with the "American Way of Life"' (Herberg 1983: 38). These three communities are the Protestant – Catholic – Jew of Herberg's title.

Herberg's analysis drew on Kennedy's (1944) study of marriage patterns in New Haven. She concluded that marriage within ethnic boundaries, such as Italians marrying Italians, was giving way to marriage along religious lines – for example, Italian Catholics marrying Polish Catholics. Her term for this pattern was 'the triple melting pot': one pot for Protestants, one for Catholics, and one for Jews. Unfortunately, a careful re-analysis of the data (Peach 1980) has demonstrated that the thesis is false. Peach found no evidence that marriage was primarily based on religious affiliation; on the contrary, she argued that the New Haven data showed an ethnic division into black, Jewish and white Gentile groupings.

The refutation of the 'triple melting pot' hypothesis does not invalidate Herberg's emphasis on religion as a source of identity, meaning and belonging in a rapidly changing society. Commenting half a century later on the 'new immigration', Ebaugh observes that religion is 'at the center of immigrants' sense of identity, and that religious institutions serve as focal points for ethnic gatherings, celebrations, and recreations of ethnic language and customs, as well as for obtaining assistance with the practical issues of finding jobs, housing, schooling, and immigration papers' (Ebaugh and Chafetz 2000: 5). Religious communities help migrants to settle in their new country.

A clash of civilizations?

The fall of communism in the 1990s has provoked intense debate about the emerging world order. Samuel Huntington's (2002) thesis of an emerging 'clash of civilizations' is particularly notable, as well as controversial, for the emphasis it places on religion as a source of cohesion and conflict.

The period between the inauguration of communism with the 1917 October Revolution and its collapse after the destruction of the Berlin Wall in November 1989 was doubly exceptional: it was a bipolar world, pivoting around a Cold War between the two superpowers; and the Communist experiment was an aberration, since an alien political philosophy had been imposed upon a disparate society, the USSR, and its subjugated satellites. The fact that communism died so quickly, and with so few mourners, shows that despite its military power, it was in every other respect fragile.

Out of the debris of the bipolarity, according to Huntington, has emerged a world made up of seven, possibly eight, civilizations: Western, Latin American, Islamic, Sinic (mainly Chinese), Hindu, Orthodox, Japanese, and (at least potentially) African. Each civilization has its own culture: its values, ways of life, language and religion, to all of which its people are deeply committed. Religion is crucial: 'To a very large degree, the major civilizations in human history have been closely identified with the world's great religions; and people who share ethnicity and language but differ in religion may slaughter each other, as happened in Lebanon, the former Yugoslavia, and the Subcontinent' (Huntington 2002: 42).

What happened to Yugoslavia is instructive, and Huntington repeatedly refers to it. After the fall of communism, Yugoslavia broke up into smaller states: Bosnia-Herzegovina, mainly Muslim but with a large Eastern Orthodox minority and a significant Roman Catholic presence; Macedonia, which is predominantly Eastern Orthodox; Croatia and Slovenia, both mainly Roman Catholic; and the Union of Serbia and Montenegro, which was predominantly Serbian Orthodox. In 2006, after Montenegro voted to secede from their union, Serbia followed by declaring its own independence. One argument for Montenegro's secession was its claim to be, in implied contrast to Serbia, a tolerant multi-faith society.

Not only did Yugoslavia fracture on religious principles; other countries rallied to the support of their co-religionists. Russia supported the Serbs, the West supported the Croats, and some Islamic countries sent aid to Bosnian Muslims. Civilizations tend to answer the call of 'their own' in a process that Huntington calls 'kin-country rallying'. 'People rally to those with similar ancestry, religion, language, values, and institutions and distance themselves from those with different ones' (Huntington 2002: 126). Equally, civilizations resist efforts by 'others' to join them, which is the obvious but largely unspoken reason why the European Union has been reluctant to countenance the membership of Turkey.

Huntington's work is prescriptive. America must reaffirm its Western identity as a Christian nation. The choice, as he expressed it in his later book on national identity (Huntington 2004: 362–6), is between the cosmopolitan vision of a multicultural America open to the word, an imperial America that seeks to dominate the world, and a national America that reaffirms its identity as a liberal-democratic Christian civilization – the correct solution, and the one desired by most ordinary Americans. What is true of America is true of every other nation-state: all should remain true to their own culture.

Such recognition of the power of religion carries a high price. Huntington paints religious cultures as homogeneous and mutually exclusive. There is no acknowledgement of mutual exchange and shared dialogue. When he writes of 'the West' and 'Islam', he is dealing in ideological counters that are, in Edward Said's words, 'better for reinforcing defensive self-pride than for critical understanding of the bewildering interdependence of our time' (Said 2001).

Huntington's view of the relationship between Western and Islamic civilization is blunt: 'The underlying problem for the West is not Islamic fundamentalism. It is Islam, a different civilization whose people are convinced of the superiority of their culture and are obsessed with the inferiority of their power.' Conversely, 'the problem for Islam is not the CIA or the U.S. Department of Defense. It is the West, a different civilization whose people are convinced of the universality of their culture and believe that their superior, if declining, power imposes on them the obligation to extend that culture throughout the world' (Huntington 2002: 217–18). A significant bipolarity therefore persists in the twenty-first century, the alleged chasm dividing the West from the Rest, above all from Islam.

It is hard to see in Huntington's discussion any serious recognition of the contribution that Islam has made to Western cultures, or any sensitivity to the elements of faith that they share.

Grassroots Christian responses to diversity

Given the fact of religious diversity in the West, how do citizens respond to it? Instead of focusing on the overheated reactions of some political commentators, it would be more productive to examine research on the grassroots, such as Wuthnow's (2005) *America and the Challenges of Religious Diversity*. Wuthnow distinguishes three broad ways in which Christians are meeting the challenge of diversity. The first of these involves embracing diversity through *spiritual shopping* – that is, trying out beliefs and practices drawn from a variety of traditions, and deciding how well they suit one's values, tastes and preferred lifestyle. This approach ranges on a continuum from serious seekership to casual dabbling. It has its ironies and inconsistencies, but those are arguably a feature of any response to diversity.

The ideas and techniques with which spiritual shoppers experiment are not demanding philosophies and disciplines embedded in a faith community that expects loyalty and exclusive commitment. Instead, they are manageable recipes presented to the shopper in a packaged form that is easy to try, and then to take or leave. Given this ethos, spiritual shoppers rarely convert from Christianity to another faith.

Consumerism underpins spiritual shopping, but, ironically, 'relatively few spiritual shoppers perceive themselves to be consumers influenced by marketing, advertising, or the attractions of the marketplace; indeed, most feel just the opposite, regarding themselves as purists in search of deeper values than those supplied by commercialism and materialism' (Wuthnow 2005: 119). When they pick and mix items from different faiths, it is not, at least in their eyes, because they are restless and rootless, but because all religions are in essence the same, and therefore equally valid.

Spiritual shopping has a limited social impact. It welcomes religious diversity, revels in it, and adds some colour of its own to the religious scene; but even so, Wuthnow concludes (2005: 129), it 'seems unlikely to bring about a new consciousness that fundamentally alters American religion'.

At the opposite pole to spiritual shoppers are people who insist on the unique truth of their faith. This *exclusivism* may appear to be a robust position, but those who take it need to invest time and effort if they are to maintain their convictions in a context of religious and cultural diversity. Although Christian exclusivists do not necessarily try to convert people who belong to other religions, they nevertheless hold disparaging and typically ill-informed opinions about their beliefs and practices. This is not engagement with religious diversity, but an effort to insulate oneself against it.

The grassroots theology of exclusive Christians is centred on Jesus, who, in line with traditional Christian teaching, is regarded as fully divine as well as human. Salvation is possible only through faith in Jesus as Lord. These beliefs are not 'extreme'; they are Christian orthodoxy. What is distinctive about exclusive Christians, as Wuthnow points out, is less their beliefs about the divinity of Jesus than the huge gulf they set between Almighty God and sinful humanity. Since only Jesus can bridge this gap for us, through his atonement for our sins, non-Christians are effectively cut off from God. The founders, prophets and gurus of other faiths fall so far short that they are scarcely worth considering. We hear the voice of Christian exclusivism in the words of one respondent who said, speaking of the Prophet Muhammad and Joseph Smith with equal indifference, that 'those men have not done anything that makes them anywhere near what Jesus Christ did for us' (Wuthnow 2005: 177).

Between the poles of spiritual shopping and Christian exclusivism stand the majority of Christians, who *accept religious diversity in the spirit of denominational pluralism*. This middle way is neither superficial nor easy; it requires a balance between a firm commitment to the Christian way and respect for the beliefs and practices of other faith communities. It also demands respect for cultural diversity within the congregation itself (Ammerman 1997: 198–228). At its finest, this balance is achieved by applying the principle of loving one's neighbour as oneself.

The middle way, the way of inclusive faith, emphasizes spirituality. God is not to be understood through creeds and doctrines, which are so often the cause of conflict among Christians and between religions. A God who is approached through a personal quest is a God who is approachable. This is not the remote God of the exclusivists, but a God who can be known and experienced by people of any faith.

2

Defining Religion: Social Conflicts and Sociological Debates

Religion and power are inseparable. Since any attempt to define religion is an act of power, all definitions provoke counter-definitions. Academics, politicians, lawyers, religious leaders and their followers: all have an interest in how religion is defined.

Debates about the definition of religion carry ethical and political implications for society and for people of all faiths and none. What is at stake is not just the definition of religion but the distinction between good and bad, and authentic and bogus. We can see this in the strongly pejorative tone of much of our vocabulary about *other people's* religion: sects, cults, brainwashing, mind control, fundamentalism.

Failure to agree on a definition of religion is an inescapable social fact. Instead of deploring the failure, we should analyse it. To do so, we need to focus on the particular: not 'religion', but *this* movement, *these* people, in *that* situation.

We begin with two examples. The first is a movement that has grown rapidly in many countries, but has also been unpopular and controversial: Scientology. The second – the Baha'i faith – raises no problems in Western liberal democracies, where Baha'is are seen, in so far as they are noticed at all, as tolerant, peace-loving people who value education and give equal rights and status to women and men. In parts of the Muslim world, in contrast, the Baha'is are treated as heretics.

Scientology: authentic religion or imposture?

Scientology grew out of the therapeutic system called Dianetics, which was developed by L. Ron Hubbard (Ron to his followers) and canvassed by him in the May 1950 issue of *Astounding Science Fiction*, before publication in book form as *Dianetics: the modern science of mental health*. Dianetics involves a therapeutic relationship between an *auditor* and the individual – the *preclear* – undergoing the therapy. The auditor asks a series of questions, and the responses given by the preclear are registered on an *E-Meter*, a skin galvanometer similar to a lie-detector. From the E-Meter's readings the auditor can identify areas of stress caused by *engrams*, traumatic experiences occurring typically in early childhood which the preclear has repressed into his or her subconscious *reactive mind*. The aim of auditing is to release the preclear from the harmful effect of these accumulated engrams by erasing them from the reactive mind, thus enabling the subject to 'go clear'. A *clear* enjoys enhanced powers, such as higher IQ, better memory, and improved mental and physical health.

Scientology built a complex cosmological and metaphysical system on the basis of Dianetics. Human beings are in essence spiritual entities, *thetans*. Immortal, omniscient and omnipotent, thetans created the universe – made up of MEST (Matter, Energy, Space and Time) – but foolishly became trapped in their own creation as they deliberately shed their powers, eventually forgetting their own origins and status as thetans. Thetans have occupied innumerable bodies during the aeons that have elapsed since the creation of MEST. The techniques of Scientology enable the thetan to recover its lost powers by elimination of the reactive mind, so that the thetan can be *at cause*, that is able to determine the course of events.

The development of Scientology from Dianetics had two crucial elements. First, Scientology adopted a centralized authority structure. Dianetics had been relatively free and easy: if a particular technique worked for you, fine – the customer was always right. As a result, various practitioners launched independently their own alternative versions of Dianetics, thus threatening Ron's authority. He responded to this by developing a bureaucratic hierarchy and an internal system of discipline, designed to prevent the emergence of rival sources of authority within the movement.

Second, Scientology increasingly defined itself as a religion. Greater emphasis was given to ritual, ministry, ethics, creed and similarities to the philosophical systems of Asian religions. Alternative practitioners and their followers were transformed from competitors into heretics.

In its short history, Scientology has been caught up in a series of clashes with the authorities in several countries. An indication of the conflicts to come occurred in 1958, when the US Food and Drug Administration seized, analysed and then destroyed supplies of Dianazene, a compound that Scientology was marketing as effective in preventing and treating radiation sickness (Wallis 1976: 190–1). Dianazene proved to be no more than a straightforward compound of iron, calcium and vitamins.

Publication in Australia in 1965 of the report of a National Board of Inquiry, chaired by Kevin V. Anderson, gave rise to hostile media coverage and government-sponsored investigations into Scientology in many parts of the English-speaking world. Anderson condemned Scientology as an evil system that posed a grave threat to family life and to the mental health of vulnerable people. In the wake of this, the Australian authorities banned the practice of Scientology. In 1968, the UK government decided that foreign nationals would cease to be eligible for admission to the UK to study at or work for Scientology establishments; many were deported.

Throughout these turbulent years, the Church of Scientology continued to affirm its identity as a religion, and frequently took its case to court in an effort to assert its legal rights and to qualify for the tax concessions granted in many countries to recognized religions.

One country, however, in which the Church of Scientology has so far failed is the Federal Republic of Germany (Boyle and Sheen 1997: 312–14). The German authorities regard Scientology as a threat to the democratic principles on which the state was founded after the defeat of Nazism. The Weimar Republic, which collapsed in 1933 when Hitler became Chancellor, is judged to have been suicidal. In particular, Weimar politicians were too relaxed about democratic liberties and too indulgent towards undemocratic elements such as the National Socialists, who cynically exploited the very freedoms they would then destroy. The Federal Republic is not about to repeat this self-destruction, but will be robust in its own defence. It takes firm measures to prevent what it sees as attempted Scientological infiltration of public agencies and private industry and commerce. Some German companies have dissociated themselves from Scientology, so that their business will not suffer. Scientologists experience widespread discrimination, ostracism and intolerance. Above all, Scientology is denied the status of a religion. The prevailing official view is that Scientology's religious claims are bogus, on two counts. First, they are no more than a smoke-screen for the movement's lucrative commercial activities. Scientology's therapies are expensive. They are sold to members who are engaged in a never-ending quest for higher states of being, a process aptly described as 'the exchange of wealth for status' (Bainbridge and Stark 1980: 134). Second, Scientology claims to be a religion allegedly in order to secure democratic freedoms that it does not merit and would abuse. In response to this accusation, the Church of Scientology has repeatedly appealed to the United Nations to intervene with the German authorities on its behalf.

Scientology has also had a mixed relationship with academic researchers. On the one hand, Roy Wallis gave graphic accounts of attempts by members of the Church of Scientology to discredit him personally and professionally, and to subvert or suppress his research findings. On the other hand, Scientology has also sought scholarly support for its campaigns for recognition. In 1996 I received, unsolicited, free copies of papers written by twenty-two distinguished academics. All of them concluded that, like it or not, the Church of Scientology qualifies as a religion.

Baha'i: world faith or apostasy?

The origins of the Baha'i faith lie in a radical religious movement within Shi'a Islam that began in Iran and Iraq in the 1840s under the leadership of the prophet known as the Bab (in English, the Gate). In some respects the Bab is to Baha'is what John the Baptist is to Christians: John prepared the way for Jesus, the Bab prepared the way for Baha'u'llah (a title meaning Glory of God). From the end of the nineteenth century, Baha'is began to spread their faith to the West, gaining converts in the United States, Great Britain, France and Germany. There are now more than six million Baha'is worldwide.

Baha'is believe that God has sent a series of prophets with a divine message for humanity appropriate to each stage of human cultural development. These prophets include Adam, Abraham, Krishna, Moses, Zoroaster, Buddha, Jesus Christ, Muhammad, the Bab and Baha'u'llah; through them the divine plan has been progressively revealed. The prophet for our own age is Baha'u'llah; his successor is not expected for another thousand years. Baha'is say that the world's great religions contain prophecies that have been fulfilled in Baha'u'llah and in the Baha'i faith, which is destined to become the major worldwide religion, uniting humanity in a shared theocratic system.

Neither the values nor the activities of Baha'is have caused any problems to Western liberal democracies (McMullen 2000). The faith is peace-loving and law-abiding, opposes superstition and racial prejudice, supports education and science, is committed to environmental protection and sustainable development, upholds family values, and promotes equality of women and men.

In many Islamic countries, by contrast, Baha'is have been seen as heretics, apostates and undercover agents for the Western powers. Persecution of Baha'is has been severe in the country where the faith had its deepest roots, Iran. The Baha'i faith is doctrinally offensive because it does not recognize Muhammad as the final Seal of the Prophets and the Qur'an as the absolute and definitive word of God that has existed for all eternity. In this perspective Baha'is are apostates; that is, they have wilfully abandoned Islam – the crime of *irtidad* or *ridda*. Although the death penalty for apostasy is not mentioned in the Qur'an, it is in the Hadith (the sayings of the Prophet and his companions) and is recognized by Islamic law.

After the overthrow in 1979 of the regime of Mohammad-Reza Pahlavi, the last Shah of Iran, many Baha'is were arrested, tortured and executed. Their property was confiscated, their institutions closed, and their burial grounds desecrated. These actions had popular support. Baha'is were considered to be not only apostates, but also unpatriotic and subversive. They were judged to have supported the Shah's programme of modernization along Western lines. Their extensive international contacts, and the location of their administrative headquarters at Haifa in Israel, were held up as proof that they were agents of the West, and not members of a genuine religion at all (P. Smith 1987: 175–8).

The cases discussed above highlight the fact that the definition of religion, and any attempt to distinguish authentic from bogus religion, is of more than scholarly interest. It can profoundly affect people's lives. It raises issues of church–state relations, the constitutional rights and liberties of religious minorities, including intolerant ones, and the prospects for international agreement on human rights.

So, before discussing some of the definitions and conceptualizations of religion proposed by sociologists, it is worth setting out the reasons why some social movements insist that they are religions, while other movements equally emphatically deny it.

Advantages of being recognized as a religion

Gaining legal protection

Religious movements are granted wide protection under the law in many countries. In the USA, the Supreme Court, as the guardian of the

Constitution, has played a crucial role in determining the context in which religious movements operate.

The unconstitutionality of any establishment of religion in the USA means that no arm of government may pass legislation singling out any particular church or religious belief for special treatment. In Thomas Jefferson's much-quoted phrase, there is 'a wall of separation' between church and state. After a protracted legal campaign – the so-called saluting the flag controversy – a decision of the Supreme Court in 1943 overturned earlier rulings and upheld the Jehovah's Witnesses' constitutional right not to salute the flag or say the Pledge of Allegiance.

Reciting the Pledge of Allegiance – *I pledge allegiance to the flag of the United States of America and to the Republic for which it stands, one Nation under God, indivisible, with liberty and justice for all* – is a regular ritual at school and at civic events. It is a normal, taken-for-granted aspect of being American. To Jehovah's Witnesses, however, it is an idolatrous act. It means worshipping the nation-state and its flag instead of Jehovah, much as the Israelites bowed down to the golden calf.

Over and above national legislation, religious movements may appeal to international organizations such as the European Union or the United Nations. At issue are basic human rights, as enshrined in Article 18 of the Universal Declaration of Human Rights, 1948: 'Everyone has the right to freedom of thought, conscience and religion; this right includes freedom to change his religion or belief, and freedom, either alone or in community with others and in public or private, to manifest his religion or belief in teaching, practice, worship and observance.'

Gaining tax benefits

Many countries grant tax concessions to officially recognized religions. Achieving recognition can therefore be an important goal. For example, the Church of Scientology's long-running campaign against the Internal Revenue Service in the USA finally succeeded in 1993, when it was granted tax-exempt status. This brought with it the additional advantage that anyone giving money to the Church of Scientology could claim tax deductions on their contributions.

In the UK, the Church of Scientology presented a similar case, but failed. The Charity Commissioners for England and Wales ruled in 1999 that although Scientology professed belief in a supreme being, its core practices – 'training' and 'auditing' – did not constitute acts of worship. Training involves intensive study of the movement's literature, and auditing takes the form of individual counselling sessions. Neither practice exhibits any of the characteristics that would mark it out as a form of worship: adoration, submission, devotion, veneration, homage, supplication, sacrifice, praise, prayer and thanksgiving. Scientology asserts that training and auditing bring practitioners closer to ultimate reality, the 'eighth dynamic' or 'the urge to exist as infinity', but the Charity Commissioners decided that to count this as worship would be to violate the normal meaning of the term. They also noted that Scientology is a controversial new religious movement whose benefits to society remain unproven.

The Unification Church (the Moonies) received a more favourable legal judgment. In the 1980s, the then Prime Minister Margaret Thatcher urged the Charity Commissioners to review the church's qualification as a religion for charitable purposes, with the tax advantages that followed. Despite the clear wishes of Mrs Thatcher and intense public hostility to the Moonies, the Attorney-General dropped the case against them, leaving their status as a religion intact. They were more unpopular than Scientologists, but more recognizable as adherents to a religion. In the USA, meanwhile, the Reverend Sun Myung Moon was successfully prosecuted and imprisoned on charges of tax evasion.

In Germany, religious organizations with public law status enjoy the benefit that the state will collect taxes on their behalf from their members. To achieve public law status, a movement must prove its durability. It is required to show that it is well organized, with a sizeable membership and sound finances. It must also have been in existence for a minimum of thirty years. The law is designed to exclude short-lived volatile 'cults', particularly those that target young people, such as the Unification Church.

Jehovah's Witnesses have been engaged in a campaign to qualify for public law status in Germany. Like the Church of Scientology, Jehovah's Witnesses are not well regarded by the federal authorities, which see their movement as totalitarian.

Shedding the 'cult' label

The position of a minority religious movement may be strengthened if it can demonstrate its ties to an ethnic community, and through that to a major world religion. This is the case for the International Society for Krishna Consciousness (the Hare Krishna movement). ISKCON was founded in 1966 by His Divine Grace A. C. Bhaktivedanta Swami

Prabhupada. Its devotees became a familiar sight in Western cities, processing in their colourful robes, the men with heads shaven to leave only a top-knot remaining, chanting the mantra *Hare Krishna, Hare Krishna, Krishna Krishna, Hare Hare, Hare Rama, Hare Rama, Rama Rama, Hare Hare* – which even became a minor hit record. ISKCON was vulnerable to derogatory classification as a 'cult', with allegations that it targeted vulnerable young people, brainwashed them, used deceptive techniques of fund raising, broke up families, and moulded members to be dependent on the movement and its semi-monastic life. To counter this image, ISKCON has emphasized the priestly functions it performs for the wider Hindu community (Carey 1987). This role derives from ISKCON's roots in the centuries-old tradition of Vaishnava Hinduism, which cultivates worship of the god Vishnu and his *avatars* (roughly, incarnations) Krishna and Rama. Bhaktivedanta Swami's mission to save the West from its materialism was not simply an end in itself, but was also aimed at India, calling on it to return to the 'truth' path of spirituality. The objective is to position ISKCON not as a 'cult', but as a component of a great world faith that deserves respect.

Respectability

As well as the specific benefits outlined above, religious organizations enjoy a degree of respect as religions. As ever, this varies from society to society. In Great Britain, for example, ministers of religion are generally regarded as men and women of integrity, the charitable work of churches is well thought of, and many people continue to look to churches to provide rites of passage such as baptism, marriage and funeral services. Perhaps all this is in decline – an issue examined in chapter 4. But even if decline is under way, the mainstream churches retain a significant degree of public esteem, and minority movements are likely to continue to seek a share of it.

One key element in respectability is to be known to perform good works for the benefit of others. This taps into deep-rooted themes in the major religions of the world. For Jews, giving material help to people in need is a cardinal principle of the faith. Traditionally, Jewish homes have a container, the *pushka*, into which members of the family drop coins for charity, usually just before the lighting of the candles at dusk on Friday, marking the beginning of the Sabbath. The Christian faith inherited this commitment to charitable giving. The third of the Five Pillars of Islam is *zakat*, alms giving (the other Pillars are *shahada*, profession of faith; *salat*, worship; *saum*, fasting; and *hajj*, pilgrimage).

Minority religious movements may gain respect through their charitable work. A long-standing example of this is the Salvation Army. The
Church of Scientology combats drug abuse through an organization
known as Narconon, and the Unification Church has had a variety of
famine-relief programmes. One reason why young people may be
attracted to movements like the Moonies is the opportunity to engage
in socially worthwhile activities.

On the other hand, minority religious movements' charitable work
may be seen as little more than a calculated exercise in public relations.
This allegation was directed at the Unification Church when its practice of 'heavenly deception' became widely known. For example, the
Moonies do not necessarily disclose their identity as Moonies either to
potential recruits or to people from whom they solicit money for charitable purposes (Barker 1984: 176–88). Their scriptural justification for
heavenly deception is the subterfuge by which Jacob passed himself off
as his elder brother Esau and stole his birthright (Genesis 27: 1–40). To
Moonies, the means justify the ends in heavenly deception, since it
carries out the divine purpose. In any case, they argue that it is Satan
rather than God who is deceived.

Disadvantages of status as a religion

Legal restrictions

The First Amendment to the American Constitution guarantees free
exercise of religion, but denies religious movements access to public
institutions, restricting their operations to the voluntary sector.
Transcendental Meditation fought unsuccessfully in the USA for the
right *not* to be recognized as a religion, so that it could be taught
in public institutions such as schools and the armed forces (Barker
1995: 146).

Brought to the West in 1958 by the guru Maharishi Mahesh Yogi, TM
was made world-famous through its adoption in 1967 by the Beatles.
Although its roots are in Hinduism, to most of its hundreds of thousands of practitioners it is a technique of meditation open to people
of any faith or none. TM tends to underline its therapeutic, medical and
scientific dimensions, particularly in marketing itself to the staff-
training managers of secular business corporations.

The separation of church and state in the USA was designed to
protect the free exercise of religion from interference by the state, and
to prevent any capture of the state by organized religion. In France, the

second aim predominates (Hervieu-Léger 2001: 31). Protecting the state from religion takes the form of monitoring and curbing the activities of religious minorities, which are pejoratively called 'sects'. The presumption is that sects are exploitative and dangerous. A precautionary principle operates: fraud and abuse are presumed to be rife in the sects, so state intervention is needed to protect vulnerable people. Safeguarding individual freedom of belief, according to France's secular humanists, means curtailing the liberties of organized religions (Richardson and Introvigne 2001: 163). A broad political consensus in France supports legislation against sects, to protect freedom of belief against the threat posed by manipulative groups. Mormons, Baha'is and Quakers: these faith communities are well established and respectable in most countries, but are treated with suspicion in France. Sects are generally thought of as fanatical groups of American origin that threaten France's principle of *laïcité* (keeping religion strictly confined to the private sphere), which was a cornerstone of the Revolution of 1789 and reaffirmed in the law of 9 December 1905 on the separation of church and state. Sects are alien imports incompatible with the nation's cultural heritage. The Catholic Church in France is in a weak position; although uneasy about the tide of secular humanism, church leaders are probably afraid that some of the church's own activities, such as the work of Opus Dei, could be attacked. In this hostile cultural climate, the priority for minority religious movements is not to claim legal status as a religion but to keep a low profile, and above all to avoid being categorized as a sect.

In Greece, recognition as a religion can bring insoluble problems. Invoking 'the name of the Holy and Consubstantial and Indivisible Trinity', the Greek Constitution (1975) affirms that 'the dominant religion in Greece is that of the Christian Eastern Orthodox Church, which recognizes as its head, Our Lord Jesus Christ'. Some 98 per cent of the population are Orthodox, at least in name. The cultural hegemony of Orthodox Christianity means that other faiths can plausibly be treated as alien (Bruce 2003: 197). Free exercise of religion is guaranteed by Article 13 of the Constitution, but with a drastic restriction: 'Every known religion is free and the forms of worship thereof shall be practised without any hindrance by the State and under protection of the law. The exercise of worship shall not contravene public order or offend morals. Proselytizing is prohibited.' The faithful may worship but not seek converts: an impossible demand not only for religious minorities such as Jehovah's Witnesses, but also for Pentecostal and evangelical Protestant churches. The constitutional justification for outlawing proselytism is, as in France, the duty to prevent religious movements from 'taking advantage of the other person's inexperience, trust, need, low intellect or naïveté'. The Orthodox Church is never judged guilty of such practices.

Identification as a cult

Although recognition as a genuine religion can confer respectability, identification as a 'cult' (in France, a 'sect') carries extremely negative connotations. In many societies the rights of religious minorities are uncertain and precarious. Anti-cult movements are able to tap into a reservoir of popular hostility, and the mass media have relative freedom to target religious minorities, who do not enjoy the level of protection granted to ethnic or 'racial' minority groups.

Freemasonry provides an illustration of the wish to avoid being labelled as a deviant religion. It emphatically denies that it is a religion at all. The brotherhood says that its rituals are not religious, that it has no sacraments, and that discussion of religion is forbidden within the lodge. Admittedly, in many traditions of Freemasonry members are required to profess belief in a supreme being – the Great Architect or Grand Geometrician. Masons assert that this is entirely compatible with monotheistic faiths such as Judaism, Christianity, Islam and Sikhism, and also with the ultimate reality – *brahman* – revealed in Hinduism, despite its apparent polytheism. Masons' self-image is that they are an ecumenical brotherhood of morally serious men whose faith in God inspires them to do good works in the world. They have therefore been embarrassed by repeated accusations that theirs is an occult faith that worships a composite deity called Jahbulon, who is different from the god of the world's great religions. Denial that Freemasonry is a religious cult is a condition of its claim to respectability.

Negative images of mainstream religion

A number of religious movements, including many that stand in Eastern traditions of faith and practice, distance themselves from religion as it is understood in Western countries with a Judaeo-Christian base (Barker 1995: 146–7). Thus the Brahma Kumaris (founded in Karachi in 1937 by Dada Lekh Raj), who practise a form of yoga known as Raja yoga, prefer to be seen as a spiritual or educational movement. Ananda Marga (meaning the Path of Bliss, founded in Bihar in 1955 by Shrii Shrii Anandamurti), whose members meditate and practise yoga as a daily regime, sees itself as a way of life or socio-spiritual organization. Subud (founded in Indonesia in the 1930s by a spiritual leader known to his disciples as Bapak) is not so much a religion as an enlightenment gained through the shared spiritual experience of *latihan*, through which practitioners seek contact with their real inner self. In traditions such as these, Western religion may be thought of as moralistic, spiritually lifeless and authoritarian.

A very contrasting movement, the Jehovah's Witnesses, do not refer to themselves as a religion, even though they demand status as a religion under the law. Jehovah's Witnesses are literally that: witnesses to God, whose name is Jehovah. Religion is the false teaching of the churches who have led humankind away from obedience to Jehovah. To Jehovah's Witnesses, theirs is not a religion, but the Truth.

Christian theology, too, can display a distaste for 'religion'. An illustration of this is the work of the Swiss theologian Karl Barth (1886–1968). Barth distinguished sharply between divinely revealed faith and humanly constructed religion. To him, liberal theologians had contaminated the Christian gospel (faith) with worldly ideologies (religion). Barth's own 'neo-orthodox' theology rejected the naïvely optimistic approach of what came to be called 'cultural Protestantism' (*Kulturprotestantismus*). Barth's commentary on St Paul's Epistle to the Romans, published in 1919, was a reaction to the fervour with which liberal Protestant theologians in Germany had greeted the outbreak of the First World War in 1914. Later, when Hitler came to power in Germany in 1933, Barth supported the Confessing Church in opposition to the German Christians, those willing instruments of Nazism who sought to purge Christianity of its Jewish elements, such as the suggestion that Jesus was anything other than an 'Aryan' hero. This dark period in German history shows that supporting modernity is not necessarily the same thing as upholding liberty, equality and fraternity. The Nazis were the modernizers. They were the ones claiming to have a programme relevant to the needs of contemporary society. Barth's conservative neo-orthodox theology asserted the Christian faith in opposition to its corruption by Nazism.

Defining people as religious

We have reviewed the advantages and disadvantages to religious institutions and movements of being categorized as 'a religion'; but what of the people who are granted or refused the label 'religious'?

Denying that native peoples have a religion has been one way in which their lack of full humanity has been 'proved' by their colonial superiors.

'We' have religion; 'they' have ignorance, fear, superstition and fraud. In his discussion of theories of primitive religion, Evans-Pritchard (1965: 6–7) refers to the distinguished Victorian explorer Sir Samuel Baker, who said in 1866 of the people of the northern Nile: 'Without any exception, they are without a belief in a Supreme Being, neither have they any form of worship or idolatry; nor is the darkness of their minds enlightened by even a ray of superstition. The mind is as stagnant as the morass which forms its puny world.' These are not just nineteenth-century views. Chidester quotes the Afrikaner anthropologist W. M. Eiselen, in whose opinion the native peoples of southern Africa had no religion (*godsdiens*) but only patterns of belief (*geloofsvorme*). This 'categorical denial of their indigenous religious heritage' (Chidester n.d.: 3) was one component of the legitimation of *apartheid*.

If denying people any claim to religiosity violates their integrity, so too does attributing to them a mode or degree of religiosity that they cannot recognize. Sikhs, Jews, Muslims, Quakers: outsiders deploy these terms as unproblematic essences, overlooking the variety of commitments to be found within any community of faith.

Taking faith seriously can have unintended consequences. In the spirit of mutual understanding, the national curriculum for British state schools emphasizes the comparative study of 'the principal religions' that are represented in the UK; these are specified as Christianity, Buddhism, Hinduism, Islam, Judaism and Sikhism. Ironically, as Nesbitt (2004) points out, comparative religion can encourage the misperception that the religions studied are monoliths. Her fieldwork among young Punjabis and Sikhs challenges the easy attribution of such labels as 'Hindu' and 'Sikh' to people whose self-identifications prove to be far more nuanced. For many people, religion is not their dominant identity, but is subtly interleaved with nationality, ethnicity, class, generation, kinship, gender and sexual orientation.

One of Nesbitt's respondents said that she was in fact a Jain, but tends to call herself a Hindu because most British people have never heard of the Jain faith, even though its origins can be traced back at least 2,500 years. Some Hindus would count Jains as Hindus: in the discourse of Hindu nationalism (Karner 2006), Jains and Sikhs – even if they refuse to recognize the fact – are 'really' members of the Hindu family. Even Christians are really Hindus, since Christ was an incarnation of Brahma, the Creator. In Baumann's terms, this is a 'grammar of encompassment', in which people are deemed to be mistaken about their identity. They may think themselves different, 'but from a higher level of consciousness, these differences are but fictions of identity politics: in reality, or rather viewed from higher-up, the self-styled others are but a subordinate part of an encompassing Us' (Baumann 2004: 26).

For individuals, as well as for social movements and social institutions, definitions of religion are not neutral, but demonstrate the power of the definer over the defined.

Max Weber: on not defining religion

One of the great founders of sociology, Max Weber (1864–1920), began his major investigation of religion, first published in German in 1922, with this statement:

> To define 'religion', to say what it *is*, is not possible at the start of a presentation such as this. Definition can be attempted, if at all, only at the conclusion of the study. The essence of religion is not even our concern, as we make it our task to study the conditions and effects of a particular type of social behaviour. (Weber 1965: 1)

Weber has been criticized for this refusal to define religion at the outset. How can we know what to include in a study of religion if we have failed to define what religion is (Robertson 1970: 34)? In any case, there is bound to be an implicit definition in operation, and it would be far better to have it out in the open for us to examine (Berger 1967: 175–6; Hamilton 1995: 11–12). Obviously, Weber himself included some things and excluded others, so he had an implicit definition that the reader can work out. The suggestion is that Weber ought to have spared his readers this trouble. For, although he said that a definition of religion might be attempted at the conclusion of a study, in the end he failed to provide one.

Although plausible, this critique of Weber can itself be challenged on several grounds. First, is it true that a formal definition of religion is indispensable? Many sophisticated sociological studies of religious movements – for example, *The Making of a Moonie* (Barker 1984) and *The Trumpet of Prophecy* (Beckford 1975) – do not include a formal definition of religion. Readers are not troubled by the omission, and probably do not even notice it.

Second, any formal definition of religion is bound to contain theoretical assumptions that are contentious. 'Religion' is a contested concept. We cannot expect to agree on a definition and then debate matters of substance, since matters of substance are built into any definition. There is not, and never will be, a universally agreed definition of religion.

Third, sociologists should ask: who is demanding a definition, why, and with what consequences? The cases discussed earlier show that the repercussions of definition can be serious. Defining religion involves an exercise of power. When sociologists are asked by secular authorities or by religious movements to define religion, it is to lend scholarly support to inclusion or exclusion: to have the Moonies de-registered as a charity, or to defend Scientology as an authentic religion, or to protect the children of Exclusive Brethren from being taught computer science in school (to them, computers are a blasphemous attempt to create life).

Fourth, society changes, and religion changes with it. Given this, surely the search for a timeless definition of religion is misguided? Looking back over two centuries, it appears unlikely that even the far-sighted framers of the American Constitution envisaged the possibility of Scientologists or Rastafarians. The explosion of new religious movements in the West in the late 1960s came as a surprise to most people, including sociologists, who had to revise their conceptualization of religion in consequence. The same might now be said of New Age religiosity. To deny that these phenomena are truly religious shows a failure to comprehend them.

Far more significant than the absence of a formal definition is Weber's statement that it is not the sociologist's task to search for 'the essence of religion'. Instead, sociologists should investigate religion's 'conditions and effects'. Weber's own work involves wide-ranging historical studies of major world religions and the role of religious leadership, discussion of key themes such as magic and taboo, and analyses of social classes and status groups as the carriers of different recipes for salvation. His sociology is clinically detached and value-free, refusing to support or oppose any particular political, moral or religious position (though he did write, most uncharacteristically, that the Book of Mormon was 'a crude swindle').

Emile Durkheim: defining religion sociologically

Weber's great contemporary, Emile Durkheim (1858–1917), insisted on arriving at a clear and distinct definition of religion as a prelude to any further analysis of it. In his last major work, *The Elementary Forms of the Religious Life*, Durkheim produced a definition of religion that is densely packed with contentious elements:

A religion is a unified system of beliefs and practices relative to sacred things, that is to say, things set apart and forbidden – beliefs and practices

which unite into one single moral community called a Church, all those
who adhere to them. (Durkheim 1915: 47)

First, and most strikingly, the definition contains no reference to God,
or the gods, or spiritual beings, or the transcendent, or another world,
or the soul, or a life after death. Durkheim apparently believed that
Theravada Buddhism (a more ancient and stricter form than Mahayana
Buddhism, and prevalent in Sri Lanka and South-East Asia), although
indisputably a religion, lacked any supernatural conceptions. Any definition of religion had to allow for this. It may be that he was wrong
about Theravada Buddhism, confusing its elaboration as a sophisticated atheistic philosophy for an intellectual elite with its operative
reality as a religion for the vast majority of the faithful, who do indeed
believe in the supernatural (Robertson 1970: 36).

Second, the core concept in Durkheim's definition of religion is the
sacred, detached from any divine origin. In a Durkheimian perspective,
it is not God who has made Lourdes or Jerusalem or Mecca a sacred
place of pilgrimage. The sacred is a social construct; sacredness is con-
ferred not by God, but by society. There is no qualitative difference
between Lourdes or Mecca, on the one hand, and Anne Hathaway's
cottage or the Tupelo shack where Elvis Presley was born. Things are
not sacred unless we treat them as such. To a believer this can seem a
shockingly misguided, even blasphemous position.

Third, and unlike Weber, Durkheim was aiming to capture the
essence of religion. To do so, he argued, it is necessary to begin by examining religion in its simplest form, which he assumed was to be found in
the simplest society in existence. This led him to focus on the totemic
religion of the native people of Central Australia, supplemented by
material from North America when it suited him. Having grasped the
essence of religion by analysing its most elementary form, we could
then progress to study the more complex, but essentially similar, religions of advanced societies. As Parkin remarks (1992: 42), 'this was not
a position guaranteed to win Durkheim many friends among the
churchly', who did not relish the attempt to derive their own 'higher'
faith from the beliefs and practices of people they saw as savages.

Fourth, Durkheim's definition places beliefs and practices on an
equal footing. He deliberately avoided the 'intellectualist' error of
assuming that the essence of religion is belief.

In some religious movements, the formal belief system is indeed
central. Jehovah's Witnesses are one example of this. They devote much
of their time to studying the Bible through the perspective of the books
and magazines produced by the Watchtower Bible and Tract Society.

Becoming a Witness involves such study, plus a commitment to go out on 'the work', 'preaching and teaching' from door to door. As students, Witnesses are required to learn the Truth, not to question it. Emotional outbursts are viewed with deep suspicion. This is not a revivalist faith in which people stand up for Jesus, or testify that they have been born again, or hug and kiss one another, or dance, or speak in tongues (*glossolalia*), or raise the roof with rousing hymns. Meetings are low-key and businesslike, and have an instrumental goal: equipping the Witnesses for doorstep proselytizing, by training them in effective presentation of themselves and their Truth.

In contrast, the Religious Society of Friends (Quakers) has consistently rejected the formulation of any doctrine, creed or dogma. Quakers are concerned to acknowledge and cultivate 'the light within', or 'that which is of God in everyone'. Practice takes precedence over belief, and belief has meaning only in so far as it is enacted in practice. The Quaker does not learn an authoritative belief system, but experiences a Quakerly way of doing things and a Quakerly mode of worship.

Fifth, for Durkheim religion is essentially social, uniting its adherents into 'a single moral community'. Individual religiosity is secondary and derivative, and Durkheim characteristically showed little interest in it (just as, in his study of suicide, he concentrated on suicide rates and refused to consider individual motivation). Durkheim similarly treated magic as secondary and derivative: the magician or sorcerer has individual clients who interact not with one another but only with the sorcerer, who provides services to them. The clients of sorcerers do not, in Durkheim's view, form a community.

Although Durkheim's definition of religion is deliberately broad, and although it is grounded in his interpretation of religion among the Aboriginal people of Australia, it remains the product of a modern understanding of religion. This may have been in part a personal matter. Durkheim's insistence that there is a gulf between sacred and profane may reflect his upbringing in a Jewish culture that divided the world into *kosher* and *tref*, clean and unclean. The crucial role of ritual in enabling profane mortals to connect with the sacred corresponds to both Jewish and Catholic sensibilities. The equally sharp distinction between religion and magic is, again, characteristically modern. Both the Protestant Reformation and the Catholic Counter-Reformation sought to curtail popular, 'magical' applications of religious practices, so that access to the sacred was controlled by the Church. 'The definitional boundary between magic and religion' is, as McGuire reminds us (2003: 130), a modern conception that 'did not exist in the Late Medieval popular imagination'.

In assessing Durkheim's definition of religion, we need to recognize that it is not neutral. His theory of religion is distilled into it. Putting it another way, Durkheim's definition is a Trojan Horse for his theory of religion. If we accept the gift, we can expect theorems to emerge from inside it. Durkheim's theory of religion will be examined more fully in chapter 4.

Contemporary sociological definitions of religion

Sociological definitions of religion can be classified into two varieties: the broader inclusive and the narrower exclusive types. The balance of sociological opinion appears to be in favour of exclusive definitions, though these are not unproblematic.

Inclusive definitions

[W]e propose that religion be defined as a system of beliefs about the nature of the force(s) shaping man's destiny, and the practices associated therewith, shared by the members of a group. (Lenski 1963: 331)

A *religion* is: (1) a system of symbols which acts to (2) establish powerful, pervasive, and long-lasting moods and motivations in men by (3) formulating conceptions of a general order of existence and (4) clothing these conceptions with such an aura of factuality that (5) the moods and motivations seem uniquely realistic. (Geertz 1968: 4)

It is in keeping with an elementary sense of the concept of religion to call the transcendence of biological nature by the human organism a religious phenomenon. (Luckmann 1967: 49)

[R]eligion is a system of beliefs and practices by means of which a group of people struggles with the ultimate problems of human life. (Yinger 1970: 7)

The fundamental criticism of inclusive definitions such as those above is simply that they include far too much. This criticism has been expressed in various ways.

First, on some inclusive definitions, all human beings are religious, even if they are professed atheists and utterly reject religion. To define religion in terms of ultimate problems (Yinger), or the forces shaping human destiny (Lenski), or the human transcendence of biology (Luckmann) is to make all of us religious whether we claim to be or not.

However, sociologists who define religion inclusively may be happy to defend the view that humanity is religious by definition. Thus Luckmann (1967: 49): 'The transcendence of biological nature *is* a universal phenomenon of mankind.' And Lenski (1963: 331–2):

> Given this definition of religion, it quickly becomes apparent that every normal adult member of any human society is religious. . . . There are some people, of course, who profess to be agnostics, but any examination of their patterns of action reveals that all agnostics *act as though* they accepted one or another of the competing systems of belief. Human existence *compels* men to act on unproven and unprovable assumptions, and it makes no exception.

Luckmann and Lenski explicitly build their sociology on a conception of humanity – a philosophical anthropology – according to which human beings are essentially religious. Although this may be challenged, it is arguably the case that all sociology depends on some sort of philosophical anthropology, even though it is not usually spelled out.

A second way of expressing the objection to inclusive definitions of religion is to say that they incorporate all sorts of secular phenomena that should be excluded. B. S. Turner (1991: 15) argues that the Durkheimian approach 'drags in a diverse catch of social phenomena from baseball to nationalism, from Celtic hogmanay celebrations to royal weddings'. Ideological systems may be included that are openly materialist and anti-religious – for example, Communism (Scharf 1970: 33). They may equally well include the beliefs and practices of the devoted supporters of a football team or the fans of a rock group (Hamilton 1995: 17).

Sociologists tend to treat religion as a very serious phenomenon. All the great figures who contributed to the early development of sociology, even the atheists, held religion to be crucially important. Durkheim, himself an austerely unfrivolous man, said that religion belonged to the serious side of life – 'c'est de la vie sérieuse'. This intellectual legacy may be one reason why sociologists of religion usually treat fandom as trivial. Is it not possible, however, that in a consumer-oriented and perhaps 'postmodern' society the once-secure distinctions between fans and worshippers, popular entertainers and charismatic leaders, leisure pursuits and religion, are being eroded? This issue will be addressed in chapter 9. As for the atheistic materialism of Communist societies, the former Soviet Union spent countless millions of roubles on the systemic promotion of a ritual system that had many of the hallmarks of a religion. This will be examined in chapter 7.

A third version of the objection to some inclusive definitions is that they prevent us from examining the question: is religion growing, stable or in decline? If virtually everything is religion, then a vital question of fact has been 'answered' only by a trick of definition. Would it not be better to treat football, royal weddings and the like as substitutes for religion, rather than the real thing?

A final point about inclusive definitions of religion is that many of them are explicitly functionalist. Religion is defined in terms of the functions it performs for individuals or society, where functions are seen as both beneficial and necessary. Religion gives people a sense of identity, purpose, meaning, hope. Religion expresses and creates shared values and the social bonds that hold society together. Anything that performs these functions is religion. Functionalist definitions of religion are often linked to the view, supremely expressed in the structural functionalism of Talcott Parsons, that the social glue holding society together is neither coercion nor the everyday necessity of earning a living – what Marx called 'the dull compulsion of economic life' – but shared norms and values.

Exclusive definitions

An institution consisting of culturally patterned interaction with culturally postulated superhuman beings. (Spiro 1966: 96)

Religious culture is that set of beliefs and symbols (and values deriving directly therefrom) pertaining to a distinction between an empirical and a super-empirical, transcendent reality; the affairs of the empirical being subordinated in significance to the non-empirical . . . [Religious action is] action shaped by an acknowledgement of the empirical/super-empirical distinction. (Robertson 1970: 47)

The set of beliefs which postulate and seek to regulate the distinction between an empirical reality and a related and significant supra-empirical segment of reality; the language and symbols which are used in relation to this distinction; and the activities and institutions which are concerned with its regulation. (Hill 1973: 42–3)

Exclusive definitions of religion are supposed to be free from the objections to the inclusive type discussed above. They are substantive, rather than functional, defining religion by what it is, not by what it does (McGuire 1992: 11–15). They claim to be closer to conventional Western understandings of religion (though there is so much variety and ambiguity about the meaning of religion that the claim is doubt-ful). They do not 'drag in' footballers, rock stars and their fans; nor do they close down the question of religion's decline or growth.

Even so, there are problems. One striking feature of the definitions given above is their avoidance of key terms and concepts that have nor-mally been thought of as core aspects of religion. Exactly as with Durkheim's much-criticized inclusive definition, there is still no refer-ence to God, or the gods, or spiritual beings, or to the transcendent, or another world, or the soul, or a life after death. These supposedly exclu-sive definitions are actually rather inclusive.

What we have instead of the supernatural is the superhuman (Spiro), the super-empirical (Robertson), and the supra-empirical (Hill). Yet these terms are themselves problematic (Hamilton 1995: 15; Willaime 1995: 120). The concept of the superhuman is not found in all cultures. Nor is it obvious who or what should be included as superhuman. Exceptional people who influenced the course of history for good or ill, such as Napoleon? Great artists such as Shakespeare, and great scien-tists such as Einstein? Fictional super-heroes such as Superman? What about the vision of the Extropians, who reject religious dogma and supernaturalism as irrational, but believe that humanity will evolve into a more advanced life-form? In all of these cases, the superhuman belongs to *this* world rather than any other, and so falls well short of the supernatural in its fullest religious sense.

Unlike the superhuman, the terms super-empirical and supra-empirical do point to another world 'over' or 'above' this one. What is less clear is how these terms are an improvement on the supernatural. Perhaps their purpose is to move discussion away from transcendence of the natural world – by, for example, miraculous interventions over-riding the laws of cause and effect – to transcendence of human culture.

The drive to include all religious traditions is the reason why socio-logical definitions of religion, even ones that claim to be substantive and exclusive, are extremely broad, incorporating abstract terms such as 'super-empirical'. There is a profound paradox here. Sociology aims to be universal in scope, and struggles to avoid parochialism and ethno-centricity. Sociologists therefore seek a definition of religion that would encompass all the religions of the world. Yet this search for a univer-sally applicable definition defeats its own purpose. Cultures are too diverse, and new religious movements continually threaten to break the mould with new modes of belief and practice. Ironically, sociologists who adopt exclusive definitions of religion have often shown themselves staunch allies of conservative theology and traditional practices. Radical theologians and liberal clerics who see the divine as immanent rather than transcendent are ridiculed by atheist sociologists for their foolish betrayal of religion.

Religion and definition in use

Whether they favour inclusive/functional or exclusive/substantive definitions of religion, sociologists have tried to avoid giving priority to any one religion. They do not start from, say, mainstream Protestant Christianity, and then see other faiths in the light of it. Because of this, sociologists have become more and more reluctant to use terms such as 'sect' and 'cult'. These terms are normally used pejoratively to imply that the religious movement in question has broken away from or fallen short of the fullness of the true faith, or even that it is not a genuine religion at all.

Durkheim was famously exercised by the example of Buddhism, as we have seen. An equally problematic case is Hinduism, which does not fit Western preconceptions about religion (Knott 1998). Western observers of India in the colonial era were frequently impressed by the philosophical and spiritual dimensions of Hinduism, but repelled by what they interpreted as superstition and worship of idols – a practice particularly repulsive to Protestants. European travellers and missionaries sent home lurid stories of the abhorrent idolatrous rituals of Hindu 'polytheists'.

Hinduism did not have a founder, and does not have prophets. It is not defined by creeds. There is no set of doctrines or practices that are essential to it. It is neither a theological nor an ethical system. Although it has sacred texts, not one of them is universally regarded as carrying unique authority. It is not organized into church-type structures. Its *brahmins* are not priests in the Western sense.

So much for what Hinduism is not; what it is also diverges from Western preconceptions. Hinduism is extremely complex and internally diverse, embracing with relative tolerance a wide range of traditions, including local village cults as well as major religious movements. It is identified specifically with India and the Aryan people who have lived there for thousands of years or, as many Hindus see it, since the beginning of time. The sacred land of India, ritually purified by the priestly class of *brahmins*, is surrounded by the inauspicious 'black waters'; traditionally, to cross these was to place oneself in peril of ritual pollution. Moving in the other direction, the sacred land has been violated by alien faiths. Contemporary Hindu nationalism expresses abhorrence for Muslim, Christian and secularizing *invaders*. At the same time, the Jain,

Buddhist and Sikh faiths are native to India, and are therefore assimilated by Hindu nationalists into 'the Hindu fold' (Karner 2006).

Hinduism is bound up with an ordering of society – the *jati* or caste system – which is linked to the scriptural division of humanity into four great classes: the *varna* (meaning colour) system, a hierarchy composed of *brahmins* (very roughly, the priestly class), the *kshatriya* (the warrior caste), the *vaishya* (the farmers and merchants) and the *shudra* (the servants and labourers). Utterly outside the *varna* system lie the untouchables, a potent source of ritual pollution to the members of the varna classes – even their shadow can pollute.

The term Hinduism is itself problematic. It might be more true to the subject to speak of Hindu *dharma* – a way of life, or even *the* way of life, grounded in the cosmological order. That is how many Hindus see it, referring to *sanatana dharma*, the eternal tradition whose origins lie outside human history. As so often happens, *sanatana dharma* may be affirming something eternal, but the origins of the term are modern (Knott 1998: 117).

Like Hinduism, Shinto, the so-called religion of Japan, lacks many of the features that Western observers expect to find in a religion. It has no founder, no creed or elaborate doctrine, no commandments, no sacred scriptures, no creator God, no concept of heaven or life after death. It has no missionaries, and is not interested in proselytizing. Its emphasis is on aesthetically precise ritual practices oriented toward *kami*, the spirits and powers that animate the world around us. *Kami* are not supernatural, but part of nature, since Shinto does not recognize a distinction between the natural world and the supernatural or transcendent.

Is Shinto a religion? This obvious question proves to be deeply politicized. Throughout Japanese history, the practice of Shinto was usually seen as perfectly compatible with membership of another faith community; in particular, Shinto and Buddhism have tended to be mutually supportive. Both have been harnessed by the state in the cause of nation building. But after the Meiji Restoration in 1868, Shinto was gradually severed from Buddhism and restructured as an officially sponsored state religion. Buddhism was downgraded and secularized, and Confucianism ceased to provide the ethical underpinning of the state bureaucracies. Shinto was in the ascendant as an integral part of a militaristic, supremacist Imperial cult.

All this changed after 1945, when Japan suffered catastrophic defeat in its 'Greater East Asia War'. Secularization was imposed on Japan by the Allied powers: the Emperor was forced to renounce his divine status, Japanese 'racial' superiority was repudiated, and as a casualty of the post-war separation of church and state, Shinto lost official status. To the Allies, Shinto had become a perverted religion manipulated by the state to legitimize military dictatorship and inspire acts of unspeakable barbarity. To the Imperial regime, Shinto was integral to a glorious vision centred on the divine Emperor, the blessed islands of Japan, and the Japanese people as descendants of the gods and rulers of the world. In this perspective, Shinto was not 'a religion', but a metaphysical system that surpassed all religions. To ask, 'Is Shinto a religion?', has not been an innocent question.

The examples of Hinduism and Shinto make the point that we might do well to follow the lead of the philosopher Ludwig Wittgenstein, and abandon the search for a set of common factors that all religions must possess (Saler 1993). This would not be as disastrous as it might at first seem. Take as a comparison the concept of 'sports'. There are many different sorts of sports – football, gymnastics, synchronized swimming, billiards, darts, angling – with no one element shared by all. A sport may or may not be competitive, involve the use of a ball, be physically demanding, or be a team game. What sports share, says Wittgenstein (1958: §67), is not common elements but 'family resemblances', which enable us to recognize them as sports, just as we can see varying similarities of physique and personality among members of the same family, without there being any one characteristic possessed by them all.

A second point emphasized by Wittgenstein is that definitions are put to use in different contexts for different purposes. If we want to know the meaning of a term, we should investigate how it is used. For example, the International Olympics Committee has to decide which sports are appropriate for inclusion in the Olympic Games. There was controversy when synchronized swimming was accepted. What about darts? Although it is not widely recognized as a sport, that may be less to do with its intrinsic characteristics than with prejudice against a working-class pursuit. How do the people who play darts see it themselves? A strength of sociology is that we go and ask them.

Is Scientology a religion? With this question, we are back where the chapter started. When Scientologists themselves are asked what they think they are doing, their replies show that they do see Scientology as a religion. Whether this should be definitive is a matter of debate. In any event, we have seen some of the reasons why the answer is important to a number of interested parties, not least the Church of Scientology itself.

Wittgenstein's emphasis on definition in use reflects the sociologist's concern with practice as a dimension of religion that is at least as salient as belief. Not all religious movements emphasize beliefs, doctrines and creeds, as we have seen from the examples of Quakers and Hindus discussed above. Not all traditions have been characterized, as Christianity has been, by schisms involving disputes over true doctrine, such as those between the Eastern Orthodox and Western Catholics, and between Catholics and Protestants.

Even within those religious movements that do have formal creeds, it should not be assumed that most participants are knowledgeable about or concerned with matters of doctrine. Rank-and-file members are not usually would-be theologians. The experience of being a Jew, or a Hindu, or a Mormon is often more about doing things than believing things: about abstaining from pork, or beef, or tea, coffee and cola drinks. Often, too, it is the doing and the not-doing that provoke hostile social reactions: Jehovah's Witnesses rejecting blood transfusions, Quakers refusing to enlist in the armed services, nineteenth-century Mormons practising polygamy.

A Wittgensteinian approach to the definition of religion is well suited to modern circumstances. Whether or not we believe that religion has lost social significance in the West – as it has, according to the secularization thesis, examined in chapters 4 and 5 – it seems hard to deny that religion has become a more controversial and less predictable force in society (Beckford 1989: 170–2). It has lost its former anchorage in stable communities of faith, becoming instead a cultural resource on which individuals and interest groups may draw for motivation and legitimacy. In Western society, religion as a social institution may have declined, but religion as a cultural resource remains potent. This deregulation of religion means that its definition has become a recurring problem in modern societies, with serious consequences both for believers and for society as a whole.

3

Varieties of Religious Movement

Church and sect

Sociological attempts to classify religious movements trace their origin to Max Weber. His distinction between church and sect as forms of social organization centred on the differences in their *membership principle*.

In Weber's account, the church is *inclusive*. Church membership is socially ascribed at birth, which means that people belong to the church unless they choose to opt out. The church, as Weber says, 'necessarily includes both the just and the unjust'. It is not a select community of the chosen few, but a gathering of repentant sinners in search of forgiveness. The church's unique spiritual assets are the sacraments, defined in the Anglican Book of Common Prayer as 'an outward and visible sign of an inward and spiritual grace'. The Catholic and Orthodox traditions recognize seven sacraments as having been instituted by Christ: baptism, confirmation, the Eucharist, penance, extreme unction, holy orders and matrimony. Most Protestant churches recognize baptism and the Lord's Supper as the only true sacraments. The church offers the sacraments to everyone within its territory, which may be either a nation-state or part of a nation-state, as with the Church of England, or the whole world, as with the Roman Catholic Church.

The church's sacraments are transmitted as an inheritance from generation to generation, in what Weber calls 'a sort of trust foundation for supernatural ends'. Given this, it is symbolically appropriate that the church administers sacraments not just to adults but to infants and children as well. Conversely, a principal way in which the church exerts its symbolic power is to withdraw sacraments from people deemed unworthy of them – for example, refusing to conduct marriage ceremonies if one party is divorced, unless their previous marriage has been annulled.

The appeal to tradition as a source of sacred authority is always powerful within the church. So it is that people within Catholic, Orthodox and Anglican churches who argue on grounds of tradition against the ordination of women to the priesthood do not regard themselves as appealing to corporate inertia or unimaginative resistance to change. For them, the enduring tradition of the church is based on divine ordinance: God wills it so for all time.

The sect, on the other hand, is *exclusive*: membership is not ascribed at birth, but is achieved in adult life. Sects are voluntary associations, funded through the subscriptions of their members and not subsidized or sponsored by the state, as churches often are. Unlike a church, a sect is a gathered community of people typically describing themselves in such exclusive terms as 'the saints' or 'the elect'. People can become a member of a sect only by choosing to join it. Since a sect is a community of committed adult believers, the churches' practice of infant baptism makes no sense at all. How can an infant profess a faith? And what sense is there in a parent professing faith on behalf of a child? Infant baptism shows just how deeply the churches are in error.

Sects have strict criteria for entry, and impose stringent performance norms. To prevent conflict within families, most sects either require or at least strongly advise endogamy – marriage within the community of faith. Members' commitment is put to the test, and people who fail to live up to the sect's demanding moral codes run a high risk of being thrown out – 'disfellowshipped' or 'disowned' – and ignored, 'shunned'.

Sects have a strong sense of their own identity and of the distinctiveness of their mission. They are protest movements. In sects whose roots lie in the Protestant Reformation, protest focuses on the alleged laxity, hypocrisy and false teaching of the churches. In many sects, however, protest is much wider, even extending to wholesale rejection of the values and lifestyles of the modern world.

We can see the tension between church and sect expressed in internal conflicts within mainstream Christianity down the centuries. The Church frequently confronted rigorist groups, such as the Donatists in the third century, who claimed that in order for the Church to remain pure, its sacraments must be administered by people who were themselves personally holy and uncompromised. Mainstream Christianity repeatedly rejected this sectarian principle. The contrasting, churchly approach is embodied in the Church of England in the Thirty-Nine Articles of Religion, the twenty-sixth of which is entitled: 'Of the unworthiness of the ministers, which hinders not the effect of the sacrament'. In contrast, some sects, such as the Salvation Army and the Religious Society of Friends (Quakers), reject the concept of sacraments altogether.

Weber's analysis of church and sect is not confined to a static description. Rather, he discusses the dynamics of social change, examining the processes through which one form mutates into another. On his account, successful sects have a tendency to evolve into churches. This is partly a function of size: sects operate most effectively as small, face-to-face, locally self-policing communities. If they succeed in attracting large numbers of new members, they find themselves inevitably pushed towards the churchly mode.

The growth of sects into churches is also linked to the process of *routinization of charisma*. The personal charisma of the movement's founder becomes diffused after his or her death into a more generalized charisma of office. In the Catholic Church, for example, Christ's charisma, derived from his unique personhood, is transmitted to the Church as the office charisma of Peter, the popes and the priesthood. Even if an individual is unworthy of the office he or she holds, the office is not thereby undermined.

As a religious movement grows, personal charisma is replaced by charisma of office, which in turn gradually shades into bureaucracy – a defining characteristic of the churchly form of social organization. Bureaucracies are rule-governed impersonal structures in which the separation of person and office is complete.

Weber's ideas on the sect-to-church process were taken up and elaborated by other writers. One example of this is H. R. Niebuhr's *The Social Sources of Denominationalism*, first published in 1929 (Niebuhr 1957). Niebuhr argued that sects are 'valid' only for one generation of members: the second and subsequent generations who are born into the movement cannot share the fervour of the original members, whose commitment was forged 'in the heat of conflict and at the risk of martyrdom'. The rugged faith of the pioneers gives way to 'easily imparted creeds'. The sect is forced to pay more and more attention to the socialization of its children, and less to its external mission in society. As the movement grows and prospers, so charisma withers, and bureaucracy tightens its paralysing grip.

The sect-to-church thesis is suggestive but false. Many sects have remained sectarian despite the passage of time. They have succeeded in socializing their children into the movement's beliefs and practices, while winning committed adult converts. They continue to enforce strict codes of conduct, and do not hesitate to expel people who fail to live up to them. Not all sects depend on charismatic leadership; in such cases, routinization of charisma is not an issue.

Some movements, of the type that Wilson calls *introversionist*, isolate their members geographically and socially from contact with the wider society. For introversionist sects, salvation is found within the sacred community of the faithful. They are pollution-conscious: religious hygiene requires that members are isolated from contaminating social contact with the world outside. They are communities in a strong sense of the word. A number of ethnic groups migrated to the New World to escape persecution in the Old, including the Amish (originally from Switzerland and Alsace), the Hutterites (from Moravia) and the Doukhobors (from Russia). All of these set themselves apart in self-contained communities that aim to be self-sufficient, not just economically, but socially and culturally. They are determined to resist assimilation.

Other movements do not isolate their members from contact with the wider society, but insulate them against contamination. Take the case of Jehovah's Witnesses. A conscientious family of Witnesses will do everything they can to guard their children against the false teachings and ungodly practices of the wider society. Their children will attend state schools, but will not participate in acts of religious worship and assembly. A strict Witness family will discourage close friendships with children born outside the faith. A Witness child will not attend birthday parties, since Witnesses do not celebrate birthdays. Christmas is a pagan festival to be studiously ignored. Strict Witnesses do not exchange gifts at all, but purchase items only when they are needed; hence the rich set of symbols, rituals and interpersonal relations expressed in gift exchange can be quite alien to Witness children. Witnesses will be wary of allowing their children to stay overnight with their non-Witness acquaintances, for fear of exposure to adolescent 'bedroom culture' with its cult of popular celebrities and its easy access to dubious materials available on television, video and the internet. Witnesses cultivate in their children the traditional virtues of self-controlled 'good behaviour', not least uncomplaining obedience to parental authority. More profoundly, childhood is treated unromantically as an apprenticeship for the adult life of a Jehovah's Witness.

The Exclusive Brethren, a sect which broke away from the wider Brethren movement in the 1840s, provide another instructive case. Exclusive Brethren are required to avoid worldly practices and to minimize contact with non-members. They are forbidden to watch television, listen to the radio, read newspapers or works of fiction, attend the theatre or cinema, use computers, mobile phones or the internet, study at university, join a trade union or professional association, and vote in a political election. Their places of worship have no windows through which outsiders might observe them, and they live in detached houses because they are not permitted to share any facilities with outsiders. If a member leaves the movement, he or she has to move out of the family home.

Social integration is double-sided. Even if a group aims for greater acceptance by, and closer integration into, the wider society, it is not necessarily granted. Some of the group's beliefs and practices may seem so bizarre or offensive to outsiders that they act as a barrier to wider acceptance. The former Mormon practice of polygamy continues to be a barrier to respectability. The Supreme Court handed down a landmark judgment in 1878 in the Reynolds case, ruling that religious belief does not justify the performance of acts such as polygamy that are contrary to the law; the First Amendment protects religious belief, not illegal religious practices. Although the Mormon Church continued to resist, the fate of polygamy was sealed. The federal authorities tightened their grip with the passing of the Edmunds–Tucker Act in 1887: more and more Mormons were prosecuted for polygamy, Mormon assets were at risk of being seized, and the Church was threatened with closure if it persisted. To most Americans, polygamy was an abomination comparable to slavery. Eventually the Church gave in, and grudgingly abandoned polygamy in 1890. Polygamy remains a symbolic problem for the Mormon Church, which is obliged to put some effort into justifying the fact that Mormons ever practised it.

Denominations and cults: tolerating diversity

Although the church–sect dichotomy has been a powerful tool of analysis, it is limited in its field of application historically and culturally. The contrast of church and sect is characteristically Christian, with some parallels, but no exact equivalents, in other traditions. It applies to an era of Christendom in which churches embraced the national population and enjoyed wide-ranging privileges granted by the state (B. S. Turner 1991: 172). In that social context, sects and churches were polar opposites.

That was never the situation in the United States. There is no national church enjoying cultural supremacy or special legal privileges. In the American context, the Episcopal Church, the Roman Catholic Church, the Methodist Church and so on are all, in a sociological perspective, denominations. The key characteristic of the denomination is that it sees itself as *pluralistically legitimate* (Wallis 1976): that is, as one of a variety of valid paths to salvation. This is in contrast to the *unique legitimacy* claimed by churches and sects, which offer themselves as the one true path to salvation.

The denominational form is ideally suited to a consumer society. Switching between denominations is very common in the United States; the 2001 American Religious Identification Survey (Kosmin et al. 2001) found that 16 per cent of the adult population had switched their religious preference or identification at least once. This does not usually reflect a conversion experience in the sense that the person has undergone a fundamental transformation of identity. It is, rather, a change of allegiance, often caused by other changes of social status, including geographical mobility, social mobility and marriage. People's religious 'preferences' are like their choice of supermarket: a question of taste shaped by socio-economic status. This has often been taken by European commentators to demonstrate that American religiosity is shallow, even 'secularized from within'. The equation of consumerism with superficiality may, however, be nothing other than the cultural snobbery of intellectuals.

In European societies, churches are gradually losing their legal privileges. They no longer have either the capacity or the desire to discriminate against other religious groups. They are more and more willing to take part in co-operative ecumenical ventures with fellow Christians and with members of other faiths as well. As in North America, there is a gravitational pull towards denominationalism.

Wallis's typology includes the cult as a distinctive form of social organization. Like sects, cults are deviant rather than respectable, but they nevertheless define themselves in a non-exclusive manner. In Wallis's phrase, they are 'epistemologically individualist', whereas sects are 'epistemologically authoritarian'. This means that the cult's members enjoy a degree of freedom to work out their own path to salvation on the principle, 'if it works for you . . .'. Cults do not necessarily have a strong definition of membership. It is easy to drift into and out of them without crossing any very clear threshold in either direction. It is also possible to be associated with several different cults simultaneously. There is a 'cultic milieu' (Campbell 1972), made up of alternative therapies, complementary medicine, techniques of divination, and a wide variety of occult beliefs and practices. Cults are not necessarily 'religious' in the conventionally accepted sense. So, for example, Transcendental Meditation is treated by most of its practitioners as a technique for relaxation and relieving stress, without reference to its origins in Hinduism.

Not all cults are fully-fledged cult movements; some are better described as either audience cults or client cults (Stark and Bainbridge

1985: 26–9), neither of which make exacting demands on the people associated with them. *Audience cults* have only a minimal level of organization, and lack an authority structure through which commands could be
issued. In any case, they have nobody to command: they do not have
members, but an audience of consumers. Audience cults spread their
message mainly through the mass media. Many New Age cults are
heavily reliant on magazines and books, supplemented by audio cassettes
and compact discs, and a loosely structured lecture circuit. *Client cults*
are based on relationships between practitioners and their clients. Here
too the level of formal organization is limited. Clients are individuals, not
a community. In the past, as Stark and Bainbridge remark, client cults
offered miraculous cures, clairvoyance and contact with departed spirits;
now the emphasis has switched towards holistic therapy and healing.

Just as there is no universal one-way sect-to-church process, so the
dynamics of denominations and cults is complex and variable. Wallis
(1976) shows how Scientology developed into a sect from the cult known
as Dianetics. In its origins, Dianetics had been a relatively open-minded
therapeutic system. Its practitioners and clients had a degree of freedom
to experiment with therapeutic techniques, pragmatically adopting those
which seemed to work and discarding any which did not. This led to
potentially damaging schisms within the movement, as rival practitioners set up their own variants of Dianetics. Hubbard established his
authority by a fierce assertion of epistemological authoritarianism. Rival
practitioners were ejected as heretics. As part of this process of transition
to sectarianism, Scientology adopted more and more the character and
trappings of a religion. It was during this period that frequent clashes
took place between the Church of Scientology and the state – in the USA,
the UK, the Federal Republic of Germany and Australia. Scientology
was far more threatening as an authoritarian religious sect than it had
been when it was an individualistic therapeutic cult.

A contrasting pattern of development is shown by the Religious
Society of Friends (Quakers). The Quaker faith arose in mid-
seventeenth-century Britain as a religious protest movement under the
leadership of George Fox. The movement rapidly developed in a sectarian direction until the middle of the nineteenth century. Quakers
objected to paying tithes – the 10 per cent of earnings that everyone was
required to contribute to the upkeep of the ministers of the established
Church of England. Quakers rejected churchly sacramentalism along
with any development of a professional ministry distinct from the laity.
In the public sphere, not only did Quakers refuse to swear oaths, they
also formulated a Peace Testimony in 1661, which for most members
signifies an unswerving commitment to pacifism.

Quakers worked to preserve their own culture. They adhered to puritanical values of thrift, hard work, deferred gratification and abstinence from extravagant worldly pleasures. They founded their own schools, through which Quaker culture was transmitted. They were marked out by what they called their 'peculiarities' – their sober attire and their special dialect with its archaic forms of address ('thees and thous', now thought of as formal, but in origin expressions of intimacy, as in the French *tu* and the German *du*). They upheld a strong membership principle, frequently disowning people for marrying out, or for attending the theatre or other unrighteous entertainments.

In the latter part of the nineteenth century the Society of Friends began to move away from an inward-turned sectarian position. One sign of this was the rise of great Quaker business enterprises such as Cadbury's, Fry's and Rowntree's (all chocolate manufacturers), the Friends' Provident insurance company, and Lloyd's and Barclay's banks. (Quaker Oats, ironically, had no connection to the Quakers.) The success of these enterprises can be seen as evidence of the relationship between the Protestant ethic and the spirit of capitalism (see pages 76–8). Their wealth needed to be justified in religious terms. Hence the concerned paternalism of Quaker enterprises, and their engagement in philanthropic projects.

In the twentieth century the Society of Friends emerged fully from its earlier inward-turned sectarianism. Elements of Quaker culture remain, but have evolved out of their sectarian setting of Quaker 'peculiarities'. Quakers no longer have a distinctive dress; even so, they typically wear plain clothes dictated by practical considerations. They do not have a tradition of 'dressing up' for meetings for worship, and are not usually fashion victims. In speech, although they have long abandoned 'thees and thous', Quakers are not enthusiasts for worldly titles and honours, preferring informal use of first names and family names unadorned. They will not take formal oaths, and do not engage in 'promises', since these add nothing: if you say you will do something, you should do it ('let your yea be yea and your nay be nay'). Most Quakers no longer avoid the theatre as a morally corrupt milieu; even so, they are unlikely to be found on ostentatious display in the expensive boxes at the opera or the ballet. Quaker schools have lost their key role as transmitters of Quaker culture; nevertheless, education and self-improvement remain core values for Quakers.

The Society of Friends has evolved into a denomination. In terms of their external conception, Quakers have achieved respectability, reflected in the overwhelmingly middle- and professional-class composition of their membership, and the good ecumenical relations that the Society

enjoys with mainstream Christian churches. As for their internal conception, Quakers do not see themselves as a people with a unique
command of the truth. On the contrary, Quakers have consistently
refused to develop binding doctrines and dogmas. They are epistemological individualists. Their emphasis is on a Quakerly approach, a
Quakerly inflection on how to do things. For example, Quaker decision
making involves a painstaking search for consensus, 'the mind of the
meeting', reminiscent of Rousseau's 'the general will'. Quaker deliberations are not adversarial debates followed by democratic voting – what
Rousseau called 'the will of the majority'. This Quakerly way presents
itself as one approach alongside and working with others – a quintessentially denominational viewpoint.

New religious movements

A startling transformation of the religious scene in the West has been
the emergence of new religious movements, particularly since the late
1960s. They include the most controversial social movements in the
modern world. Some have even shown themselves to be life-threatening
to the wider society (the Manson Family and Aum Shinrikyō, for
instance) and to their own members (the Peoples Temple and Heaven's
Gate). In complete contrast, movements such as Transcendental
Meditation have a large clientele of respectable people and business
corporations, who use TM as a technique to achieve personal and career
goals in this world. Clearly, as with long-established religions, new religious movements are not all alike.

An influential classification of new religious movements was proposed by Wallis (1984). His aim was to develop a classification that
would be useful in analysing new religions in the West since the Second
World War; he was not aiming at a set of universal categories beyond
space and time. His classification is rooted in the social, economic and
cultural conditions in which new religious movements have emerged,
conditions that determined the resources available to them. He distinguished three ideal types: world-rejecting, world-affirming and world-
accommodating.

World-rejecting

Examples of this type are the International Society for Krishna
Consciousness (Hare Krishna), the Unification Church (the Moonies),

The Family (formerly known as the Children of God); the Peoples Temple, the Manson Family, and Heaven's Gate. This world-rejecting category includes the most controversial new religious movements, many of which have been prime targets of anti-cult pressure groups.

World-rejecting new religious movements are the ones that most closely resemble the epistemologically authoritarian sect. They and they alone have the truth. They impose uncompromising standards of conduct on their followers, standards which they demand in the name of an emotionally remote personal deity – a God more of judgement than of love. Human beings are seen as sinful creatures whose salvation can be achieved only through obedience to God's commandments. The price of membership is high – literally so in cases such as The Family and the Peoples Temple, where followers were encouraged to surrender their assets to the movement. Members must show uncritical obedience to the leadership and enthusiastic commitment to the cause. This entails ascetic, self-denying lifestyles, sometimes in the context of communal life in a temple, an ashram or some other form of religious community.

The community holds that there is no salvation outside the faith. Non-members are often branded with derogatory terms – for example 'Karmies', which for devotees of the Hare Krishna movement signals that those outside are locked in the karma–samsara cycle: that is, a life of karma (action) followed by death and rebirth with no hope of release.

Stigmatization of outsiders is sometimes used to justify exploiting them – for example, by asking for donations to 'charity' while concealing the movement's true identity. To Moonies, this misrepresentation is known as 'heavenly deception'. It is justified by their dualistic conception of the world as a battlefield in the war between God and Satan. The same thinking lay behind The Family's 'flirty fishing' – the practice of women members offering sex to powerful outsiders in return for conversion or financial and political support.

In general, apart from the sale of cheap trinkets to raise money, and an occasional show of charitable work, world-rejecting movements do not offer goods and services to the wider society.

Millenarian movements are important instances of the world-rejecting type. These are movements that expect an imminent apocalyptic collapse of the existing world order and its replacement by a perfect, new dispensation. In the Christian tradition this involves active belief in the Second Coming of Christ. A Muslim parallel is belief in the Mahdi. In Shi'a Islam, the Mahdi is the 'hidden imam', the religious leader who will reappear and establish a reign of peace and justice according to the will of Allah.

Many contemporary millenarian movements are what Wilson (1970: 93–117) calls revolutionist. Members are not active revolutionaries participating as political agitators or armed combatants in the war against ungodliness. Instead, they are waiting for God to bring about the apocalypse. Jehovah's Witnesses are one example of the revolutionist stance. They are good citizens, not seditionists. It is Jehovah who will wage the war of Armageddon against Satan; the Witnesses' task is to obey Jehovah's commandments and to bring the Truth to as many people as they can before it is too late.

What categories of people have been attracted to world-rejecting movements? Wallis (1984: 120) specifies two factors. First, these movements appeal to people who are marginal to their own society or have been marginalized by it. This factor by itself is not decisive, for many disprivileged groups – the poor, old people, ethnic minorities – are repelled by world-rejecting new religions. The latter are not, in Lanternari's (1963) phrase, 'the religions of the oppressed'. Their appeal has been mainly to white, middle-class, well-educated young people (though the Peoples Temple is an exception to this). The second factor is that world-rejecting movements attract people whose values are at odds with those of the wider society. They offer an invitation to 'drop out'. Because of the rigours of life in world-rejecting movements, for many members their stay is a temporary one. Movements such as the Moonies have always had a very rapid turnover of members, as Barker (1984: 141–8) clearly demonstrates.

Putting Wallis's two factors together, it becomes clear why world-rejecting movements have attracted young white adults from economically comfortable backgrounds. These are the people for whom 'dropping out' may be not only appealing but also feasible, with good prospects of re-entry back into society after the period of 'time out'. Even here, it is only a minority of young people who are attracted in the first place. For all the public concern, media coverage and political rhetoric, world-rejecting religions have a tiny membership.

Whatever efforts these movements may make to cultivate political support – as the Moonies did in the USA – they are unlikely to receive it for long. They are often deeply unpopular with the public and have few friends in high places. No politician would make the mistake of thinking that votes could be won by supporting them. Their survival depends on the civil liberties they claim for themselves under the Constitutions of Western democracies; significantly, they do not flourish in undemocratic societies. The rhetoric of world-rejecting movements, and occasionally their reality, provokes widespread concern about the threat they pose to society and to their own members. Evil purposes are attributed to them, together with sinister techniques of 'brainwashing' or 'mind control' (see chapter 8) .

World-affirming

World-affirming movements, as Wallis's term implies, find much to value in the world. People are seen not as sinful but as blinkered, restricted, held back. What they need is liberation, and this is primarily individual, rather than collective. Although expressed in all manner of different ways, the mission of world-affirming movements is essentially the same: to enable us to unlock the potential that lies hidden in us all. Implicit in this is an optimistic philosophy of human perfectibility. Examples of such movements are Transcendental Meditation (TM), *est* (Erhard Seminars Training), Scientology, and the Human Potential Movement.

The ethos of world-affirming movements is individual self-realization. They offer a set of techniques that virtually anyone can use to improve their mental, spiritual and physical powers. The techniques can be taught painlessly. No special talent is needed to practise TM or Scientology. Practitioners do not cut themselves off from contact with friends and family, withdraw from college, or abandon a promising career. On the contrary, personal relationships, educational achievements and career goals are all supposed to benefit. Because of this, world-affirming movements are seldom accused of breaking up families or causing people to drop out.

Bruce (1995: 98–9) points out that there are two varieties of world-affirming movement. On the one hand, there are those which have added a spiritual dimension to Western secular psychotherapies. Bruce's example is Insight, a movement that became fashionable in Britain in the late 1970s. Insight's training aimed to liberate people from fear, guilt, anxiety and the clutter of negative self-images, thereby empowering them to take responsibility for their own lives. On the other hand, there are movements that have taken an Eastern religious-philosophical system and adapted it to Western sensibilities. Bruce's example here is Transcendental Meditation.

Wallis identifies three related themes in world-affirming movements. First, they claim to help people not only to succeed but also to cope with the stress of individual achievement in a competitive capitalist society. Sometimes people are advised to lower their expectations to a more realistic level – a prominent theme in *est*. Wallis (1984: 30) quotes *est*'s founder, Werner Erhard: 'Happiness is a function of accepting what is.'

This means that people should abandon any false hopes of greener grass elsewhere. Simply changing your job, your home or your partner is unlikely to deliver what you hoped for. As Bruce says (1995: 101), 'movements which promise empowerment often actually deliver acceptance of the status quo'.

Second, world-affirming movements emphasize the 'true' self. People are encouraged to cast off the social constraints of convention and tradition and the personal shackles of repression and inhibition. 'Authenticity' and 'spontaneity' are valued and cultivated.

Third, world-affirming movements offer strategies for coping with the loneliness of modern life. Their emphasis on self-discovery often goes together with a quest for intimate contact and authentic relationships with other people, usually in the supposedly 'safe' emotional environment of the movement.

Most of the people who use the services of world-affirming movements do so as consumers. The consumer is at the opposite pole from what Weber called a religious *virtuoso*. Religious virtuosity involves rigorous discipline suitable for only a few exceptional individuals. For example, the celibacy of Catholic and some Orthodox priests is virtuoso religion. It is not expected of rank-and-file members of the faith; on the contrary, their vocation, traditionally, is to marry and have children. In church-type organizations, religious virtuosity is forbidden to the majority. A graphic example of religious virtuosity in the Christian tradition is provided by the stylites of the fifth to tenth centuries. These were ascetics who spent the whole of their life on the top of a pillar. Food and drink were supplied by their disciples. The stylites devoted most of their time to prayer and contemplation. They also provided services to others, such as reconciling quarrels and adjudicating theological disputes. Their inspiration, St Simeon Stylites, was a renowned champion of orthodoxy against heresy. Even in the warmer regions of Christendom, theirs was a harsh existence.

World-affirming movements have an inner core of committed members – devotees or adepts – who practise more advanced techniques. In the case of Transcendental Meditation, these techniques, known as *sidhis*, include yogic flying (levitation). The ordinary consumer of TM is not required to participate in the *sidhis*, and may not even know about them.

World-affirming movements often have the organizational structure and managerial style of secular multinational corporations. The goods and services they provide are efficiently marketed as commodities. In line with their commercially inspired customer orientation, they arrange their courses and seminars at times convenient to clients. Since the mass market in the West is urban rather than rural, the 'good life' they celebrate is not a back-to-nature rural idyll, but a more urban and cosmopolitan success story.

In the spirit of a consumer service, Transcendental Meditation describes itself as 'a simple, natural, effortless procedure' that requires 'no effort or concentration, no special skills, and no change of lifestyle'. It conveniently takes only two twenty-minute periods of mediation per day. Everybody can benefit; students, for example, are promised more efficient learning, enhanced creativity, higher IQ and better grades. These results, the movement claims, have been demonstrated by independent scientific research.

Movements of this kind are not overtly 'religious' as religion is conventionally understood in the West. Some of the signs of religion that the state looks for may be lacking: consecrated buildings, collective worship of a deity, an ethical code, a set of divine commandments, or a formal theology with dogmas and creeds. Because of this, their status as religions is often contested.

In contrast to world-rejecting movements, they draw their membership not from the socially marginal but from the socially integrated. These are the very people whose material success and prosperity leave them caught in the pressures of contemporary capitalism. It is precisely to such a constituency that world-affirming movements pitch their message.

On the face of it, world-affirming movements are the ones most in tune with the modern world, but that has not prevented controversy. The absence or attenuation of features that are conventionally expected of religions leaves them open to the accusation that they are not 'really' religions at all. Their claims to religious status may be thought to reflect their desire to secure respectability, legal protection and tax advantages. At worst, they may be thought of as no more than fraudulent schemes to raise large amounts of money from gullible people. The fact that Scientological auditing is a never-ending and expensive process is taken by its critics as proof that it is no more than an elaborate swindle.

The second major problem facing world-affirming movements is that their system for releasing human potential may bring them into conflict with well-established professional groups. Scientology again provides an example. It has campaigned aggressively against ECT (electroconvulsive therapy), psychosurgery and the medical use of psychotropic drugs such as Prozac (Barker 1995: 174). Scientological literature on psychiatry is uncompromisingly hostile. Psychiatry is characterized as a pseudo-science lacking any evidential basis for its pretentious theories and barbaric treatments. It is a massive and dangerous deception perpetrated on vulnerable people by powerful vested interests. Psychiatrists routinely misdiagnose physical ailments as psychiatric conditions. Frail elderly people are particularly at risk of being subjected to ECT, and the reason, at least in the United States, is financial: Medicare (US government medical insurance) will pay. ECT and psychosurgery are social control in the guise of treatment; their primary effect is not to cure patients but to render them docile.

More profoundly still, the Church of Scientology accuses psychiatry of being not merely a pseudo-science but a crude anti-religious substitute for religion. Psychiatry is a conscious conspiracy: it has targeted religion as the enemy, and has sought to infiltrate irreligion into the educational system. Psychiatry has corroded personal morality and social order. No wonder, the Church says, there is so much mental illness among psychiatrists themselves. Here is a vivid example of a minority religious movement reflecting back to society the very accusations that are made against the movement itself.

World-accommodating

Examples of world-accommodating religious movements are Subud, ECKANKAR, the Aetherius Society, Western forms of the Japanese movement Sōka Gakkai, and neo-Pentecostal movements such as charismatic renewal. Wallis has relatively little to say about movements of this type, on the ground that they have been less important than the others (Wallis 1984: 5). Some writers such as Bruce (1995, 1996) omit the world-accommodating type altogether, though this seems an unnecessary loss of conceptual precision.

World-accommodating movements are largely content with, or at least indifferent to, the world. Instead, they are concerned to cultivate their members' interior spiritual life through collective forms of worship or spiritual exercise. Members of ECKANKAR, for example, engage in a spiritual quest for direct personal experience of the Light and Sound of God. One outcome may be that members perform their secular tasks more effectively. But that is not the goal. As Wallis says, such worldly consequences are unintended, rather than designed.

Unlike the world-rejecting type, these are not movements of social protest. They do, however, express a different form of protest, one which is less against the world than against religious institutions that are held to be spiritually lifeless. Thus charismatic renewal aims at reinvigorating the spiritual life of Christians, and in particular restoring to contemporary Christianity its long-lost access to charismatic blessings such as *glossolalia*. Christian congregations have found themselves bit-terly divided into supporters and opponents of charismatic practices. Dancing, hugging and kissing, speaking in tongues, faith healing, exor-cism, non-traditional forms of worship, abandoning the organ and switching to the guitar and the tambourine: all these have aroused deep passions. They are, however, domestic troubles. Unless an individual is demonstrably harmed (as occasionally with exorcism), the mass media are not interested, and fewer and fewer people outside the churches either know or care about them.

World-accommodating movements typically have a mainly middle-class membership. They do not attract socially marginal groups, and joining them does not involve 'dropping out'. Members are free to decide whether or not to reveal their religious identity to outsiders. Involvement can therefore be unobtrusive, and may have little impact on a member's lifestyle or life chances. This is shown by the case of the Aetherius Society, which was founded in the 1950s by George King (Wallis 1975: 17–34). The society claims to have established the con-nections between yoga, unidentified flying objects, and the theology of all the great religions. In alliance with Cosmic Masters such as Aetherius, who inhabit the higher planes of other planets, the society's members take part in esoteric rituals in a cosmic battle against the forces of metaphysical evil. Their mission as cosmological warriors on behalf of the human race and planet earth does not prevent them from return-ing unremarked to conventional work roles.

It is not hard to see why world-accommodating movements are seldom controversial. Their members, who are mostly middle class and respectable, are not prevented from carrying out their secular work; nor are intimate relations with family and friends under any obvious threat. World-accommodating movements are not protesting against the world; at worst, they are indifferent to it. Their overriding concern is with the spiritual life of their members. This means that they are not engaged in what could be construed as political activity threatening major social institutions or even the state itself.

When, rarely, world-accommodating movements attract controversy, it tends not to become politicized. Spiritualism, for example, has been dogged from the outset by persistent accusations of fraud. Margaret and Kate Fox are often seen as among the founders of the modern Spiritualist movement in the United States. Their public demonstrations and seances persuaded many people that they were genuine mediums who possessed the power to contact the spirits of the dear departed, conveying reassuring messages to their loved ones here on earth. Then, following intense public scrutiny and a destructive addiction to alcohol,

Margaret confessed in 1888 that Spiritualism was a sham. As young girls, she and her sister had mischievously produced strange noises in the house to frighten their mother. The reality behind the noises was banal: Margaret and Kate used to tie an apple to a piece of string and bump it on the floor. Because the children were so young, adults naïvely believed they were incapable of fraud. (In the twentieth century, similarly, some parents of adolescent children were more inclined to believe in poltergeists than in teenage personality problems.) Later in their career, the Fox sisters developed slightly more sophisticated techniques, not least the ability to make the joints of their toes crack, producing unusual sounds whose origins appeared mysterious.

Three years after making her confession, Margaret Fox retracted it, claiming that the confession, and not her spirit mediumship, was bogus. This pattern of confession followed by retraction, which is not uncommon, has supplied both true believers and sceptics with material to support their case, so controversy never ends. Despite this, Spiritualism has not provoked fear or loathing, but at worst mockery.

The categories world-rejecting, world-affirming and world-accommodating are put forward as ideal types. Any given religious movement may well exhibit features of more than one type, and this can give rise to bitter internal conflicts. One example is the Divine Light Mission, which originated in India in the 1930s as part of the Radhasoami movement, an offshoot of Sikhism (Wallis 1984: 81–3; Barker 1995: 176–8). The Divine Light Mission was consolidated as an independent movement in the 1960s, and brought to the West in 1971 by the founder's youngest son, the thirteen-year-old Guru Maharaj Ji. Initially, the movement stressed its world-rejecting, ascetic origin. It sought to recruit young people disillusioned with the counterculture. Devotees ('premies') were invited into the spartan and celibate communal life of the ashram, or 'premie house', where they would be instructed by senior practitioners known as 'mahatmas'. Guru Maharaj Ji was seen as a saviour, the Satguru or Perfect Master, who would usher in the millennium. But after the dismal failure of its sparsely attended Millennium 73 festival in the Houston Astrodome, the movement adopted a world-affirming position. It offered 'the Knowledge', in the form of techniques of meditation, to a diverse clientele who were not expected to join an ashram. The trappings of an Asian faith were abandoned as the movement became overtly Westernized. One symbol of this was that the guru married a white American and broke with his Indian family of origin. He repudiated any claims to divine status, discarded traditional Indian dress in favour of business suits, and abandoned the title Guru Marahaj Ji, preferring to be known either as Marahaji or by his family name, Prem

Rawat. The name of the movement was changed to Elan Vital, the ashrams were dissolved, and the terms 'premie' and 'mahatma' were dropped. The erstwhile divine guru was repackaged as 'an inspirational speaker'.

Prem Rawat claims to offer practical methods by which anyone can achieve spiritual tranquillity. Originally he aspired to bring about world peace, but now he focuses on the needs of the individual, which he says take priority over the demands of society. Elan Vital has sought to move out of the spotlight of adverse publicity (Barker 1995: 178), and has gravitated toward the world-accommodating type of religious movement.

The limits of classification

Wallis presents his typology as addressing a particular cultural context: the rise of 'new religious movements' in Western societies in the 1960s and 1970s. Surprisingly, though, he does not explain why his approach is so well suited to those movements in that period. I would argue that the typology reflects Western societies' concern with the apparent 'newness' of these movements, where newness connotes two things: the 'alien' religious movements, which were particularly problematic if they rejected the wider society's norms and values, and the 'invented' quasi-religions, which zealously endorsed Western values but proposed deviant methods of fulfilling them. Young people in particular were thought to be at risk from both types of movement.

Western preoccupations in the twenty-first century have changed. The focus is now on a different challenge: not new religious movements, but minority communities of the major world faiths. The problems of Western youth have been displaced by the dilemmas of multiculturalism.

We shall never arrive at a universally agreed classification of religious movements that will stand for all time. The reason for this is exactly the same as the reason why no final definition of religion is possible. Society and culture change, and religion changes with them. Thus the classic church–sect dichotomy was useful in analysing Christian societies when a particular church was closely associated with the nation-state. This church–state dichotomy never fitted the American religious scene, and has less and less relevance even in Europe. Hence the emergence of the concept of the denomination. In the late 1960s, however, the church–denomination–sect trichotomy came under increasing strain because of the unpredicted rise of new religious movements, many originating in

Eastern faiths. This led to a period of theoretical ferment, in which the concept of the 'cult', variously defined, was widely deployed to explain the so-called new religious consciousness. More recently still, as will be discussed in the final chapter, existing categories of analysis have been called into question by a 'cultural turn' from religion to spirituality.

4

Secularization: The Social Insignificance of Religion?

There is a strong case for saying that a concern with religion was at the very heart of classical sociological theory (Wilson 1982: 9). What is problematic is to assess the legacy of classical theorizing to the contemporary sociology of religion. A key issue is that the majority of the founders of the discipline of sociology were personally atheists and professionally preoccupied with the *decline* of religion and its eventual replacement by other social institutions and modes of thought (Beckford 1989: 42). Their work laid the foundation for the contemporary secularization thesis.

The majority of classical theorists were also rationalists, not simply in the weak sense that they held reason to take precedence over other means of acquiring understanding, but in the strong sense that for them reason was the only path to knowledge. This meant denying that knowledge can come through divine revelation. It also tended to encourage a triumphalist celebration of Western scientific progress, together with a judgement that Western civilization is superior to all others. The value of the classical legacy to contemporary sociology is therefore problematic.

Auguste Comte and the Law of Three Stages

In his monumental *Cours de philosophie positive* ('A Course in Positive Philosophy'), published in six volumes between 1830 and 1842, Auguste Comte set out a grand theory of the evolution of society and human understanding. It was formulated as the Law of Three Stages, which he conceived as a necessary and progressive evolutionary sequence.

In the *theological* stage, phenomena are explained as the actions of fictitious gods and spirits, supernatural beings who are similar to humans though far more powerful. The theological stage can be subdivided into three phases: first, fetishism, in which each individual object is thought to be inhabited by an indwelling spirit; second, polytheism, in which the world is peopled by spirits operating in particular spheres – gods of the forest, of the field, of the waters and so on; and third, monotheism, the phase of the great salvation religions of the world. In the theological stage, society is organized hierarchically, with power shared between the priesthood and the military.

In the *metaphysical* stage, phenomena are explained in relation to the operation of abstract entities and forces such as Nature. Religion as conventionally understood is gradually displaced. Society is governed by churchmen and lawyers. This stage is, as Comte said, only a modification of the theological stage, and thus merely transitional.

In the *positive* stage, explanations are liberated from religion and metaphysics to become truly scientific. Science rests on observation, and aims to discover the laws governing the operation of the natural and social worlds. Scientists are not encumbered with religious or metaphysical baggage, and do not address unanswerable questions about the purpose of creation or the meaning of life (Comte's legacy to the logical positivists of the twentieth century is evident here). Society is ruled by experts, the latter-day equivalent of Plato's philosopher-kings, with sociologists at the top of the scientific hierarchy. Their guiding principle is summed up in Comte's formula: *savoir pour prévoir et prévoir pour pouvoir* – 'knowledge for foreknowledge and foreknowledge for action' (Thompson 1976: 15).

In Comte's scheme the positive stage is the end-point of history. Although science will of course develop, there will be no fourth, post-positive stage – for what could such a stage be, other than a regression to irrationality?

Comte's grand three-stage scheme of societal change also applies to the development of scientific disciplines. Each of the sciences undergoes a transition from a theological, and therefore fictive, beginning, through an abstract metaphysical interlude, to the positive scientific goal. Sciences develop at different rates. Those that have 'simpler' subject matter, such as mathematics, physics and chemistry, develop sooner than more complex sciences such as biology and sociology. Individuals also go through the same three stages. Comte asks us to examine our own biography: 'Now does not each one of us, when he looks at his own history, recall that he was successively a *theologian* in childhood, for his most important ideas, a *metaphysician* in his youth, and a *physicist* in his maturity?' (Andreski 1974: 20). The history of the individual replicates the history of the species, or, in scientific terms, ontogeny repeats phylogeny.

The Judaeo-Christian world-view, like the Islamic, treats history as linear. The dominant macro-sociological theories of social change advanced by Western sociologists share the Judaeo-Christian perspective. Thus Comtean positivism, Parsonian evolutionism and Marxian dialectical materialism all incorporate a linear philosophy of history. History marches onward to a goal, and we are expected to march optimistically with it. The goal – whether the Kingdom of God or the various secular visions of the good society – is a glorious end-state of which we are usually told very little, except that it will neither be overthrown nor evolve into something else. Arguably, then, the appeal of these sociological theories is that they resonate with the Jewish and Christian faiths, of which they are secular reworkings. They are convincing because they conform to a template laid down over the centuries. Although they relocate the Kingdom of God from heaven to earth, we can still recognize it as the Kingdom.

For Comte, religion fails as a system for understanding the world, natural or social. Nevertheless, the question remains: does religion perform useful functions in society? Here the answer is less clear-cut. Comte expresses a concern that has been echoed by countless successors: that religion distracts human attention away from action in this world and reorients it towards a transcendent order to which this world is supposedly subordinate. Appeasing the non-existent gods becomes more important than altruistic action towards our fellow humans. Religion threatens scientific progress and weakens the social fabric. It is perhaps worth noting that Comte is famous for having invented two words. One was 'sociology', the other 'altruism'.

Comte argued that religion as conventionally understood would have to be replaced by a positive religion with sociologists as its high priests. We need to love something greater than ourselves, and society needs spiritual power. Religion meets these individual and social needs. Hence Comte's proposed religion of humanity, which drew heavily on medieval symbols and rituals, and celebrated collectivism and humanity in the abstract (Beckford 1989: 26–7).

To those who read him today, Comte's proposals for the religion of humanity seem absurd, and the role assigned to sociologists at worst vainglorious and at best laughable. As Nisbet (1967: 228) says, 'it is often hard to remember that we are reading the works not of a theologian but of a self-proclaimed scientist'. His vision is sometimes excused as the product of the mental illness that periodically assailed

him. Yet there may be at least one point in its favour – its universalism. Raymond Aron, who was no disciple of Comte, defended him
against his sternest critics (Aron 1968: 108). Comte celebrated the best
in humanity. He did not select one particular tribal faith and insist
that it be imposed on everyone else. And at least he did not hold
up any existing or imaginary socio-economic order as the object of
veneration.

Karl Marx and the projection theory of religion

Karl Marx (1818–83) was born in Trier into a Jewish family living in
a Catholic region of Germany. Although both his parents' families
had a strong rabbinical tradition, his father Heschel was a cosmopolitan intellectual influenced by Voltaire, Rousseau and other rationalist Enlightenment philosophers. Heschel converted somewhat
reluctantly to Protestantism in order to be able to continue practising
as a lawyer, changing his name to Heinrich in the process (McLellan
1973: 1–8).

Throughout his adult life, Karl Marx was an unswerving atheist. He
was a socialist who consistently rejected Christian socialism. Thus,
when Hegel died in 1831, Marx aligned with the radical Left (or
'Young') Hegelians in opposition to the politically and religiously conservative Right (or 'Old') Hegelians. McLellan (1973: 1) begins his
study of Marxism and religion with an ironic account of the experiences of a delegation of Left Hegelians, including Marx, who went to
Paris in 1843 to join forces with French socialists. The German dele-
gates thought that, since they were now in the land of the French
Revolution, they would be mingling with the avant-garde of progressive atheism. They were soon to be disillusioned. Their French
counterparts shared Robespierre's hatred for godlessness. To them,
Christianity was simply socialism in practice, with Jesus the first
Communist.

Hegel himself was a practising Lutheran. Religion plays a progressive role in his philosophy of history, and Protestant Christianity – the
religion of truth and freedom – is held up as the culmination of
humanity's spiritual quest. Martin Luther's challenge to the corrupt
practices, sterile rituals and rigid dogma of the medieval Church was,
according to Hegel, the dawn of the reconciliation of God and
humanity. This implied that before the Reformation, Christianity, like
Judaism and Islam, had constructed a God who stood over and
against his creation. The result of any religion that alienates us from

God is 'an unhappy consciousness', a state in which we are divided against ourselves.

Marx believed that religion had been fully explained once and for all by the Left Hegelian Ludwig Feuerbach in his influential book *The Essence of Christianity*, which was first published in German in 1841 and translated into English in 1854 by Marian Evans (the novelist George Eliot). Pushing Hegelian themes further than Hegel was willing to go, Feuerbach argued that God is a projection of humanity, and Christianity a form of wish-fulfilment. Hegel's 'unhappy consciousness' is the outcome of *all* religions, including Lutheranism. An ideal of human perfection – perfection of knowledge, power and love – is projected outside this world on to a fictive being, God. The properties of omniscience, omnipotence and benevolence are attributed to this being. Belief in life after death is the projection of our aspirations and ideals into another, non-existent world. Religion is a delusion not just of the human intellect, but of the human will and the human heart, and is therefore something far deeper than an intellectual error or a priestly fraud. In projecting our human qualities outward, we impoverish ourselves, creating a God who proceeds to coerce us with his imperious demands. Feuerbach held that religious faith encourages dogmatism, intolerance, arrogance and illiberality, and thereby legitimizes the persecution of unbelievers and heretics. His atheism presents itself as a liberation from this dehumanizing bondage. Humanism implies atheism, since atheism restores to us our true dignity as humans. Atheism will transform us from 'religious and political lackeys of the heavenly and earthly monarchy and aristocracy into free, self-confident citizens of the world'.

Perhaps the greatest twentieth-century exponent of a projection theory of religion was Sigmund Freud (1856–1939). His atheism was pessimistic and stoical, rather than joyous. Freud equated religion with empty consolation, and science with informed resignation (Rieff 1965: 298). The God postulated by theologians and philosophers is an irrelevance; the God who is truly operative in the human psyche is a jealous, oppressive father. Religious faith belongs, therefore, to an infantile stage of personality development, persisting in adults only as an obsessional neurosis. Dispensing with God is necessary to full maturity as a human being.

This was one of the key issues on which Freud's former pupil, Carl Gustav Jung (1875–1961), departed from Freudian orthodoxy. From Jung's perspective, Freud overemphasized the pathological side of life, generalizing from neurotic states of mind to the whole of human experience. This is the case with Freud's diagnosis of religion as obsessional

neurosis. Jung, in contrast, attaches a positive value to all religious traditions. He says that among all his patients in the second half of their
lives – by which he means everyone over thirty-five – 'there has not been
one whose problem in the last resort was not that of finding a religious
outlook on life' (Jung 1961: 264).

Marx regarded Feuerbach's critique of religion as philosophically
definitive, and therefore wasted no time elaborating it. He compared
Feuerbach's analysis to the Copernican revolution: 'Religion is only the
illusory sun which revolves around man so long as he does not revolve
around himself.' Marx would reject inclusive approaches to religion that
see it as a core component of culture and even of human nature.

Feuerbach addressed a public of bourgeois individuals, making an
appeal simply to their powers of reason. This was not the way to change
the world. Thus Marx wrote in 1845 in his *Theses on Feuerbach*: 'The
philosophers have only interpreted the world in various ways, the point
however is to change it.' Capitalism carries within itself the seeds of its
own destruction. Although it depends on religion to maintain social
order, it is nevertheless an agent of secularization. The proletarian
masses would mobilize (or be mobilized) to overthrow the system that
oppressed them, after which they would have no further need of religion.

Religion is, then, a distraction from effective political action in this
world, offering the spurious consolation of a life to come. Religious
movements are measured against the norm of class-based movements,
only to be found deficient (Scott 1990: 39). Religious protest is merely
pre-political, at best paving the way for class action, at worst siphoning
energy from it.

In Marx's famous dictum, religion is 'the opium of the people'.
Religion is an opiate not because it causes euphoria, but because it is a
pain-killer. It is not only that the ruling class cynically promotes religion
in order to keep the masses in check, which is where Lenin placed the
emphasis. The masses turn spontaneously to religion to relieve their
burden. Religion is not a cultural universal, a necessary component of
the human condition, but a product of class society. It is also an epiphe-
nomenon – that is, an effect, but not an independent cause. Religion will
wither away when the conditions that give rise to it are eliminated. In
this respect it is unlike other cultural forms such as the arts and sciences.
They suffer under capitalism, but will be set free under socialism,
whereas religion is irredeemably reactionary.

The Marxian legacy to contemporary sociology is thus double-
edged. On the one hand, religion is a this-worldly phenomenon, a
cultural product open to sociological investigation. Its claims to a tran-

scendental basis are radically debunked. On the other hand, it is hard to escape the conclusion that religion has little significance, being merely a minor element in the ideological apparatus of the state.

Emile Durkheim and the social functions of religion

Emile Durkheim (1858–1917) was born in Epinal in the Vosges. Like Marx, his family had a rabbinical tradition. Also like Marx, he remained an atheist throughout his adult life. His approach was likewise rationalistic. He too believed that religion as a cognitive system is false, and that we arrive at the truth through the natural and social sciences. Despite this, he insisted that religion cannot be written off as a tissue of illusions or a collective hallucination. There is indeed a reality in and behind religion, though it is not what the faithful imagine it to be. The reality is not God, but Society. Religion fulfils important social and psychological functions. Hence, like Comte before him, Durkheim saw the need for social institutions that would fill the role vacated by religion.

Durkheim's definition of religion was discussed above in chapter 2. For him a religion is 'a unified system of beliefs and practices relative to sacred things, that is to say, things set apart and forbidden – beliefs and practices which unite into one single moral community called a Church, all those who adhere to them' (Durkheim 1915: 47).

Durkheim saw religion as essentially social in character. Religion integrates individuals into 'one single moral community'. An individual's religious faith is ultimately derived from the faith of the community. Religion centres on the sacred, and this is a social construct. The power of religion is generated within the community, as men and women signal to each other through symbols and ritual activity that they hold the same things sacred.

Lukes (1973a: 462–77) distinguishes three aspects of Durkheim's theory of religion. First, there is the *causal* aspect. Durkheim argued that religious commitment is generated in social situations characterized by 'collective effervescence', when emotions are bubbling over. Symbolically charged acts of collective worship are the settings in which religious beliefs and imagery are produced, reinforced and made vibrant for the believer. Durkheim's thinking here may have been influenced by contemporary theories of crowd psychology, though without the implication that crowd behaviour is inherently pathological or disruptive.

Durkheim's causal approach extended to examining the ways in which social structure shapes the content of religious beliefs and practices. He sought to show that even the fundamental categories of thought – such as our ideas of time, space and causation – are socially determined. It was a sociological rendering of Kant, a bold attempt to give an empirical sociological answer to key problems in philosophy.

Second, Durkheim's theory of religion has an *interpretative* aspect, offering an explanation of the meaning of religious beliefs and practices. Religion is a kind of mythologized sociology, providing us with categories of thought through which we understand and interpret social life. Religion expresses, symbolizes and dramatizes social relationships. Here then is the heart of religion: through it, society is represented to itself. If a society lacked religion, it would, Durkheim held, also lack a proper consciousness of itself (Parkin 1992: 47). A society without religion, would be profoundly pathological.

Durkheim typically ignores the potentially dysfunctional consequences of religion. Surely religion can involve *mis*representation of one's own society and its relationship with others? What else is the terrible history of Christian anti-Semitism? Or consider the European explorers who 'discovered' the native peoples of the Americas. Europeans had a pressing need to explain who these people were, how they got there, and how 'we' should relate to them. Among the resources that the explorers and the Church drew on was the Bible. The answers to the questions were diverse, but they all implied the superiority of the Christian Europeans to the natives, who were categorized as 'sub-human animals, monsters, degenerate men, damned souls, or the product of a separate creation' (Leach 1982: 74). Religious categories provided a warrant for their elimination or subjugation.

Third, Durkheim's theory has a *functional* aspect. Religion promotes social integration by strengthening the bonds between the individual and the society of which he or she is a member. Religion also performs positive functions for the psyche; quite simply, it is good for us – a point diametrically opposed to Marx's view. Durkheim wrote that the believer 'who has communicated with his god is not merely a man who sees new truths of which the unbeliever is ignorant; he is a man who is stronger (*un homme qui peut davantage*)' (Durkheim 1915: 416). Participating in the cult of the faith brings peace and joy, serenity and enthusiasm.

Durkheim maintained that religion could not possibly be founded on an illusion: 'the unanimous sentiment of the believers of all times cannot be purely illusory' (Durkheim 1915: 417). Were it so, the normal processes of evolutionary selection would have put paid to religion long ago. It is on these grounds that Durkheim rejected the animistic theory put forward by Edward Tylor and the naturistic theory advanced by Herbert Spencer. In both of these theories, religion is bound up with a phantasmagorical world dreamed up by the human imagination.

Despite his declared position, most of Durkheim's readers have concluded that his own account makes religion out to be at least partly an illusion. After all, his famous aphorism is that religion is 'society worshipping itself'. That is certainly not what the believers of all times have thought they were doing. Evans-Pritchard (1965: 63–5) pointed to the paradox: 'if Durkheim's theory of religion is true, obviously no one is going to accept religious beliefs any more; and yet, on his own showing, they are generated by the action of social life itself, and are necessary for its persistence'. Worse, as Aron argued, society's self-worship is surely the height of idolatry. Aron (1970: 68) puts the point more strongly than most of Durkheim's critics: 'To suggest that the object of the religious feelings is society transfigured is not to save but to degrade that human reality which sociology seeks to understand.'

Durkheim's position is similar to Jung's. For Durkheim the reality of religion is social, whereas for Jung it is psychological. Like Durkheim before him, Jung believed that his theory was not reductionist. The psyche is real; hence to say that the truths of religion are psychological is not to rob them of meaning but to endow them with it. It was in this sense that Jung declared, in a famous television interview late in his life, that he did not *believe* in religion but *knew* it to be true.

Durkheim's theory stresses religion's positive impact on the individual and its function in building social cohesion. He offers no account of a dark side of religion for individuals or society. The part that religion can play in stimulating social conflict and legitimizing inequality and oppression is ignored. So too is the role of religious leaders – priests, prophets, preachers, sorcerers, mystagogues, shamans and so on. Durkheim pays no attention to the strategies through which religious entrepreneurs mobilize scarce resources. His focus is on the demand side rather than the supply side of religion – a focus replicated in contemporary approaches to secularization.

Unlike many of his contemporaries, Durkheim was searching for a middle way, as Lukes puts it (1973a: 482), between 'the facile rationalism of the anti-religious and the explanations or justifications of the religious'. Few of his successors think he succeeded. Although he did not judge it feasible to create an artificial surrogate religion, as Comte had tried to do, Durkheim was preoccupied with the fate of religion in the modern world. Just as religion was not founded on an illusion, so 'there is something eternal in religion which is destined to survive all the particular symbols in which religious thought has successively enveloped itself' (Durkheim 1915: 427). Society will always need religion in the sense of a cult of the faith. Durkheim believed that the religion of the future would celebrate individualism. This would not be

individualism as self-indulgence and freedom from social restraint, but
an individualism based on human dignity and moral responsibility.

Very few contemporary social scientists share Durkheim's concern to
ensure that religion has a future. One exception is Ernest Gellner.
Gellner examines two major currents in the modern world, religious
fundamentalism and postmodernism, neither of which he is disposed to
endorse. Fundamentalism is irrationally dogmatic, postmodernism
frivolously irrational. In Durkheimian style, Gellner is searching for a
middle way between them which will preserve the sane inheritance of
the Enlightenment. His outline proposal is an accommodation between
science and religion based on an analogy with the political settlement
achieved in constitutional monarchies such as the UK (Gellner 1992:
91–6). Constitutional monarchs retain the rituals and symbols of true
monarchies, but have transferred effective political power to secular
politicians. Similarly, religion might retain its symbolic role in representing and legitimating the social order, leaving to science the cognitive function of understanding the world.

Although on the face of it this is a Durkheimian approach, Gellner
departs from Durkheim in one critical respect, as Beckford (1996: 43)
points out. Gellner concedes that his so-called constitutional religion is
'an ironic, non-serious faith, disconnected from genuine conviction
about how things truly stand' (Gellner 1992: 93). It is a self-conscious
fantasy, rather like adults sentimentally play-acting a belief in Santa
Claus. Gellner's solution involves a curious concession to something he
despises: the frivolous spirit of postmodernism. It is completely at odds
with Durkheim, for whom religion was concerned with serious matters.
To divorce symbolism from the serious side of life leaves religion poorly
placed to deal with questions of meaning, purpose and evil.

Durkheim's agenda for securing the future of religion reflects his own
age rather than ours. The anxieties of contemporary sociology of religion are to be found in the work of Durkheim's great contemporary,
Max Weber.

Max Weber and the disenchantment of the world

Max Weber (1864–1920) described himself in a letter he wrote in 1909
as 'religiously unmusical'. Although many commentators gloss over
this as if it were a casual or even flippant remark, it may be a profound
and perhaps devastating comment on Weber's inner life. Some writers
suggest that it may have prevented him from understanding the nature
of religion. What are the limits of a musicology undertaken by an

unmusical person? Thus Joachim Wach (1944: 3) said that 'the great scholar's understanding of religion was somewhat impaired by his critical attitude toward it'.

In Weber's perspective, modernity is characterized by rationalization. This is not the same thing as the liberating triumph of enlightened reason. Weber's vision is a long way from Comte's celebration of positivism. Weber's mood is one of resigned and fatalistic pessimism – a mood acutely summarized in Gouldner's (1955) phrase 'metaphysical pathos'. In Weber's view, modernity brings the rule of experts, but these are not benign Comtean scientists. They are bureaucrats. Their outlook on life is summarized by Weber (2001/1920–1: 124) as follows: 'Specialists without spirit, sensualists without heart; this nullity imagines that it has attained a level of civilization never before achieved.'

Rationalization means the spread of legal-rational systems of domination at the expense of both traditional and charismatic systems. In *traditional* systems of domination, rulers claim authority on the basis of the sanctity of customs and traditions handed down to a people from time immemorial – 'the authority of the "eternal yesterday"', as Weber called it (1948: 78). Typically, the tradition is seen as God-given, so that the ultimate answer to the question 'Why should I obey traditional authority?' is that 'God has willed it so'. Traditional leaders govern by right – for example, the Divine Right of Kings, or the right of the eldest son to succeed his father – and obedience takes the form of loyalty and pious deference to them. Traditional domination involves personal relationships between leaders and their subjects. It is the form of authority exercised by monarchs, sultans, feudal lords, patriarchs and tribal chieftains. Their assistants are not office-holders, still less elected representatives, but dependent subordinates (slaves, family members, vassals, barons, courtiers and the like) whose well-being, advancement and even life itself depend on the leader's favour. Although personal in character, traditional authority is not arbitrary, since the leaders are expected to abide by the canons of the sacred tradition, and risk revolt, usurpation or palace revolution if they are seen to depart too drastically from it.

Charismatic systems of domination also involve personal relations between leaders and led. In popular speech *charisma* is used diffusely, referring to individuals who possess qualities that make them photogenic, or sexually attractive, or persuasive, or generally plausible. Weber meant something much more specific. He borrowed the term *charisma* from the Christian tradition, in which it means a divine 'gift of grace'. Charismatic leaders demand obedience in order to transform their followers' lives. They have the authority to determine things that are normally considered matters of private choice: how you dress, how you do your hair, whom you marry. They can dictate such matters very suddenly and, as Barker remarks (1993: 182–3), without a lot of explanation.

The commands that charismatic leaders give often violate the requirements of tradition and the dictates of the law. Charismatic leadership is therefore a source of cultural innovation. Here Weber refers to Jesus's characteristic injunction, 'It is written . . ., but I say unto you'. Charismatic authority implies discipleship, the whole-hearted devotion of followers to the charismatic leader. Faith, not critical evaluation, is the appropriate response. The leader and his or her disciples avoid administrative routine and the mundane activity of earning a living through regular employment. They typically do not have jobs, but depend instead on voluntary donations from the public to whom they minister (Jesus), or sponsorship by wealthy patrons (Krishnamurti), or robbery and extortion (Charles Manson). Charismatic leaders also typically escape the routines of domestic life. Some, like Jesus, are celibate, while others, like Jim Jones, are promiscuous. Avoidance of conventional sex lives and routine ways of earning a living are two of the key ways in which the exceptional qualities of charismatic leaders are symbolized. These people are demonstrably not like the rest of us.

Legal-rational domination is embodied in bureaucratic systems of administration. Authority is impersonal and vested in rules. Commands are obeyed not because of the personal authority of a traditional or charismatic leader, but because they have been issued by the appropriate office-holders acting within their official remit and following approved procedures. Devotion to traditional or charismatic leaders is replaced by meticulous implementation of regulations in conformity to the chain of command within the organization. In contrast to traditional and charismatic systems, legal-rational authority structures separate the person from her or his office. When offices fall vacant, the former incumbent has no say in who should be appointed. A systematic search is undertaken for the person best qualified to fill the post.

In Weber's account of history, the process of modernization makes traditional authority structures obsolete and pushes charismatic systems to the margins of society. Weber's mood in writing of the march of rationalization is not triumphant but resigned. Bureaucracy is described as an 'iron cage' in which we are imprisoned. It stifles human creativity. Legal-rational systems are not necessarily rational in the sense that they involve, in Comtean fashion, the application of scientific expertise for the benefit of humanity. Nor are they necessarily economically efficient. Their rationality is mundane, involving calculation, prediction, measurement and control. If the supreme virtue in a bureaucracy is consistency, the greatest evil is anomaly.

Weber's writings on rationalization have been the inspiration for Ritzer's (1996) concept of 'McDonaldization'. Fast-foot outlets such as McDonalds are, he argues, a paradigm case of rationalization in the era of globalization. Efficiency, calculability, prediction and control are the principles on which they are organized – a modern version of Weberian bureaucracy. Fast, big, standardized and automated: McDonaldization substitutes quantity for quality as the criterion by which goods and services are to be judged.

In true Weberian fashion, Ritzer's analysis is despairing. It is hard to escape from McDonaldization, since more and more sectors of social life have been colonized by it. Its origins lie in twentieth-century American capitalism, but it has fanned out aggressively and is now global in scope (Ritzer 2004). We are doubly ensnared in McDonaldized organizations, both as their seduced consumers and as their alienated employees. Dehumanization of social relations – the ultimate 'irrationality of rationality' – is the essence of McDonaldization. We collaborate as its victims. Having acquired a debauched taste for McDonaldized goods and services, we are fearful of taking the risk of trying something more colourful. Even if escape were possible, most of us would not attempt it. Ritzer's analysis, like Weber's, may ironically become part of the problem, since their cultural pessimism may help to bring about the very thing they deplore: the fatalistic collapse of any resistance to rationalization.

The operation of legal-rational authority structures does not depend on religion for its legitimation. The dominance of bureaucracy is, therefore, at the root of the declining social significance of religion in the modern world. Weber wrote of 'the disenchantment of the world' (*die Entzauberung der Welt*), in the sense that the world has had magic and mystery driven from it. Our forests are managed, not enchanted.

Charismatic leadership and legal-rational systems of domination stand at opposite poles. Charismatic leaders are unpredictable, their lifestyles chaotic, their moods labile, and their commands often unfathomable. The authority of charismatic leaders depends entirely on the support of their followers. If the followers lose faith, the leader is left with no power of command. For this reason the charismatic leader's position is precarious (Parkin 1982: 84). In movements with a charismatic leadership, great effort is devoted to what Barker (1993) calls 'charismatization': socializing people to recognize and orient to charismatic authority. Charismatization is achieved through the accumulation of elements, many of them apparently minor but all of them tending in the same direction, to render charismatic claims plausible. Barker points out that the Unification Church has developed an elaborate 'Moonology' similar to Christology, underpinning the belief that

Moon is Lord of the Second Advent. References to Reverend Moon pepper Moonie discourse, and in Moonie establishments his photograph is everywhere.

In principle, followers have a duty to acknowledge the leader's charismatic quality, so if they are hesitant or doubtful, it is a failing on their part, and one which the leader may come to resent (Bendix and Roth 1971: 175). Lacking the shelter of a bureaucratic office or the sanctity of tradition, the charismatic leader must be ready to perform miracles to satisfy the followers' craving for proof of their leader's charismatic endowment, and to keep them motivated in the face of persecution by the authorities and mockery by unbelievers.

It is therefore a mistake to think that charismatic leaders simply issue commands that followers automatically obey. Leaders may meet resistance, as Muhammad did initially from the people of Mecca, who refused to acknowledge him as the Prophet. Alternatively, leaders may face demands that they are unable or unwilling to satisfy. In the New Testament, Jesus is shown as reluctant to identify himself as Messiah, despite being acclaimed as such by the people (Wach 1944: 338).

The tragedy at Jonestown in 1978 (discussed below in chapter 8), where more than 900 people lost their lives through suicide or execution, can be seen as an instance of the precariousness of charismatic leadership (Johnson 1979). The charismatic leader of the Peoples Temple, the Reverend Jim Jones, felt increasingly insecure. He feared persecution by the US authorities and betrayal from within. As the movement developed, members were propelled into a relationship of ever greater dependence on Jones and his entourage. Total commitment was expected, and found its most graphic symbol in the 'white nights', in which members would enact a collective suicide ritual as a test of their faith. The decisive step was Jones's decision to set up a community in virgin territory in Guyana. Members who moved there became utterly dependent on the movement. They expected Jones to perform miracles – which he faked. Pressure increased as the community struggled to become self-sufficient, and as the US authorities demanded that Jones allow his followers to return to the USA if they wished. According to Johnson's account, Jones was caught in a vicious circle. His followers were more and more dependent on him, and he on them. They brought one another down.

If the authority of charismatic leaders is precarious during their own lifetime, the survival of a charismatic movement after its leader dies is also a challenge. In particular, the question of succession is problematic. It is symbolically inappropriate for the movement to advertise a vacancy and interview the applicants, as if they were seeking a new marketing manager. That is not the way charisma is transmitted. Other means are deployed (Hill 1973: 170–1). They are typically ritualized and rich in symbolism, involving such elements as consulting oracles, praying for divine guidance, and elaborate initiation ceremonies. Weber distinguished three ways in which charisma can be passed on. First, the transmission of charisma can be based on symbolically charged criteria that guarantee the outcome. An example of this is Tibetan Buddhism, which mounts an organized search for the boy child who bears charisma, the new Dalai Lama. Second, the leader may designate his or her successor, sometimes making a surprising choice. Jesus designated Simon (whom he renamed Peter, the rock), a fallible man who would deny him three times. Finally, the leader's close disciples may designate the successor. In essence, this is how the Catholic Church elects a new pope. Cardinals are summoned to Rome, and are secluded in conclave behind locked doors. They are shielded from all communication to or from the outside world, and the whole area is checked for bugging devices. The voting procedure takes place in the Sistine Chapel and is highly ritualized. The world-famous sign that the cardinals' deliberations have reached a conclusion is the emission of white, rather than black, smoke from the chimney – white being an auspicious colour, and one of the papal colours (the other is yellow). Despite the comparative efficiency of information technology, it can safely be predicted that the traditional convergence on Rome is not about to be replaced by e-mail or teleconferencing.

Whatever the method of selection, the duty of the faithful is to acclaim the new leader, who governs by right. Over time, charisma may come to be regarded as hereditary, as in monarchies, thus evolving into the traditional mode of domination.

The death of a charismatic leader can unleash a succession crisis. This happened to ISKCON when its founder, His Divine Grace A. C. Bhaktivedanta Swami Prabhupada, died in 1977. He had entrusted the spiritual well-being of the movement to eleven gurus. Within ten years of his death, many of these had either left the movement or been expelled from it (Barker 1995: 185).

The divisions within Islam turn on the question of succession to the Prophet. In the majority Sunni tradition, Muhammad's successors were caliphs: that is to say, guardians of the faith, its sacred rites and its traditions. Caliphs were not charismatic leaders. Muhammad is the Seal of the Prophets, so no successor can partake of his divine inspiration. After the first four caliphs, who were held to have known Muhammad personally, the caliphate became dynastic until its eventual abolition by Kemal Ataturk in 1924. In the Shi'a tradition, by contrast, Muhammad is held to have appointed Ali as his successor, the first in a line of exemplary prophets or imams, who through divine inspiration are able to interpret the Qur'an infallibly. Hence the continuing influence of a charismatic element in Shi'a Islam, as shown by the authority wielded in Iran by the ayatollahs. Shi'a also embraces a powerful millenarian expectation. The majority among Shi'ites are Imamis, or 'twelvers'. For them the twelfth imam is the Mahdi, the 'hidden imam' who did not die but mysteriously departed, and who will come again to rule in accordance with the will of Allah. In the course of history several charismatic leaders have claimed to be the Mahdi. A minority within the Shi'a tradition are the Isma'ilis, or 'seveners', one branch of whom are followers of the Aga Khan. The Isma'ilis believe that after the death of the sixth imam, his elder son Isma'il, and not Isma'il's brother, should have been designated the seventh imam. Like other branches of Islam, the Isma'ilis have developed their own body of religious philosophy and practice. The example of Islam shows that crises over the theology and practicalities of succession can arise and persist long after the death of the charismatic leader.

For Weber, charismatic leadership tends to become routinized. The life of a charismatic band of disciples is hard. As the movement gains new members and spreads geographically, so pressure mounts to institutionalize practices into formal procedures. When the leader dies, something of his or her charisma dies too. The vibrant and innovative personal charisma of the founder mutates into charisma of office – as with the papacy. This, in turn, gradually shades into traditional authority or bureaucracy. Even so, charisma remains *latent* within the movement as a potential resource for revivalists (Hill 1973: 172). For example, the claim of charismatic renewal within mainstream Christian denominations is to restore to the faithful the gifts of the spirit – in Christian terms, the *charismata* – which were given to the apostles at the first Pentecost. Speaking in tongues, interpretation of tongues, prophecy, healing – these gifts are available to Christians *now*. The charismatic foundation of the Church is thus a resource on which ginger groups can draw to shake the Church out of what they see as its bureaucratic inertia. After all, Weber presented traditional, charismatic and legal-rational forms of domination as ideal types. Any given empirical situation will normally contain a mixture of elements, and these are resources to be argued over and activated.

Even though Weber's best-known work, *The Protestant Ethic and the Spirit of Capitalism* (2001/1920–1), proposes a complex link between Calvinism and modern capitalism (Marshall 1980, 1982), it also carries the implication that contemporary societies have moved beyond the stage of dependence on religion.

Weber was specifically concerned with the rational form of capitalism. Other forms of capitalism exist, but they are not the object of his thesis (Parkin 1982: 41). They are *booty capitalism*, in which wealth is acquired through war, plunder and speculation, as with merchant adventurers; *pariah capitalism*, in which economic activities are undertaken by socially marginalized groups, for example money-lending by Jews in medieval Europe; and *traditional capitalism*, entailing large-scale economic activities which are not, however, designed for the continuing pursuit of profit. Modern *rational capitalism* involves a formally free market in labour, a disciplined labour force, laws of contract, a money economy and a banking system, double-entry bookkeeping to ensure accurate accounting, and the systematic pursuit of profit over the long term.

Weber believed that most of the world's religions have stood in the way of the development of the spirit of rational capitalism. They give too much scope to magic, mystery, superstition and other-worldly concerns.

Buddhism, Hinduism and Taoism all promote *other-worldly* asceticism: withdrawal from the world rather than engagement with it. Confucianism produces benignly paternalistic societies that give little stimulus to innovation. Islam, in Weber's view, is essentially a warrior religion, seeking conquest rather than the disciplined pursuit of profit. Judaism lacks ascetic values, and is therefore best adapted to medieval adventure capitalism. Only ascetic Protestantism, particularly in its Calvinist form as developed not by Calvin himself but by the Puritans in the late seventeenth century, was well suited to the spirit of rational capitalism. In part, this was because Protestantism placed few barriers in the way of capitalist development. Weber goes beyond this, arguing controversially that ascetic Protestantism actually *stimulated* rational capitalism – though this was an unintended and paradoxical consequence of Calvinism.

The Calvinist doctrine of predestination, Weber argues, induces 'salvation anxiety'. Our fate is sealed before we are born: we are predestined to be either among the elect who are saved or among the damned. Sacraments administered by a priesthood cannot change this. Nor can we know which category we are in – an intolerable psychological burden, Weber says. People inevitably cast around for signs that they are among the elect, and find these in material prosperity. They draw the theologically invalid but psychologically satisfying conclusion that God will favour with material prosperity those whom he has chosen. As Parkin comments (1982: 45), the doctrine of predestination, which might have encouraged passive acceptance of one's unalterable fate, is transformed into a belief that spurs people to work systematically and single-mindedly in the pursuit of profit, in order to prove to themselves and others that they are among the elect.

Calvinism is characterized by Weber as a form of 'this-worldly asceticism'. Other-worldly retreat into contemplation and mysticism is rejected: God requires us to act in this world to secure the benefits of the next. Our acts must be self-denying, displaying self-control, sobriety, thrift, frugality and deferred gratification. Work is a vocation, a calling from God. Calvinism is not self-indulgent – that is an orientation more suited to booty capitalism. The fruits of one's labour are not squandered, but invested.

Weber is clear that modern capitalism no longer depends on religion. Ascetic Protestantism has done its work, and capitalism today is powered by a secular dynamic. Inner-worldly asceticism as a value-system can survive the death of God. It does not matter whether we are Protestants, Catholics, Jews – or atheists. Religious affiliation is no longer relevant. As Weber remarked, in a characteristically bleak diagnosis, 'The Puritan wanted to work in a calling, we are forced to do so' (Weber 2001/1920–1: 123).

Georg Simmel: an alternative classical view

> For the Enlightenment would be utter blindness if it were to assume that with a few centuries of criticism of the content of religion, it could destroy a yearning that has dominated humanity from the first stirrings of its history, from the most primitive indigenous people to the supreme heights of culture. (Simmel 1997: 9)

So wrote Georg Simmel (1858–1918) in an essay published in 1911 and entitled 'The problem of religion today' – one of many essays he devoted to the sociological and philosophical discussion of religion. Unlike other classical sociologists, Simmel was a man of faith (Flanagan 2001). He focused on the spirituality of the individual and the human orientation to religion, which he regarded as having priority over religions as objective systems of belief and practice.

An inescapable feature of social life is the implicit trust we place in others. We can never be certain about other people's actions and motives; instead, we have faith in them. Without faith, society would disintegrate. The demand for certainty, for proof, is normally impossible to meet, and although it might appear rational, it is profoundly pathological. (Hiring a private detective to verify one's partner's activities is a sign of a relationship on the point of disintegration.) This means that faith is robust, and can withstand apparently contrary evidence: 'That we still can retain our faith in an individual in the face of reasonable contradictory evidence or appearance, no matter how obvious, is one of the strongest of the ties that bind human society' (Simmel 1997: 110). Simmel immediately draws this conclusion: 'Now, this faith is certainly religious in character.' Faith in other people is analogous to faith in God – a complex mixture of knowledge, emotion and practical activity. This is why rationalist 'refutations' of the existence of God simply miss the point.

Simmel is not saying that religion existed first, and that faith in other people is derived from faith in God. The process is the reverse of this; social ties arise through social interaction, and find their abstract expression in religious faith. Dependence on God is congruent with dependence on other human beings, including our ancestors as well as our contemporaries (Simmel 1997: 115). Crucially, however, this is not a reductionist theory. Offering a sociological account of the wellsprings of faith does not explain it away or in any way diminish it; on the contrary, it is a tribute to its power. Simmel's sociology is founded on the conviction that religion is not alien to us, but part of our social being.

Throughout history, at least until the dawn of the twentieth century, humanity had experienced religion as a *need*. The pressing question is: is any religion capable of meeting that need under the conditions of modernity? 'Until now', he wrote, 'religion has survived the religions as a tree survives the constant plucking of its fruit. The real gravity of the current situation is that not this or that particular dogma but the object of transcendent faith per se is characterized as illusory' (Simmel 1997: 9). *Characterized* as illusory; Simmel does not say that religion *is* an illusion. For example, Christian belief in the Virgin Birth and the bodily resurrection are no less plausible now than they were in the thirteenth century or the first. Neither science nor philosophy have refuted religion; nor have they rendered religious faith untenable.

The crisis of religion is one element in the crisis of modernity. In his seminal essay written in 1903, 'The metropolis and mental life', Simmel diagnosed this crisis as the subjugation of the subjective spirit to objective culture. The latter, embodied in things and in knowledge, has vastly outpaced the capacity of individuals to cope with it. Metropolitan life is restless, frenetic and bordering on the meaningless, bombarding us with an excess of dissociated stimuli, which forces us into a dehumanized, *blasé* attitude of studied indifference and even aversion to our surroundings and to other people. One common but pathological way of coping with the pressures of modernity is to retreat into an inner world of self-absorbed subjectivity.

In this modern predicament, religion, like art, offers hope. Instead of starting his analysis with objective culture – the creeds, dogma, commandments and authority structure of a religion – Simmel focuses on the emotionally charged practical activities in which the faithful engage. One example is the practice of praying for faith, which from a strictly rational viewpoint appears to be totally illogical (Simmel 1997: 130–3). Prayer can be addressed only to a God in whom one already believes; but if one believes in God, then surely praying for faith makes no sense? Against this, Simmel argues that praying for faith is an effort to bring together the objective content of a religion with the spiritual yearnings of the individual. People who pray for faith are seeking to achieve not simply an intellectual acknowledgement of the existence of God, but an inner spiritual and emotional transformation based on their relationship with God.

Religious faith, like art, has the capacity to resolve the crisis of modernity by creating a bridge between objective culture and subjective life. For Simmel, a society without religion is scarcely possible; if it did exist, it would be pathological.

Defining secularization

Although the definition of religion is contentious, the definition of secularization is not. Debates about secularization are preoccupied not with the meaning of the term but with the evidence for and against the social process to which it refers.

One widely cited definition is Berger's: secularization is 'the process by which sectors of society and culture are removed from the domination of religious institutions and symbols' (Berger 1967: 107). It operates at three levels. One is *social-structural*: in the West, Christian churches have lost functions that are now performed by secular agencies. Equally important for Berger is the *cultural* aspect. The religious content of Western art, music, literature and philosophy has drastically declined. Meanwhile the triumphant natural and social sciences have promoted a secular perspective on the world. Finally, secularization of society and culture is accompanied by a secularization of *individual consciousness*. Fewer and fewer people think in a religious mode. The faithful are a cognitive minority.

Another definition is proposed by Bruce: secularization is a

'social condition manifest in (a) the declining importance of religion for the operation of non-religious roles and institutions such as those of the state and the economy; (b) a decline in the social standing of religious roles and institutions; and (c) a decline in the extent to which people engage in religious practices, display beliefs of a religious kind, and conduct other aspects of their lives in a manner informed by such beliefs. (Bruce 2002: 3)

Neither Berger nor Bruce match Wilson for conciseness; he defines secularization as 'the process whereby religious thinking, practice and institutions lose social significance' (Wilson 1966: 14).

These definitions have important features in common. First, they presuppose an exclusive definition of religion, the argument being that such definitions make it possible to decide on the basis of the evidence whether or not secularization is taking place. If religion is defined very broadly, its persistence is not a discovery about the world, but a mere trick of definition.

Second, they treat secularization as a multi-faceted process. This means that, in principle, secularization might be proceeding rapidly on one dimension but not on others. Despite this logical possibility, secularization theorists tend to see the levels and dimensions of secularization as so intimately connected that, at least in the long run, secularization is thought to take place on all of them.

Third, the secularization thesis focuses on the demand for religion, rather than its supply. Demand is not a constant; it rises and falls as a result of social and cultural changes that make religion more or less plausible and desirable (Bruce 2002: 3–4). Putting it bluntly, these theorists are arguing that secularization is caused not by the inadequacies of the 'firms' (the churches and other religious organizations) that supply religion, but by the dwindling appeal of the product itself.

Six major themes in secularization theory are discussed below: secularization from within; the decline of community; the marginalization of charisma; cultural amnesia; pluralization, relativism and consumer choice; and reason, rationality and science.

Secularization from within

Marx and Engels famously argued in the Communist Manifesto of 1848 that the capitalist system nurtures the seeds of its own destruction: it depends upon its own 'grave-diggers', an increasingly class-conscious industrial proletariat that will bring about the revolutionary overthrow of the system that produced it. In a similar vein, Hegel, Schopenhauer, Nietzsche and Weber claimed that the Judaeo-Christian tradition contains, paradoxically, elements that lead to secularization.

Weber argued that the origins of the disenchantment of the Western world lie in ancient Judaism (Weber 1952; Zeitlin 1984). Like Protestantism, but unlike the great Asian faiths, the religion of Israel was this-worldly. Theologically, its key feature was the utter rejection of any form of polytheism, a refusal that had profound social and cultural consequences.

Dictionary definitions of polytheism as the belief in and worship of more than one god, though apparently straightforward, conceal the full implications of polytheism as a cultural system. Polytheistic deities are fundamentally limited:

- They do not reign supreme, but are subject to impersonal forces – the Latin fates, the Greek *moira.*
- None of them is omniscient or omnipotent, not even Zeus or Jupiter.
- They did not create the universe, but were themselves born out of it.
- They can be manipulated and coerced by human magic.
- They are dependent on worship and sacrifices.
- They are the victims of their own urges, lusting for one another and for humans.
- They war among themselves.
- Humans can become demi-gods, sometimes even gods.

The strict monotheism of Israel had no truck with any of this. God is a creator who proclaims a unique covenant with his people. Israel's duty is unswerving obedience to God's commandments. In return, God promises a strikingly this-worldly salvation: wealth, fertility, conquest, deliverance from bondage to Egypt, and dominion over Canaan. This is not a god who can be manipulated by mortals: no sorcery or magic can bend God's will. Nor are there any other entities who can influence him: he stands alone. The crucial point about other gods, such as Baal or Dagon, is that they do not exist.

Magical coercion of the gods, a foolish expression of human arrogance, is replaced by the duty of obedience to the creator. Miracles can be performed only in the name of God, and only if God wills them. Evil is transferred from the realm of mythology to that of ethics.

Monotheism, in Weber's opinion, had powerful consequences. It liberated humanity from dependence on mythology and magic, while at the same time forcing us to confront ethical choices. The natural world had the spirits driven from it, and became an arena for human endeavour in the service of God.

For Berger, as for Weber, disenchantment of the world begins in the religion of ancient Israel (Berger 1967: 110–25). The exodus from

Egypt was more than a political emancipation. It marked Israel's break with an entire universe of meaning. The religion of Israel repudiated the cosmological world-view of Mesopotamian civilizations. In this world-view, the empirical and the super-empirical are continuous with one another. The human world is embedded in a cosmic order, so that everything that happens in society has its analogue on the level of the gods. To illustrate his point, Berger gives two examples. First, he cites disobedience to the God-King of Egypt. As well as having political and ethical implications, disobedience upsets the cosmic order. It may jeopardize the annual flooding of the Nile or national security against foreign aggression. Punishing the individual offender is not just a matter of appeasing a wrathful king; it is crucial to restoring a right relationship between Egyptian society and the cosmic order on which it rests.

Berger's second example of the cosmological world-view of Mesopotamian cultures is their practice of sacred prostitution. This is not just the satisfaction of lust by the world's oldest profession, though that was doubtless part of it. Sacred or temple prostitution was *sacramental*. Through an ecstatic act, it put human beings in touch with the divinely suffused cosmos. That is why it was rejected by the religion of Israel. To Israel, the world was not divine, but a divine creation.

On Berger's analysis, Israel's rejection of the cosmological world-view had three motifs: transcendentalization, historization and the rationalization of ethics.

Transcendentalization   The God of the Hebrew Scriptures stands outside the cosmos that he has created. He is radically transcendent, totally other, and not to be identified with any element in nature or culture. Strict monotheism means that he is alone and self-sufficient, lacking parents, companions or offspring. He is not a tribal divinity naturally tied to Israel. Nor does he need Israel's support. He cannot be manipulated by magic. Even when he demands sacrifices, he does not depend on them. He is the universal God who has chosen the Israelites as his people and who makes demands on them.

Historization   The Hebrew Scriptures are rooted in history, more so than any other sacred writings of a world religion, even including the Christian New Testament. All of the books of the Hebrew Scriptures (except Ecclesiastes and Job, which are among the later texts) have a historical orientation. The world is not populated by mythologized divine entities and forces. Instead, it is the arena of the actions of human beings and of the mighty acts of God.

Rationalization of ethics   The God of Israel is not like the gods of Greece and Rome, a capricious deity whose erratic behaviour may be influenced by human flattery or deceit. God's commandments are self-consistent ethical laws that have to be obeyed. Both the priestly and the prophetic elements in the religion of Israel had ethical rationalization as a dominant motif. The priestly ethic entailed a formalization of religious law governing everyday life, and the elimination of magical and orgiastic rites. The prophetic strand insisted that life be devoted to the service of God, which again entailed a rationalized ethical structure guiding all human activity.

In its origins, and in its Western development in Catholicism, Christianity reversed two aspects of the secularizing thrust of the religion of Israel, while retaining its emphasis on history. First, the doctrine of the Incarnation and its theological elaboration into the doctrine of the Trinity significantly modified Judaism's radical monotheism and the transcendentalization it expressed. To the offence of monotheistic Judaism and Islam, God has a Son. Catholicism proliferated a host of angels and saints and a wealth of devotions to the Virgin Mary. The world was re-enchanted, and repopulated with semi-divine entities mediating between God and humanity.

Catholicism also put ethical rationalization into reverse. Unlike Judaism, whose numerous ethical laws apply to all the faithful, Catholicism institutionalized virtuoso religion in monastic orders – a calling not suitable for ordinary people. The piety of the Catholic laity depended not on a rationalization of ethics, but rather on their acceptance of the authority of the priesthood as stewards of the mysteries of God.

The Protestant Reformation reasserted the secularizing dynamic which had been temporarily halted by medieval Catholicism. Protestantism divested itself of mystery, miracles and magic, which meant 'an immense shrinkage in the scope of the sacred' (Berger 1967: 111). Sacraments lost many of their supernatural and magical associations; some movements (Quakers and the Salvation Army, for instance) rejected sacraments altogether. In Protestant Christianity, guardian angels no longer watch over us. Saints and the Virgin Mary do not intercede for us. The Virgin ceases to be an object of veneration. There are no sacred places of pilgrimage where miraculous cures may be expected. Reality is polarized between a radically other deity and a fallen world of rather lonely men and women. In Weber's phrase, the world is disenchanted.

In Berger's view, the Protestant Reformation put religion at risk. It reduced the relationship between humanity and the divine to one narrow channel: the Word of God, the uniquely redemptive action of God's grace. As long as this connection remained plausible, religion continued to flourish. But as soon as it was severed, secularization proceeded unchecked. That is the modern condition, and Protestantism played an unintended but decisive part in bringing it about.

Decline of community

Religion is always primarily a communal, as distinct from a societal, institution. Its operation is always essentially local. The basic commodity that religion purveys – reassurance about salvation – must be available wherever its agents operate. (Wilson 1976: 89)

For Wilson, religion and fellowship are inseparable. Religion requires particularistic and affective relationships between people who treat one another as whole persons. Priests need close personal relationships with their congregations, gurus with their devotees, and charismatic leaders with their followers. Wilson made this point succinctly in discussion with colleagues in a forum set up as part of the consultation process involved in the Second Vatican Council. He said: 'I interpret religion very largely as necessarily a face-to-face, person-to-person phenomenon; when religion ceases to be that, it loses a great deal of its vigour and of the power it holds over the individual. In our role-articulated world, face-to-face relationships in the community have ceased to be the principal context of people's lives' (Caporale and Grumelli 1971: 177).

The latent functions of religion, Wilson argues, depend upon stable local communities enduring over time. The rise of the nation-state brings *societalization*, the end of locality: 'Local crafts, local products, local customs, local dialects have all shown a rapid diminution in our own times' (Wilson 1982: 154). Urbanization and suburbanization leave religion with little to celebrate in terms of community spirit (Wallis and Bruce 1992: 13). Religion has less and less scope to supply an overarching system of transcendentally grounded values.

Societalization replaces personal ties with rule-governed contractual relations between role-performers – managers and workers, salespeople and customers, bureaucrats and the public. Personal trust gives way to abstract expert systems, and goodwill yields to formally codified rights and duties. People are judged by their performance in achieving secular goals. Morality is replaced by calculation, so that personal virtue counts for very little, often proving to be a liability rather than an asset. Societalization entails that human activities are increasingly coordinated by merely technical controls, rather than by morally charged

social bonds. It means demoralization, in the sense that moral judge-
ments are replaced by causal explanations. At its bleakest, this is a consumer culture that has ceased to believe in responsibility or guilt.
Echoing Daniel Bell's (1979) analysis of the cultural contradictions of
capitalism, Wilson argues that the Protestant ethic 'would be dysfunctional were it to continue to command adherence in the consumer
society' (Wilson 2001: 49). Such a society requires self-indulgence, not
self-denial. In this demoralized consumer culture, humanity no longer
needs to be reconciled to evil and suffering. The concept of 'salvation'
is therefore drained of all meaning, and religion loses its *raison d'être*.

As societalization proceeds, so the traditional symbols and rituals
that expressed and maintained community life come to lose all
meaning. A telling British instance of this is the terminal decline of the
rite of passage known as the churching of women (Wilson 1992: 197).
Although churching is 'officially' an expression of thanksgiving to God
after childbirth, in practice it was treated as removing ritual unclean-
ness. Women who had given birth were not supposed to go out of doors
until they had undergone the rite of churching. The practice had not
shed its origins, which lay in the Jewish rite of purification. Churching
was a rite integral to pre-industrial community life, and survived until
the 1950s in the 'urban villages', the vibrant, close-knit, working-class
communities that flourished in all major cities. Thus Young and
Willmott's (1957: 39–40) celebrated study of working-class life in
Bethnal Green, a community in the East End of London, pointed to
churching as a vital ingredient of family and community life. Young and
Willmott's respondents in the early 1950s referred to the rite as traditional, old-fashioned and superstitious. Even so, more than 90 per cent
of the women in their study had been churched after the birth of their
last child. It is a measure of how secular we have become that churching has faded to the point where few people have even heard of it.

Once societalization is complete, the social system operates without
reference to religious institutions or to the religious orientations of individuals. Religion retreats into the private sphere. People may continue
to evince a religious faith, but it is increasingly a matter of personal
taste, a private choice that has no impact on the operation of the social
system. Religious movements therefore face an unavoidable dilemma.
To have any impact in the modern world, they must accommodate to
the forces of rationalization and societalization, but in doing so they
undermine the reason for their own existence.

The United States is not an exceptional case, but one that, Wilson
claims, proves his thesis. He draws heavily on Herberg's (1983) argument that religious affiliation is a means by which migrants affirmed an

American identity, while harking back nostalgically to their origins in the rural communities of Europe. The crucial point for Wilson, however, is that religious values in the USA are not independent and autonomous. Instead, they are derived from national secular values and are subservient to them. Going to church is part of the American way of life, requiring only a superficial commitment and making few demands on those who do go. Churches offer 'synthetic' community life (Wilson 1966: 115), not the 'natural' communities of the old country. As a condition of their acceptance by the secular state, Wilson contends, religious denominations have virtually abandoned any distinctive commitments of their own.

Wilson's case for the secularization thesis rests on a sharp distinction between *Gemeinschaft* and *Gesellschaft*, community and association, as Robertson (1993: 2), Beckford (1989: 109–10) and Bruce (2002: 12–14) have observed. His contention that religion can flourish only if it is rooted in local communities is, I would argue, questionable on three grounds.

First, he defines community as a social formation that is localized in a particular place; alternative forms of community are discounted. His approach is derived from classical sociology, but contemporary sociology has drawn attention to the limitations of the classical view (Delanty 2003: 3). Instead of seeing community as a form of social interaction within a geographical location, sociologists now focus on community as a source of meaning and identity. Community is a matter of imaginative identification with a people, a nation, a tradition, a culture. Such identifications are not necessarily local; many are cosmopolitan. Roman Catholics, for example, belong to a worldwide communion: in theological terms, the Church as the Body of Christ, that transcends local and national territorial boundaries. Muslims are members of the *umma*, the community of the faithful wherever they may live. Jews, Sikhs and Hindus have an ethnic identity that has survived diaspora from their homelands. Individual members of faith communities have available to them a complex set of potential identity markers, only some of which depend on the local community.

Second, although he rejects the possibility that religion can flourish in the *Gesellschaft*, it is not clear that he is right to do so. World-affirming movements do not depend upon face-to-face interactions in a local community; instead, the services they offer are aimed at individual self-realization. Although they typically have a core of fully committed devotees, most of their members are consumers. As consumers, their involvement in a world-affirming movement does not necessarily clash with or take priority over their other social relations; but this does not mean that *gesellschaftlich* forms of religious affiliation can be discounted as less authentic or less meaningful than their traditional *gemeinschaftlich* counterparts.

Third, the Wilsonian concept of societalization is linked to the rise of the nation-state. It implies, controversially, that the nation cannot be the primary source of meaning and identity, but is necessarily secondary and dependent upon ways of life that are locally rooted. Even if that were so, nation-states and the process of societalization have been challenged by globalization. Religions are being reconfigured and revitalized (Karner and Aldridge 2004). In a globalizing world, religion has demonstrated its capacity to provide discourses of political resistance, mechanisms for coping with anxiety, and networks of solidarity and community.

Marginalization of charisma

The impersonality of a detraditionalized world leaves little room for personal charisma. Wilson sees charisma as quintessentially a property of *pre-modern* societies: there and there alone is belief in charisma widespread and credible. In these societies – Wilson calls them 'simpler' – social relationships and social organization are interpreted in personal terms. This is true of traditional authority as well as charismatic leadership (Wilson 1975: 20–6). In both, power is anthropomorphized, residing in great men and great women. Given this, it makes sense to place faith in a charismatic leader as someone who will transform the world. Gautama Buddha, Jesus Christ and the Prophet Muhammad did just that. Nowadays, charisma survives as little more than a romantic idea from the remote past. It can be reactivated, but only in small social movements operating at the periphery of society, and with no capacity to change anything of significance except perhaps the lives of a few followers. Collectively they have never added up to a counterculture; instead, they are 'random anti-cultural assertions' (Wilson 1976: 110), as diverse as they are ineffective.

One symptom of the marginality of charismatic movements in the modern world is the redefinition and even trivialization of the concept of charisma itself. On Shils's (1965) account, *all* leadership has a charismatic quality. This applies not just to religious prophets, but to politicians and chief executives of major business corporations. By redefining Weber's concept in this way, Shils turns charisma from a social force opposed to bureaucratic rationalization into its very embodiment. More commonly, the concept is debased into a personality trait manifested by

Hollywood stars, rock musicians and other entertainers with a mass public of fans. In the Weberian sense, however, charisma is not a trait of personality, but a complex relationship between a leader and a following. Fans are not followers, and entertainers are not leaders seeking to transform society. Except for a hard core of true devotees, fans are in it for fun – and they know it. Fandom is 'time out' from the stresses of modern life, not a radical challenge to it.

Mainstream Christian churches, both Protestant and Catholic, have felt the influence of neo-pentecostal 'charismatic renewal', involving exuberant worship, *glossolalia* and miraculous healing. Here again the concept of charisma is being adulterated. What is missing is the key element of charismatic leaders transforming tradition and legal-rationality (Wilson 1975: 121–4). Paradoxically, the charismatic movement's leaders are not charismatic leaders. Their authority rests not on new revelations, but on revitalizing the faith and restoring its blessings. Successive generations of evangelists, even those who are aligned with charismatic renewal, such as Oral Roberts and Morris Cerullo, have been revivalists who preach the Word, not prophets who challenge it. Evangelists often avoid political engagement, but when they do enter the political arena, their stance is typically conservative. They do not say, 'It is written, . . . but I say unto you'. Theirs is a 'derived charisma' (Wilson 1975: 116–19), since everything they do is in the name of Jesus.

Contrary to Wilson's analysis, it is worth noting that charisma remains powerful even when it is derived; that Pentecostal and charismatic movements have experienced explosive growth (see pp. 128–30 below); and that the personality cult of autocratic political leaders such as Hitler (pp. 158–60) suggests that charisma is not incompatible with modernity.

Cultural amnesia

'One of the chief characteristics of modern societies is that they are no longer societies of memory, and as such ordered with a view to reproducing what is inherited' (Hervieu-Léger 2000: 123). *Cultural amnesia*, the loss of collective memory, raises a general problem that is particularly acute in the case of religion: what beliefs, norms and values shall we pass on to our children?

In her analysis of the French case, Hervieu-Léger invokes themes similar to those in Wilson's work on the decline of community. For centuries in France, the parish was the social milieu through which memory was cherished and transmitted. Anamnesis – committing the past to memory – was achieved through the rituals of parish life. The vision of a religious society, a Catholic France, was based on two key elements: the traditional extended family, through which the faith was transmitted from generation to generation, and a rural society in which heaven and earth were reconciled. Keeping the faith through life's travails offered the assurance of eternal bliss in the life to come. In this harmoniously ordered world, the Church and the priesthood wielded authority over a deferential, loyal flock.

It is a world that France has lost. Rural depopulation is irreversible, the extended kinship system has given way to consumption-oriented nuclear families, and the priesthood has become an ageing fraternity of pastors with diminished authority over their dwindling congregations.

The fact that fewer and fewer Catholic parents feel obliged to transmit 'the Faith' to their own children is a telling instance of a wider phenomenon. Such parents believe that they ought not to put pressure on their children, but should bring them up to make their own decisions. Taken to an extreme, this can mean that what is transmitted from one generation to the next is not an inherited culture that enriches the lives of citizens, but a set of skills required by consumers. A persistent complaint in affluent societies is that young people are pathetically ignorant of their own history and culture. It shows, in Hervieu-Léger's stark assessment, that 'the collective memory of modern societies is composed of bits and pieces' (2000: 129). Cultural memory is fragmented, anomic and increasingly incoherent. Secularization is to be seen as one instance of a wider challenge: how to forge a chain of memory connecting past, present and future.

Pluralization, relativism and consumer choice

The key feature of contemporary Western societies, according to Berger, is their pluralism. Modernity involves a move from fate to choice, including choice of religion. Religious movements operate now in a competitive market-place. One theme in Berger's writing is that this can generate a shallow consumerist approach to religion, in which religious firms, like the manufacturers of detergents, market their products to consumers who are fastidious and fickle. The market, in this dystopian vision, is a meeting-place for self-interested consumers and manipulative producers.

Berger's critique of modernity goes much deeper than an intellectual's denunciation of consumerism. Pluralism undermines objectivity. Not only do we make choices, we know that we are doing so. Relativism is a fact of society and of our consciousness. Bruce makes precisely the same point, emphasizing that religion has been undermined 'by the general relativism that supposes that all ideologies are equally true (and hence equally false)' (Bruce 2002: 117).

In religion, relativism is a guilty secret. The Israelite covenant has been reversed: God has not chosen us, we have chosen a god, or even no god at all. Modernity brings a widespread loss of innocence. Even conservative forms of faith, so-called old-time religion, are self-conscious strident revivals lacking the pristine vitality of the originals. They too are an option. We cannot escape modernity by opting into protest against it, since such protests are themselves thoroughly modern phenomena.

All belief systems are grounded in what Berger calls a *plausibility structure*, by which he means a set of social institutions and social networks whose functioning and day-to-day reality render belief plausible. It is a Durkheimian insight: religion depends on a practising community, and there is no such thing as a literally private religion. The mistake that Durkheim made was to presume that religions and plausibility structures are necessarily society-wide. In the modern world, most nation-states embrace a plurality of sub-societal religions and plausibility structures. Claims to absolute authority in this competitive situation are hard to enforce and, worse, hard to credit. When religion no longer holds a monopoly, it faces a far more difficult problem of social engineering. Religion can no longer construct a sacred canopy over everybody, a common culture in which we all share. The problem of 'other religions' breaks free from its confines in theology, and poses a set of practical problems for nation-states and their citizens. There is also a pressing problem for religious institutions themselves, in that modernity forces them increasingly into the sectarian defence of a cognitive minority.

Berger's thesis has been carefully unpacked by Beckford (2003: 73–102), who draws attention to the multiple meanings of pluralism and the ways in which it manifests itself. Beckford distinguishes three meanings: pluralism as the *fact* of religious diversity, as the *public acceptance or recognition* of diversity, and as the social *value* placed on diversity.

The fact of religious diversity can be measured in various ways, taking into account such factors as the representation of the major world faiths within a society, the number of separate religious organizations and faith communities, a head-count of their members, or even the degree to which individual believers combine the elements of more than one faith into their own personal beliefs and practices. However it is measured, the crucial point, against Berger, is that the mere fact of diversity does not destabilize faith.

It is true, of course, that some people find their personal faith shaken by the existence of diversity. It may provoke the suspicion: if there are so many different religions, all preaching different truths, then perhaps they are all false – or, at the least, man-made rather than divinely revealed. It may lead to scepticism about the claims advanced on behalf of, say, the Prophet Muhammad or Joseph Smith; people may question the authorship of the holy Qur'an or the Book of Mormon that the faithful believe were delivered respectively to these prophets.

It may; but it may not. Religions supply the faithful with an account of other faiths, which may be cast as fellow-travellers, or junior partners, or lacking in the fullness of the faith, or regrettable breakaways, or seriously flawed sects, or deviant cults, or apostates, or blasphemers, or the agents of evil. No faith community is embarrassed by the existence of rivals; on the contrary, a community is partly defined in opposition to these others.

Moving beyond the existence of diversity to its public acceptance and recognition, we can recognize a continuum, ranging from grudging tolerance to acceptance as worthy partners or competitors. Acceptance can, as Beckford points out, take many forms: arbitrary concessions to favoured religions; legal and constitutional provisions conferring rights and exemptions; and informal understandings and arrangements that grant representation and a voice to some faith communities, but not others.

Acceptance and recognition shade at the positive end into the encouragement of diversity. This, Beckford suggests, is the most productive meaning of pluralism. It goes to the heart of the dilemma with which Berger grappled. Is a multi-faith society to be welcomed? Is it best secured if the state is secular? Does it mean that people should be free to choose their religion, to move from one faith to another, and to combine elements from different faiths into their own preferred mix of religious ingredients? What if the liberties of individuals conflict with the culture of the faith community of which they are part? These are controversial and potentially explosive issues, and the subject of ongoing debates in societies that are supposedly secular.

Reason, rationality and science

For centuries the Church played an extremely reactionary role and fought pitilessly against the scientific conception of the world and against the democratic and socialist movement. But the development of natural science inevitably caused more and more breaches in the religious and idealistic outlook. That is why the founders of Marxism considered scientific and materialist propaganda as the most powerful weapon in the fight against religion.

So wrote the anonymous editors of a collection of classic writings by Marx and Engels on religion, published in the Soviet Union with the endorsement of the Communist Party and the Institute of Marxism-Leninism (Marx and Engels 1957: 9). The statement may be crude, but it is not unfaithful to the substance and tenor of Marx and Engels's thought.

Very few social theorists in the Marxist tradition have departed from the position that religion is essentially a reactionary force: obscurantist, dogmatic and intolerant. Among those who have questioned elements of Marxist orthodoxy, Max Horkheimer is arguably the most interesting case. He accepted the Feuerbachian 'projection' theory of religion, and appeared to agree with Marx that religious illusions would vanish in the socialist future. Socialist men and women would abandon all fantasies of martyrdom, with their promise of rewards in heaven, in favour of self-sacrificing work for future generations living in this world – a quintessentially Soviet theme, optimistic and heroic.

Yet Horkheimer also wrote this: 'In a really free mind the concept of infinity is preserved in an awareness of the finality of human life and of the inalterable aloneness of man, and it keeps society from indulging in a thoughtless optimism, an inflation of its own knowledge into a new religion' (Horkheimer 1995: 131). Suddenly, the triumph of socialism appears bleak, rather than bright, and religion, with its reference to the transcendent, gives meaning and hope where atheistic ideologies reveal themselves as shallow quasi-religions that peddle totalitarianism in the guise of liberation.

Horkheimer's view that absolute truth is impossible to achieve without God provoked Jürgen Habermas into mounting a sophisticated defence of the main line of Marxist criticism of religion (see in particular Habermas 2002: 95–109). His argument is that truths are established not by reference to religion but in 'the ideal speech situation'. In this ideal (and idealized) situation, people participate in debates on an equal basis; their motives are open to inspection; they do not seek to manipulate one another; and their contributions are judged on merit rather than on the status of the participant. Since communication is not distorted by irrational drives or by the exercise of power, the quality of the arguments is what determines the outcome of any debate. Truths are arrived at procedurally through rational discussion; they are therefore provisional, and can legitimately be replaced when fresh information and stronger arguments are brought forward. That is exactly how science operates, through a rational process described by Popper (1963) as one of conjectures and refutations. Running through Habermas's work until very recently (see pp. 221–2) was a conviction that religious beliefs and the faith communities in which they are nurtured are incompatible with the rational exchange of ideas that characterizes the ideal speech situation.

In opposition to Habermas, Michele Dillon (1999) argues against the claim that religion is necessarily inimical to rational critical discourse. She suggests that he misguidedly treats religion as a pre-modern belief system that is monolithic, static and impervious to critique. He fails to see that reason plays a critical role in theological discourse. As for the rank-and-file members of religious communities, they are not necessarily committed to official dogma, bound by tradition, or subservient to the dictates of the hierarchy. The image of a unified and unchanging tradition may be propagated by the hierarchy, but it is a fiction.

Dillon's evidence is based on an acid test case, the Catholic Church. She focuses on institutionally marginalized Catholics in the United States: lesbians and gays, advocates of women's ordination to the priesthood, and people arguing for the right to choose abortion. These Catholics contest official Church teachings and the underlying principle that interpretative power in the Catholic Church resides solely in the hierarchy. Their aim is not merely to overturn official Church teaching that delegitimates the policies they advocate. Their project is, in Habermas's own terms, emancipatory, because 'they seek to reconstruct an inclusive, egalitarian, and pluralist church wherein these identities are validated' (Dillon 1999: 12).

Crucially, this is a challenge from within the Catholic Church. Pro-change Catholics do not base their case on secular themes, such as the rights of the individual. Instead, they draw on symbolic resources provided by the Church's own doctrinal and institutional history; 'they defend their vision of Catholicism using arguments squarely grounded in the Catholic doctrinal tradition' (Dillon 1999: 24). That tradition emphasizes the compatibility of faith and reason; Catholicism rejects biblical literalism and the irrational 'blind leap' view of faith. The debates that took place during the Second Vatican Council provide a rich supply of symbolic resources that support the construction of an emancipatory Church.

Habermas's conception of the ideal speech situation is, obviously, a benchmark against which we can measure any given reality. We should strive for the ideal, though we can never attain it. The core difficulty with his approach is that the actors who take part in the ideal speech situation have been shorn of their identity; class, gender, ethnicity and religion are all regarded as obstructions to rational debate. The problem with Habermas's ideal speech situation is not that it is idealized, but that it is 'devoid of real people' (Baert 2001: 91).

The real people in Dillon's study are Catholics who are loyal to the Catholic tradition, identify strongly with it, and have no desire to leave. They are not rootless; nor are they constructing their own privatized religiosity. As good Catholics, they are not simply consumers of Catholicism, but producers of it. The implication of Dillon's work, contradicting Habermas, is that their Catholic identity, far from being a constraint to the project of emancipation, is what motivates and inspires them to strive for it.

Religion, Habermas argues, is irredeemably authoritarian and reactionary. (He has subsequently softened his position, as explained at the end of this book.) Religion can serve as a resource for resistance to, and withdrawal from, oppression; but it lacks the potential to emancipate us from it. Taking Habermas's approach, it is hard to avoid the conclusion that these marginalized Catholics would be better advised to leave the Catholic Church, which, given its inherent dogmatism and massive authority structure, cannot possibly come anywhere near the ideal speech situation. We should shed our illusions about religion; its primary task is not to seek the truth, but to legitimize inequality, injustice and oppression (Habermas 1987: 188–9). As Outhwaite tartly puts it, 'its ideological message is wrapped up in a mishmash of sacred and profane beliefs' (Outhwaite 1994: 93).

Outside the Marxist tradition, a lack of concern with intellectual challenges to religious faith is a remarkable feature of contemporary sociological approaches to secularization. Although the secularization thesis divides sociologists of religion, they are virtually unanimous in denying that it is a matter of rational scientific challenges to the basis of faith.

Bruce addresses the issue at length, with the stated aim of setting the record straight (2002: 106–17). He distances sociologists from the folly of liberal Christians, some of whom think that modern science and technology make belief in the transcendent impossible for 'modern' people. Science and religion are not in a zero-sum game, where one must gain at the expense of the other. Some classical sociologists may have thought that way, but contemporary theorists emphatically do not. Bruce correctly points out that neither Wilson, nor Berger, nor Martin, nor Wallis, devote much attention to science, and do not see it as a direct cause of secularization. Few people are truly knowledgeable about scientific procedures and discoveries; facility in playing computer games does not prove otherwise. The social impact of science is indirect: it creates in us a sense that technology frees us from being at the mercy of fate.

Conflicts between science and religion – over, say, the origins of the universe, the emergence of our planet, the dating of fossils, and the descent of human beings – are, on the accounts offered by Bruce and other theorists, local skirmishes. Bruce makes light of them: they show only 'an apparent clash' between specific scientific findings and 'the traditional teachings of the Christian tradition' (Bruce 2002: 111–12), not a real war between science and religion. On the contrary, the cognitive styles of science and religion have much in common, Bruce argues. He presents scattered but persuasive evidence to show that scientists are often attracted to conservative forms of religion precisely because they find in them the same concept of objective truth that prevails in the sciences.

Having established that scientific rationality presents no fundamental challenge to religion, Bruce attacks the equation of secularization theory with militant secularism, made by David Martin in a much-quoted essay (Martin 1965). Martin suggested that the secularization thesis was a tool of counter-religious ideology, and ought to be erased from the sociological dictionary. His article was intentionally provocative, and is better read as an attempt to open up a debate rather than banish a word (Martin 1978: p. viii). In his later work, he sought to clarify the concept of secularization and to identify the social and cultural conditions that advance or inhibit it.

The charge of anti-religious secularism can certainly be sustained against Comte and Marx, who openly opposed religion in the name of science. As an accusation levelled against Wilson and Berger, it is wildly implausible, as Bruce (1992: 1–3) has pointed out. Both these authors have been influenced by Weber's pessimistic account of the modern world. Berger's work testifies to his lifelong struggle to reconcile his calling as a Lutheran with his profession as a sociologist. As for Wilson, there is evidence throughout his work of a distaste for many aspects of secular society, and a profound sense of loss of the religious values that once underpinned community life. Their work cannot sensibly be read as a joyous celebration of secularity.

The sociological consensus is that secularization has not been brought about by the progress of scientific rationality. I would make two observations about this. First, the consensus draws a very sharp line between the theoretical explorations of intellectuals and the beliefs of ordinary people. As Chadwick puts it, 'Enlightenment was of the few. Secularization is of the many' (Chadwick 1975: 9). There is no hint here that theories and concepts might spread from intellectual giants through interpreters to a wider public without being mangled. Instead, the public – particularly in the work of Berger and Martin – is regularly painted as ignorant and gullible.

Second, the reconciliation of science and faith requires a huge cultural effort, and is potentially unstable. Any implication, as in Bruce, that the clash of science and religion is an easily rectified misunderstanding, does little justice to the struggles that have been played out in secular and ecclesiastical courts of law, and in schools and universities, between the rationale and findings of sciences and the dogmatic teachings of religions. Perhaps it is time to revisit at least some aspects of the Marxian critique of religion?

A consensus on dystopia?

If we follow the accounts put forward by contemporary secularization theorists, we might conclude that they have converged on a remarkable consensus. Drawing on the diverse but harmonious perspectives of the classical sociologists – while conveniently overlooking Simmel – they have erected a consistent thesis that has overwhelming empirical support. This has been achieved without recourse to rationalist ideology. Believers, agnostics and atheists have joined forces, despite their divergent faith positions, in building a massive consensus.

It may be so; but there are problems. The various themes discussed in this chapter – secularization from within, decline of community, marginalization of charisma, cultural amnesia, pluralization, scientific rationality, and privatization and institutional decline – are not an intellectual package deal. To adopt a phrase favoured by Bruce, we can pick and mix them. The secularization thesis is less coherent than its proponents claim. Even more damagingly, the irreversibility of secularization is tied to a theory of modernity that is beginning to look out of date.

Although secularization cannot be dismissed as anti-religious ideology, the vision of an alliance of believers and unbelievers united in endorsing the secularization thesis is too optimistic. The thesis appeals mainly to secular intellectuals. The outstanding example of a believer committed to secularization was Berger – but he has changed his mind. Few believers find the secularization thesis persuasive, and that is not merely because they have a vested interest in faith. Religion offers meaning and hope in the face of chaos; secular belief systems struggle to match this achievement, and lack mass appeal even when, as in the former Soviet empire, they receive the backing of the state. There is, as Durkheim observed, 'something eternal in religion'.

In its nineteenth-century heyday, atheism challenged the oppressive, reactionary and corrupt practices of the Christian churches and the irrational superstitions they cultivated. The cumulative effect of the work of Comte, Feuerbach, Marx and later Freud was to present atheism as politically, scientifically, culturally and psychologically liberating. A Copernican revolution appeared to be under way, with humanity displacing God at the centre of our moral and spiritual universe. To all these thinkers, atheism was the natural fulfilment of our humanity; religion needed to be explained and overcome as a degrading pathology.

It is clear that their arguments were logically circular, assuming what had to be proved. None of them showed that atheism was the truth of religion; they simply assumed it to be so, and argued from that premiss that religion should be consigned to humanity's past: to the theological and metaphysical stages (Comte), to class society (Marx), or to our psychic infancy (Feuerbach and Freud). None of these writers proved that organized religion was incapable of reforming itself; they simply took it for granted that all religions were dogmatic, superstitious and intolerant.

At the beginning of the twenty-first century, organized atheism is in a sorry state (McGrath 2004). As an ideology, it presents as antiquated, dull, moralistic and, ironically, pious. Its rationalism addresses the intellect, but ignores our emotions, senses and imagination. It speaks of liberation, but commands the adherence only of a small number of intellectuals. It attributes to organized religion a power that it no longer possesses, and assumes that believers are dupes who would benefit from being set free. Its claims to be liberating have proved to be not universally valid, but historically contingent. Although it may be unfair to judge atheism by the performance of the Soviet Union and its satellites, the fact is that politicized atheism has never been popular. McGrath pointedly marks the rise and fall of atheism by the destruction of two brutal physical structures that expressed the power of a society that affirmed religion and one that denied it: the Bastille, stormed by the people in 1789, and the Berlin Wall, torn apart by the people exactly 200 years later.

Although the Marxist atheist tradition revels in the supposed death of religion, the majority of secularization theorists, as we have seen, portray secular society as a dystopia. Secularity is not the triumph of science and the intellect set free from the bonds of clerical authoritarianism and irrational superstition. Secular society is dehumanized and demoralized. Cultural amnesia has delivered us over into a banal, restless, profoundly unsatisfying consumerism.

If so, secular society is not a liberation, but a prison. And if that is so, then perhaps it cannot endure for ever.

5

Secularization Challenged: A New Paradigm?

A secularization theorist recants

My point is that the assumption that we live in a secularized world is false. The world today, with some exceptions to which I will come presently, is as furiously religious as it ever was, and in some places more so than ever. (Berger 1999: 2)

So wrote Peter Berger, one of secularization theory's greatest exponents. His change of mind appeared so momentous that it is regularly said that he 'recanted'. This word is normally used in the context of religious faith; it suggests that Berger has renounced his belief in secularization, and is publicly confessing his sin in having espoused the heresy. How could modernity eliminate 'the religious impulse, the quest for meaning that transcends the restricted space of empirical existence in this world' and which has been 'a perennial feature of humanity'? (Berger 1999: 13).

Berger does not deny that there are secularizing tendencies within modernity. His point is that there are also powerful countervailing forces. Secularization is not the dominant trend; instead, there is a complex interplay between secularization and desecularization. Among religious movements, those that reject secularization and robustly affirm supernaturalist beliefs and practices are, significantly, on the upsurge almost everywhere.

The one setting where secularization is entrenched is among 'an international subculture composed of people with Western-type higher education, especially in the humanities and social sciences' (Berger 1999: 10). Its members, few but influential, are prominent in defining reality through education, the media and the legal system. This secular intelligentsia assembles at international conferences, where like meets like. Their global travels may suggest that their outlook is cosmopolitan, but Berger claims that they are in fact a self-regarding subculture, insulated against wider cultural currents and the common people.

In his earlier work, as we saw in chapter 4 (pages 80–1), he distinguished three dimensions of secularization: social-structural, cultural, and the level of individual consciousness. As is typical of secularization theorists, he saw the dimensions as so closely interconnected that secularization proceeded unchecked along all three. Now, however, he insists that they be pulled apart. Secularization is apparently most obvious at the social-structural level, particularly in the Protestant countries of Europe, where levels of church attendance have plummeted. Yet, even in Europe, the situation is ambiguous and nuanced: formal membership and active participation have fallen, but religious institutions and symbols continue to play an important part in social, cultural and political life.

Believing without belonging

Secularization theorists typically make two crucial assumptions: they posit a sharp divide between the public and private spheres, and they see the private sphere as having secondary importance. As religion becomes an increasingly private matter, so it loses social significance.

Both these assumptions are questionable. Religions frequently contest the conventional public/private boundary, seeking to place on the public agenda issues about identity and culture that others would like to keep confined to the private sphere. And the assumption that the public world of work and politics takes primacy over the private world of home and family, leisure and friendship, is not one shared by the vast majority of people.

Declining participation in religious institutions is, Grace Davie suggests (2002), part of a wider reluctance to engage in voluntary and civic activities. In a series of publications beginning in the 1990s, Davie launched a significant challenge to the secularization thesis. She introduced the pregnant phrase 'believing without belonging', which was designed to capture the profound changes taking place in people's response to religion in contemporary societies.

Even if believing without belonging is eventually judged not to be the best way to describe the trends, we need some means, she argues, of understanding the persistence of the sacred despite the undeniable decline in churchgoing. In the British case, hard evidence of declining church attendance goes back at least to the 1851 Census in England and Wales. At that period, on any given Sunday over half the adult population attended church; 150 years later, this figure had fallen to less than one twelfth (Voas and Crockett 2005: 17).

Davie has always insisted that 'believing' and 'belonging' need to be interpreted subtly and should not be taken too literally: 'The disjunction between the variables is intended to capture a mood, to suggest an area of enquiry, a way of looking at the problem, not to describe a detailed set of characteristics. Operationalizing either or both of the variables too severely is bound to distort the picture' (Davie 1994: 93–4).

What she means by operationalizing them too severely is using crude measurements, such as opinion polls and raw behavioural data, which sacrifice the nuances of human life to the quantitative demands of statistical procedures.

Davie's account of believing without belonging is intended to apply to mainstream Christianity, particularly in Europe and most noticeably in countries with a Protestant inheritance, above all the UK and the Nordic countries. Her thesis is not directly concerned with major world faiths other than Christianity, or with minority religious movements.

At its strongest, believing would refer to the core tenets of the Christian faith as expressed in creeds and other statements of doctrine. Davie is not arguing that belief in this strong sense is flourishing in contemporary Europe. She recognizes that more and more people have assembled a set of personal beliefs and orientations from a variety of sources, not all of them sanctioned by official Church teaching. Nor is it only a matter of belief in the sense of giving assent to a set of statements; 'believing', as Simmel saw, encompasses sensitivity, emotion, and an openness to the transcendent.

To critics of Davie's analysis, the content of belief has become diffuse, the choice of what to believe is now a matter for the individual consumer, and the meaning of believing has been fatally weakened, all of which raise serious doubts about the status of her thesis. Voas and Crockett (2005: 12) claim: 'The defensible interpretations of the phrase assert little; the bold versions have high empirical content but happen to be false. Proponents of BWB tend to want both the stature of a strong claim and the self-evidence of a weak one.' Her thesis is either significant but false, or true but trivial.

Analysing data from the British Household Survey from 1991 to 2000, and from the British Social Attitude Surveys since 1983, Voas and Crockett conclude that there is no mismatch between the figures on believing and belonging. Both are falling, and at a similar rate. It has been a long-term process, stretching back to well before the cultural turmoil of the 1960s. Crucially, this pattern of decline is largely a generation effect, with each succeeding age cohort being less religious than its predecessor. It betrays a crisis in religious socialization; whether we look at active participation, passive affiliation or levels of belief, the hard truth is that, with each passing generation, 'young British adults are half as religious as their parents' (Voas and Crockett 2005: 22).

All participants in the debate recognize the crucial issue of the long term. Is believing without belonging sustainable? If each succeeding generation is less committed to religious faith and practice than its predecessor, at what point will the cultural transmission of religion break down?

There is nothing remarkable about the erosion of Christian beliefs, Bruce argues, given the crises afflicting the institutions that carry them. 'Ideologies do not float in the ether. They need to be preserved; mechanisms must exist to acquaint the next generation with those beliefs' (Bruce 2002: 72–3). What corrodes both believing and belonging is the pervasive individualism of a consumer society. Robust faith has lost ground to diffuse, low-salience, 'pick-and-mix' religion, which lacks social significance and threatens to have less and less meaning at the personal level too. Bruce insists that pick-and-mix religion has little significance for people, and is as trivial as most of the 'choices' facing consumers. This is why believing does not entail belonging: religious belief has become so diffuse, individualistic and unimportant that people are unwilling to invest money or time in religious practices and institutions.

For all its impact, the phrase 'believing without belonging' has been criticized as seriously misleading. The two key terms, 'believing' and 'belonging', are open to multiple interpretations. Worse, the attempt to divorce believing from belonging is deeply problematic from a sociological perspective. There may well be a strong case for abandoning the phrase altogether, as Voas and Crockett suggest (2005: 25): ' "Believing without belonging" was an interesting idea, but it is time for the slogan to enter honourable retirement.' The chances of this happening are exactly the same as they were when David Martin proposed in 1975 that the term 'secularization' be erased from the sociological dictionary: zero. Too much intellectual capital has been invested in the phrase, and its popularity shows that it has captured something elusive.

Davie is not a slave to her famous phrase; other ways of formulating the issues at stake are no less important. Thus she argues that a 'culture of obligation' has been superseded by a 'culture of consumption'. This does not imply disaffection from the churches; on the contrary, people expect their services to be on offer as an option to be taken up as and when required.

Linked to this is the concept of 'vicarious religion' (Davie 2001) – that is to say, religion carried out by a minority on behalf of the majority. In some cultural settings, particularly in the Lutheran societies of northern Europe and also in the UK, the general population has in effect delegated religious activity to the mainstream churches, particularly the established or state churches. These churches and their professional ministers are viewed as a kind of Spiritual Health Service that offers a service free at the point of delivery to all citizens; it is this, and not hostility, that makes people reluctant to pay the full economic cost of services rendered. Affection for church buildings, and the sense that they belong to everyone, is an expression of these sentiments. So too is people's recourse to churches for major rites of passage such as birth, marriage and funerals, and at times of national crisis. Davie argues that Europeans are typically appreciative of these services, rather than resentful of the cultural position that churches occupy. Only a small minority of secularists are hostile to the churches' cultural privileges. Vicarious religion is a pervasive cultural phenomenon, and not to be dismissed lightly as somehow lacking in social significance.

A new paradigm

According to Stephen Warner (1993), we are witnessing the birth of a new paradigm in the sociological interpretation of contemporary religion. This paradigm is emerging in the work of a few leading scholars who have drawn on a variety of theoretical approaches, including economic analysis and rational choice theory. Dissenting from sociological orthodoxy, they have declared the secularization thesis ethnocentric, empirically unsafe and intellectually bankrupt.

The new paradigm is rooted in the social reality of American religion, which has two key features distinguishing it from religion in Europe: disestablishment and institutional vitality. Curiously, European sociologists have treated the United States as if it were deviant from the European norm. On this view, religion stands out as the one field of social life in which Europe shows America its future, rather than the other way round. Hence the charge of ethnocentricity.

If one is looking for a classic source of the new paradigm, it must surely be Alexis de Tocqueville's *Democracy in America*, published in two volumes in 1835 and 1840 and based on the young Frenchman's extensive travels in the new republic. The significance of religion in

Tocqueville's analysis cannot easily be exaggerated. The condition of religion in America was, he said, the first thing that struck him. He could hardly fail to notice the separation of church and state, and the citizens' freedom of conscience, worship and assembly. The democratic politics of the American republic were paralleled by the democratic plurality of religious sects and denominations. Underlying these parallel institutional forms is something more profound: a vital link between the spirit of religion and the spirit of liberty. Contrary to militant secular thought, a republic needs religion even more than a monarchy does. Or, more sharply, 'Despotism may govern without faith, but liberty cannot.' In a purple passage cited by Aron (1968: 199), Tocqueville celebrates the affinity of religion and liberty. On the one hand, since religious organizations do not aspire to political power they are all the more socially significant: 'religion never more surely establishes its empire than when it reigns in the hearts of men unsupported by aught beside its native strength'. Liberty, in reply, 'considers religion as the safeguard of morality, and morality as the best security of law and the surest pledge of the duration of freedom'.

Religion is therefore necessary to maintain social integration in societies where citizens have been set free from subservience to an authoritarian state. In the French republic, by contrast, an *intégriste* Catholic Church (one seeking to fuse church and nation) is opposed by a secular anticlerical Left – a cultural rift with profound consequences for the social order, manifest today in the tensions over France's Muslim community.

Critics of Tocqueville contend that his analysis of the European scene applies only to Catholic countries such as Italy, Spain and his native France. This has misled American commentators into exaggerating the extent of religious persecution in the Protestant nations of Europe. Thus Bruce (1996: 132–5) says that Dissenters in Britain were free to leave the Established Church and join sects and denominations. Religious persecution of British Dissenters has been greatly exaggerated by Americans who idolize the Pilgrim Fathers. Perhaps it has – though not all 'Dissenters' or 'Nonconformists' would have agreed. Bruce adds that Tocqueville's intellectual descendants have also exaggerated the degree of religious choice actually available in the USA. Parts of the USA are dominated by one or a few denominations; thus 'Utah is as Mormon as Spain is Catholic' (Bruce 1996: 134). Choice is further restricted by the fact that many local churches are in practice ethnic churches.

The new paradigm treats American religiosity as authentic. Notions that religion in America is 'secularized from within', infected by shallow consumerism, and a vehicle of ethnic identity rather than genuine spirituality – all these are rejected as unfounded and condescending. As Stephen Warner pointedly remarks (1993: 1068): 'Since the new paradigm recognizes the historic popularity of American religion, it is more generous than the old paradigm in crediting such forms as genuinely religious.'

A basic shift of focus is involved in the transition to the new paradigm. Instead of seeing religious movements as engaged in an embattled effort to shore up plausibility structures, attention switches to the strategies by which religious institutions are built and resources mobilized to help them grow. The emphasis is on the rise of successful religious movements (e.g. Mormons) rather than the decline of old movements (e.g. Methodism) or the marginality of the feeble new ones (almost all the cults). Alongside this is a concentration on the entrepreneurial activities of individuals – preachers, television evangelists, wealthy sponsors, aspiring politicians and rank-and-file members – rather than on the decline of the clerical profession as manifested in the state-subsidized churches of Europe.

This emerging paradigm has been labelled 'the new voluntarism'. People have choices: they can reject their old allegiances outright, convert to a new identity, or return assertively to the faith of their parents. Religious affiliation is typically chosen, rather than ascribed for all time at birth.

Choice is valued positively: people ought to arrive at their own beliefs for themselves. That is, after all, one of the core values of Protestantism. Choosing a faith is increasingly a self-conscious reflexive process – which does not mean, as Berger believes, that religious allegiance is precarious. Choosing one's religion is the privilege not of selfish materialistic consumers but of mature citizens acting as autonomous individuals. People who switch their allegiance do so for serious reasons. Here is a positive affirmation of consumer society – an issue examined later in chapter 9.

Voluntarism according to Talcott Parsons

The new voluntarism is a development of the 'old' voluntarism of Talcott Parsons, which has been unfashionable since the 1960s. Parsons mounts a full-blooded challenge to the secularization thesis. For Parsons, religion provides a transcendental grounding for a society's ultimate values. All our rules of conduct, folkways, mores and social norms are derived in the final analysis from these ultimate values.

In a sweeping overview of the history of Western Christianity, Parsons (1967) argues that religion has gained in social significance, not lost it. He rejects the bleak Weberian vision of a disenchanted world governed by utilitarian individualism and imprisoned in the iron cage of meaningless bureaucracy (Robertson 1991: 147–8). Parsons's argument is almost the exact opposite of Berger's account of the secularizing principle inherent in Christianity. In the normal course of social evolution, Parsons says, religion has become differentiated from other social institutions. It has lost functions it once had – in education, the legal system, the political order and economic production. In this it resembles the kinship system, which has also conceded functions to other agencies. The shedding of secondary functions, however, does not mean that religion, or kinship, has declined. Rather, they have been liberated. Religion's primary function is to address the problems of meaning in adult life, answering the core questions of the human condition. 'The cognitive meaning of existence, the meaning of happiness and suffering, of goodness and evil, are the central problems of religion' (Parsons 1960: 303) – a view which is exactly the same as Berger's.

Religion's answer to these questions is far more than a neat solution to an intellectual puzzle. In a similar vein to Berger, Parsons (1991: 163) observes that 'death cannot be treated with indifference'. Parsons, like Durkheim before him, sees a powerful motivational outcome of religion. The religious actor is *un homme qui peut davantage*, a man (or woman) who is empowered to contribute more than he (or she) otherwise would to the functioning of society. This is what is implied in Parsons's somewhat opaque statement that religion's core function is 'the regulation of the balance of the motivational commitment of the individual to the values of his society' (Parsons 1960: 302). Religion is a compensatory mechanism that keeps us motivated in the face of evil. No social system is so well integrated that *all* legitimate expectations are fulfilled. Virtue is not always rewarded, vice often goes unpunished, and innocent people suffer. As Parsons says (1991: 164), 'The moral economy of a human society never has perfectly balanced books.' We are back with the theodicy problem. Religion provides a transcendental *Ausgleich*: that is to say, an ultimate balancing of the moral books.

Parsons's account of the rise of Christianity is a story of the progressive differentiation of religion from other social institutions, the emancipation of the autonomous individual, and the suffusion of religious values throughout society. The process was set in train when the early Christian Church made its decisive break with Judaism. Christianity constituted itself as a religious system, whereas Judaism was the culture of a people. The religion of Israel was the whole of culture, not a differentiated part of it. Christ's formula in respect of the Roman Empire – 'Render unto Caesar the things that are Caesar's' – epitomized Christianity's refusal to claim jurisdiction over secular society (unlike Ayatollah Khomeini's Islamic Republic). The church was not the whole of society, but a distinct voluntary community concerned to order its own affairs in accordance with God's will and to spread its message throughout the world. Christianity is individualistic at its very core: Christian churches recruit individuals, not necessarily families, tribes or nations. Individualism does not, however, imply anarchy. Christian churches are normally tightly disciplined, at times fiercely so, as demonstrated by the persecution of heretics.

What, though, of the Holy Roman Empire? Surely the coronation of Charlemagne by Pope Leo III on Christmas Day 800 marked the subordination of the secular powers to the authority of the Western Church? Not according to Parsons, who interprets the coronation both as a religious legitimation of the differentiation between the secular and the sacred, and as signalling their common commitment to shared norms and values. Western Christianity, in Parsons's evolutionary framework, has been more effective than its Eastern counterpart. The Eastern Orthodox Church emphasizes monasticism and other-worldly spirituality, and the subordination of the church to secular authority (Robertson 1991: 155). This may be at the root of Eastern Orthodoxy's inability in our own times to profit from the collapse of Communism. In Russia, the Eastern Orthodox Church has been forced to call upon the post-Communist state to erect protectionist barriers against the evangelical missionary endeavours of Western denominations.

Throughout the medieval period, the Church struggled to avoid being absorbed into the secular state. Religious orders played an important role in this. They were dedicated to cultivating personal piety and preserving the integrity of religion as an institution differentiated from the rest of society. Priestly celibacy was a symbol of this differentiation. Religious orders were power-houses of scholarship, first in the monasteries and later in the universities of medieval Europe. Although the medieval Church was capable of setting its face against science – as in the censure of Galileo – it allowed far more room for the development of an independent intellectual culture than any other religion did in the medieval period. The contrast with the medieval Islamic stranglehold over intellectual life is striking.

For Parsons, unlike most secularization theorists, the Middle Ages were not the high point from which religion has lost social significance, but simply one phase in the evolution of religion. He rejects Troeltsch's view that medieval Catholicism was the last truly Christian form of society (Robertson 1991: 147). Instead, Parsons insists that the Protestant Reformation carried further the principles embedded in Christianity's break with Judaism. Protestant reformers challenged the tutelage of the Catholic Church and the high authority of the priest-hood as guardian of the sacraments. The individual was enfranchised and placed in a more direct relationship with God. Structures of medi-ation between the profane and the sacred – priests, saints, the Virgin Mary – were demoted, or had their functions redefined, or were swept aside. Protestantism gave to individuals the responsibility for their own salvation through faith. This is not secularization, but an opening up of the secular world as a field of Christian endeavour and opportunity.

America's denominational pluralism is seen by Parsons as a further extension of the process unleashed by the emergence of Christianity and carried forward by medieval Catholicism and the Protestant Reformation. People are not born into churches. Instead, they choose their denominational affiliation as autonomous adults. They decide what to believe and which denomination to join. Implicit in the volun-tary principle is religious tolerance. Against secularization theorists, many of whom see tolerance as a sign that religion means very little, Parsons interprets it as an authentic unfolding of the Christian faith.

Underlying the diversity of denominational pluralism is a shared commitment to society's ultimate values. Parsons speaks, controver-sially, of 'the societal community' (Parsons 1977) – a phrase which for some sociologists is a contradiction in terms, since communities are inherently local and cannot be society-wide. In the United States, the core value system centres on mainstream Protestantism, but extends to encompass Catholicism and Judaism. Religious values are highly gen-eralized – but this does not mean that they are empty of meaning. Despite conflict, consensus is real. Parsons asserts that 'To deny that this underlying consensus exists would be to claim that American society stood in a state of latent religious war' (1967: 414) – which would be absurd. Acknowledging that he risks the charge of complacency, he goes on to say that 'in a whole variety of ways modern society is more in accord with Christian values than its forebears have been' (1967: 417).

The demand for religion: a rational choice?

The most controversial expression of the new paradigm in the sociol-ogy of religion is the rational choice theory developed by Stark and Bainbridge (1996). It involves a new mode of discourse about religion and a total reconceptualization of sociological theory. It marks a complete break with Parsonian voluntarism, embracing as it does a style of economic analysis which the whole of Parsons's sociology was designed to refute.

Two fundamental concepts in the Stark–Bainbridge theory of religion are *rewards* and *compensators*. Rewards are anything that people desire, but they typically carry costs – that is, anything that people seek to avoid. People will pursue a reward only if they expect that the benefit they derive from it will exceed the cost they incur in doing so. If a reward is forgone, that counts as a cost; conversely, avoiding a cost is counted as a reward.

Some rewards that people seek are scarce or unavailable. Faced with this, people are willing to accept *compensators* instead. A compensator is a substitute for a reward. It may involve the promise of a future reward if gratification is deferred, and an explanation of how the reward can eventually be obtained. People accept compensators only if rewards are not available.

Among the rewards that people desire are some that are so great and so general that only a religion – that is to say, a supernatural belief system – can produce credible compensators for them. Examples are immortality and enlightenment, which are not obtainable in this life by anybody, or by only a few. We all die, and so doctrines of an afterlife appeal to us all: everyone has a strong motive for being religious. Stark and Bainbridge define religions as *systems of general compensators based on supernaturalist assumptions*.

Their theory is a modern version of Pascal's famous wager, in which belief in God is a sensible bet (or a prudent investment). If God exists, the investment made by the faithful yields them an infinite profit, while the unfaithful bear heavy losses – in purgatory or hell, for example. Conversely, if God does not exist, the faithful have lost very little, and the unfaithful have still gained nothing. The unfaithful always lose, whereas the faithful stand at least a chance of winning.

It follows that naturalistic belief systems, however well grounded in science, simply cannot compete with supernaturalist religion when it comes to the provision of credible compensators for the supreme rewards. Hence the failure of belief systems such as scientific humanism and Marxism-Leninism to appeal to more than a few intellectuals. It also follows that any organization that seeks such rewards as immortality or enlightenment will gravitate towards supernaturalist beliefs, since only supernaturalism can supply sufficiently powerful compensators. Scientology is a case in point: originally a therapeutic system, its religious dimension has become so pronounced that it now campaigns vigorously to be recognized as a religion.

The concept of compensator and the distinction between rewards and compensators are crucial to Stark and Bainbridge's theory. Both are deeply problematic, however. On Stark and Bainbridge's account, there are three aspects to compensators: they are a form of reward; they hold out the promise of future rewards; and they provide an explanation of how such rewards may be obtained. The theory slips continually between these three things.

If compensators are a form of reward, then Stark and Bainbridge cannot claim, as they repeatedly do, that people often 'mistake' compensators for rewards. Nor can it be true that people 'prefer rewards to compensators and attempt to exchange compensators for rewards' (Stark and Bainbridge 1996: 37), since compensators *are* rewards. What the claim amounts to is that people prefer material rewards to spiritual ones. There is no reason to accept this materialistic theory of human motivation.

If, on the other hand, compensators are promises and explanations, then they are not inferior substitutes for material rewards. The choice, as Wallis and Bruce (1984) point out, is not between rewards and compensators, but between secular promises and explanations and religious promises and explanations. It is obvious that we face such a choice; on this point, rational choice theory has not told us anything new.

To treat religion as a system of compensators is not to justify it, but to render it irrational, since a compensator is not a real compensation. Ironically, rational choice theory provides a poor explanation of the rationality of religious faith. For a coherent treatment of faith, we might return to the old voluntarism of Parsons. Religion provides emotional and cognitive resolution of fundamental problems (Parsons 1954, 1991; Kunin 2003: 29–30). The problems are universal, but they bear on people in different ways, and the manner of their resolution varies from one faith tradition to another. There are secular ways of addressing the fundamental problems of meaning, but they are, at the least, not demonstrably superior to religious promises and explanations – also known as hope and faith.

The supply of religion: the benefits of competition?

Berger famously argued, as we saw in the last chapter, that pluralism undermines faith. The very fact of religious diversity introduces doubt: why should one particular faith be the truth and command our allegiance when there are so many others, each with its own truths, vying for acceptance? It is hard, Berger says, to avoid the relativist conclusion that one's faith commitment, or lack of it, is simply a product of accidents of birth and socialization. 'Fundamentalists' may claim a monopoly of the truth, but fundamentalism is a self-conscious effort to will modernity away. The reality of diversity, and therefore of choice, is the guilty secret that corrodes religious faith.

The new paradigm challenges the notion that pre-industrial Europe was an 'age of faith' that reached its zenith in the thirteenth and fourteenth centuries. Ordinary people went to church and took part in religious observances not willingly, but because they had little alternative. In any case, the evidence shows that patterns of observance in pre-industrial societies have been grossly exaggerated. Iannaccone (1997: 41) puts the case forcefully: 'Europe's so-called "age of faith" was in fact an era of widespread religious apathy.' The modern era is the true age of faith, where people participate in religion because, in a healthy competitive market, they freely choose to do so.

One way of putting the point is to say that the religious market-place has suppliers and consumers, as any market does. Secularization theory typically concentrates on the consumer, who supposedly is less and less inclined to demand religious goods and services. In contrast to this, rational choice theorists of religion draw attention to the capacity of religious suppliers to stimulate and satisfy demand for their product. The basic proposition is that free competition is highly desirable. Conditions of monopoly or oligopoly, typically with state subsidies and barriers to entry, breed lazy religious institutions that lack the incentive to market their services effectively. In a competitive market, in contrast, religious firms seek to maximize their profits by increasing their membership and other material resources. If there is no state regulation or state subsidy – both of which distort the market – the success of religious firms will depend on their ability to satisfy their customers. Inefficient firms will eventually be driven out of business. As Iannaccone (1997: 27) bluntly puts it: 'In a highly competitive environment, religions have little choice but to abandon inefficient modes of production and unpopular products in favour of more attractive and profitable alternatives.'

Much of the evidence in favour of the hypothesis that competition benefits religion comes from the United States. For example, Finke and Stark (1992: 22–108) put forward a supply-side explanation of two periods of religious revival in American history. The First Great Awakening, which began in the late 1730s, saw tens of thousands of people flock to hear the preaching of an Englishman, the 'Calvinist Methodist' George Whitefield, just as the Second Great Awakening from the 1790s saw popular enthusiasm for the revivalism of the American-born Charles Finney, a Presbyterian turned Congregationalist, in the

Burned-Over District of Western New York and Ohio, together with a rapid growth of Baptism and Methodism. The standard explanation of these Great Awakenings is that they were a response to an explosion of demand. Against this, Finke and Stark argue that the root cause was an increase in the supply of religion made possible because the colonial establishment was gradually losing its grip on the regulation of the religious market-place. Nostalgic and patriotic images of universal piety during the colonial period are untrue to history. The churching of colonial America faced two major impediments. On the demand side, the American frontier presented all the social problems of a transient population. There were indeed virtuous Puritans, as depicted in American iconography, but there were also apathetic people and irreligious scoundrels. On the supply side stood the mainline established churches of the Old World, the Congregationalists, Episcopalians and Presbyterians. The Congregationalists were legally established in New England, and the Episcopalians in New York, Virginia, Maryland, North and South Carolina, and Georgia. These churches made a poor fist of evangelism. Their genteel ministers, schooled in theological intricacies at Harvard and Yale, were out of touch with the grassroots, unlike their Baptist and Methodist competitors.

The two Great Awakenings are a story of the failure of anaemic, established churches to compete in the emerging free market in religion. Deregulation unleashed competitive energy. The new religious entrepreneurs sold their product hard: the crowds who came to hear George Whitefield did not just materialize or drift in, but had been stimulated by a well-organized advance publicity campaign. In this respect Whitefield was a precursor of evangelists such as Billy Graham and Morris Cerullo.

American experience from the 1960s provides two telling examples of the significance of the supply side. The first is the rise of television evangelism (Hadden and Shupe 1988). In the 1950s, as television became standard equipment in all but the poorest homes, religious broadcasting was dominated by the mainstream Protestant denominations, in alliance with the Catholic Church and Jewish organizations. In order to fulfil the terms of their licence, under which they were required to provide programmes that served the public interest, television stations and networks allocated free airtime to be shared out among the mainstream bodies. It was an arrangement that suited all parties: the networks were able to comply with their legal obligations without any trouble, while the liberal mainstream enjoyed a virtual monopoly of religious broadcasting, effectively excluding the sects and the evangelicals (Christiano et al. 2002: 283–4).

This comfortable compromise rapidly fell apart after 1960, the year in which the Federal Communications Commission ruled that the public interest could be served by commercially funded programmes as well as by programmes benefiting from free airtime. The implication was clear: the networks had an incentive to sell airtime to the highest bidder. Within a decade, free airtime for religious broadcasting virtually disappeared. In the new commercial situation, as Hadden and Shupe document, it was not the mainstream liberal churches but the evangelical and fundamentalist preachers, with no strong ties to any particular denomination, who were willing to take the enormous risks of purchasing airtime and making the other investments needed to produce programs for a mass audience. (The spectacular fall of Jim and Tammy Bakker's *Praise the Lord* network demonstrates that the financial basis of such ventures could be precarious.) Conservative evangelicals now control at least six national television networks and almost all the religious radio stations (Blake 2005). The rise of the televangelists was not so much a response to new consumer demands as the result of a change in public policy that radically altered the conditions under which religion was produced for a mass audience.

Television evangelists have been enthusiastic advocates of 'the prosperity gospel'. God wants humanity to enjoy health and wealth; therefore, the faithful can expect to do so. Prayers to God are confident demands for tangible rewards, not tentative aspirations for vague blessings. There is no place in the prosperity gospel for modesty and self-effacement. In some cases, notably among televangelists, the proposition is that God will reward you in proportion to your giving to the cause. A famous example is Oral Roberts's concept of 'seed-faith': 'You Sow It, Then God Will Grow It.' The seed is, of course, a donation to Roberts's organization. In an earlier phase of his ministry he offered the 'Blessing-Pact', which put divine intervention on a predictable footing: subscribers who donated $100 were guaranteed their money back if they had not already received it from an unexpected source within one year (Coleman 2000: 41–2). Fund raising, as Hadden and Shupe point out (1987: 66), has been transformed from an incidental to an integral activity; no longer a means to an end, it is an end in itself.

The second American example that illustrates the significance of the supply side is the impact on 1960s counterculture of Asian faiths, including Hare Krishna, Transcendental Meditation, the Divine Light Mission, the Unification Church, 3HO (the Healthy, Happy, Holy Organization), Meher Baba and numerous others. This apparent turn to the East was interpreted by many commentators as a rejection of Western consumer culture. The Western version of modernity was thought to be in deep crisis. Against this, Finke and Stark (1992: 239–44) make three main points. First, the phenomenon was scarcely new, since Eastern faiths and philosophies had attracted interest in America for more than a century. For example, the influential Theosophical Society (Wilson 1970: 157–60) was founded in New York in 1875. Its founder, Madame Helena Petrovna Blavatsky, had received her teaching in Tibet from spiritual masters who revealed to her the hidden secrets of the cosmos and the human condition. In its heyday Theosophy became fashionable, and influenced other metaphysically oriented belief systems; in our own times, Theosophical ideas have influenced a number of UFO cults (Partridge 2003). Second, for all the debate surrounding them in the 1960s, the Asian faiths in the USA have always had tiny memberships – typically a few hundred members each. The controversy they provoked is out of all proportion to their membership. If we are looking for growth religions, we should turn not to the East, but closer to home – to the Mormons, Jehovah's Witnesses, Seventh-day Adventists and Christian Scientists. Third, and most important of all, is the history of American immigration laws. After the First World War, immigration quotas were calculated on data from the 1890 Census, which favoured migrants from northern and western Europe. Eastern religious teachers and gurus were admitted for only brief visits on tourist visas. The crucial turning-point came in 1965, when US immigration quotas were recalculated in such a way that migration from Latin America, the Caribbean and Asia dramatically increased. Religious entrepreneurs responded quickly. Before the year was out, His Divine Grace A. C. Bhaktivedanta Swami Prabhupada, founder of the International Society for Krishna Consciousness, had taken up residence in New York. He then shrewdly moved the headquarters of his operation to the symbolic capital of the counterculture, San Francisco. As Melton (1992: 10) puts it, 'For the first time Asian faiths became a genuine option for religious seekers in the West.'

Levels of rank-and-file participation in religious organizations are high if and only if the market is competitive. This is shown by the striking contrast between the high participation rate in the USA and the low rates in European countries such as Sweden, with its state-subsidized liberal Protestant churches. It is also shown by the revival of religious participation in the USA. On Finke's evidence, whereas in 1850 only one-third of Americans belonged to a church, by 1980 the figure had increased to almost two-thirds. High rates of religious participation in the USA are not some irrational survival of ethnic identity, but the result of a free market. Over the past century, the USA has witnessed a process of 'churching'. Contra the secularization thesis, a similar revival of religious participation would happen in Europe if the state withdrew its subsidies, forcing religious organizations into competition for customers.

One example where this appears to have happened is Italy (Introvigne and Stark 2005). The year 1984 was a watershed: in that year, the government negotiated a new financial relationship with the Catholic Church, in which parish priests ceased to receive a salary from the state. Instead, Italians were required to pay a new tax, the *otto per mille* (meaning 0.8 per cent). Each year, taxpayers can choose whether this tax goes directly to the state for humanitarian purposes, or to their personal choice from a list of participating religious bodies, of which the Catholic Church is one. The result, say Introvigne and Stark, has been 'an intense, very public, yearly competition to persuade taxpayers to give their taxes to one religious "firm" rather than another'. The impact has been cultural as well as financial: Italians are reminded annually that there is a vibrant market in religious services competing for their support. The Italian religious economy has been transformed, and Italy has experienced a religious revival from which, despite – or rather, because of – competition from Protestant denominations, the Catholic Church has been the chief beneficiary.

Outside Europe and the United States, the flowering of religious activity in Japan since 1945 has been cited (Finke 1997) as a further example of the benefits of deregulation. Before the Second World War, the imperial Japanese state exercised tight control over religious practice. It subsidized Shinto, associating it with the identity and destiny of the nation, and repressed alternative religions. Post-war reconstruction of Japan as a modern democratic nation brought with it deregulation of religion, including disestablishment of Shinto. In this favourable, deregulated market-place, vigorous movements like Sōka Gakkai have flourished. All of this stands in contrast to Germany, also defeated in the war, but which has retained a strong state regulation of religion in order to defend democracy against the threat of authoritarian movements. Unlike Japan, Germany predictably presents us with the familiar picture of apparently irreversible secularization.

The supply side of religion is obviously important, and new paradigm theorists are justified in emphasizing it. It has not been proved, however, that deregulation necessarily unleashes healthy competition, and therefore increases the vitality of religion. Many new paradigm writers are 'market fundamentalists' (Stiglitz 2002): they assume, as a matter of dogma, that deregulation is a necessary and sufficient condition for promoting a competitive market and thereby providing consumers with what they want. Conversely, in the eyes of market fundamentalists, a regulated market cannot but produce lazy firms, poor-quality goods and services, and disaffected consumers.

Reviewing a large body of research, Chaves and Gorski (2001: 275) conclude that 'there are some contexts in which pluralism and vitality are positively correlated, some in which they are negatively correlated, and some in which the correlation is null'. There are also problems in the analysis of the statistical evidence, suggesting that the apparent link between competition and vitality is a statistical artefact, not a causal relationship (Voas, Crockett and Olson 2002).

Key terms such as 'pluralism', 'vitality' and 'competition' are notoriously difficult to measure. A feature of new paradigm approaches has been the tendency to focus entirely on quantitative measures of aggregate attendance and participation as the indicators of vitality and success. This reflects a commitment to *methodological individualism*, a prescriptive doctrine that holds that all sociological explanations are reducible to facts about individuals and individual behaviour (Lukes 1973b: 110–22). Methodological individualists do not see religious culture as anything more than the sum of the religiosity of individuals.

A crucial message of Stephen Warner's 1993 article was that sociologists could work within the new paradigm without needing to buy into rational choice theory. Utilitarian rationality, methodological individualism and market fundamentalism: we can dispense with them all, and still understand the continuing appeal of religion and its impact on individuals and society.

The Mormons: a new world faith?

Membership statistics published annually by the Church of Jesus Christ of Latter-day Saints show apparently unstoppable growth. The Book of Mormon, a sacred text standing alongside the Bible, has sold 120 million copies, and is currently available in 106 languages.

The church's rate of growth has been impressive throughout its history. At its foundation in 1830 it had a few hundred members. After a turbulent period, thousands of Mormons made the great trek to Salt Lake City in Utah from 1846 onwards. When Utah became a state in 1896, the Mormon Church already had a quarter of a million members. Since the end of the Second World War it has doubled its membership roughly every fifteen years, which implies an average annual growth rate of about 5 per cent. It had one million members in 1947, two million in 1963, three million in 1971, four million in 1978, and stood at more than twelve million in 2005. As Stark (1990: 205) points out, its highest rates of growth are now not in its most mature market (the USA, where 46 per cent of all Mormons live) but elsewhere, particularly South America, Central America and Mexico. It is worth adding that one feature of the LDS Church is its diligence in assembling accurate statistics – an indication of its efficiency as a thoroughly modern organization.

How can this success be explained? In Stark's original model, there are eight factors that contribute to the success of new religious movements. I have reorganized them into two broad categories.

Effective mobilization of resources

Strong leadership has always been highly valued by the Mormon Church. It encourages all members to participate actively in its affairs, and requires them to tithe a tenth of their income to the Church. It is constituted as a hierarchy similar in many ways to that of the Roman Catholic Church, with wards (i.e. churches) headed by bishops (equivalent to priests) and organized into stakes (dioceses). At the apex of the movement is a quorum of twelve apostles, two counsellors and the President, who is endowed with prophetic powers and open to new revelations from God. Obedience to authority is expected. As in Catholicism, women are excluded from leadership roles in the Mormon Church's chain of command. A crucial difference from the Catholic Church, however, is that Mormons have a lay priesthood. Not only does this imply active lay involvement, it has also meant that the LDS church escaped one of the critical problems facing Catholicism and liberal Protestantism: the serious decline in men coming forward with a vocation to the priesthood.

Movements that fail to retain their own children in active membership will inevitably decline, since they will not be able to recruit enough committed new people to replace those they lose through the normal processes of attrition. Mormons are fertile people who devote time and effort to effective socialization of their children. Mormon priesthood is divided into two separate orders, the lower Aaronic and the higher Melchizedek priesthood, each of which is subdivided into three grades. The result is an objective career structure through which all Mormon males are expected to advance (O'Dea 1957: 174–85). Mormon children are involved at an early age in the organizational structures of the faith – boys through their incorporation into the priesthood, girls through their role as helpers and facilitators of their menfolk.

Mobilizing family values and kinship networks plays a vital part in the church's success. Mormon views on family life are conventional and conservative, with the man securely installed as head of the household. His wife is subject to his authority, and is charged with particular responsibility for the upbringing of their children, who are expected to be well behaved and obedient. Procreation is valued, since it enables a new spirit to enter this life; hence neither celibacy nor voluntary childlessness are valid options. The family is at the heart of human life in this world and the next. Sacred ordinances that Mormons perform in the temple enable them to seal their marriages for all eternity. They also perform baptisms on behalf of their ancestors, so that they can be reunited with their forebears after death. Consistent with this, Mormon proselytizing is oriented towards recruiting families rather than individuals. Exogamy (marrying outside the faith) carries a heavy spiritual penalty. Only couples whose marriage is sealed in a Mormon temple will enjoy eternal marital bliss in the next life. Mormons who marry outside the faith will be divorced at death, and will not be able to attain the celestial kingdom.

Managing cultural identity and difference

New religious movements can succeed, Bainbridge says (1997: 411), if they are 'deviant but not too deviant'. If they are not offering anything new, why should anyone incur the cost of transferring allegiance to them? On the other hand, if they are too deviant, most people will judge the cost of conversion to be simply too high.

In the early years of its history, the LDS Church existed in a high state of tension with the wider society. Mormons made no fewer than four failed attempts to build their own city. Violent clashes were frequent, culminating in the murder of Joseph Smith and his brother Hyrum by an armed mob in 1844. The great Mormon trek began two years later under the leadership of Smith's successor, Brigham Young. In a supreme expression of the pioneering spirit, they struggled across Iowa and into Nebraska, before embarking on an arduous 1,300-mile trek to the Valley of the Great Salt Lake. They saw themselves as re-enacting the exodus of the people of Israel from captivity, and their experiences stamped them with a profound sense of ethnic identity as a 'people' (O'Dea 1966: 70).

The violent confrontations between Mormons and the wider society had complex causes, including the practice of polygamy (more precisely, polygyny – plural wives), which was a symbolic affront to Christian and humanistic values. As the century drew on, the federal authorities passed increasingly punitive legislation outlawing plural marriage. Repeated requests that Utah be granted statehood were flatly rejected; polygamy was the chief obstacle. Finally, under mounting pressure, the Church's new president, Wilford Woodruff, issued an official statement in 1890 formally abandoning polygamy. This signalled the end of Mormon 'separatism'. Six years later, Utah became the forty-fifth state of the Union. Ever since its drastic about-turn on polygamy, the church has totally repudiated fundamentalist splinter groups – 'hold-outs' – which continue to recognize plural marriages. Within contemporary Mormon thought, polygamy 'has retreated to the limbo of theological relics' (O'Dea 1966: 140).

For most of its history the LDS Church excluded men 'of African lineage' from the priesthood. The theological justification given for this was the argument that Noah's son Ham and his descendants had been cursed by God with a black skin, just as the North American 'Indians' had been. This argument, widely used by anti-abolitionists to justify slavery, was absorbed into Mormon theology. With the growth of the civil rights movement in the 1960s, the Mormon Church stood accused of overt racism. Protests were directed at key symbols of Mormon achievement and respectability, including the Mormon Tabernacle Choir and sports teams representing Brigham Young University. Mormon missionary efforts in Africa were hampered by the closure of the priesthood to black Africans. The Church faced further problems in Brazil, a racially mixed society in which racial lineage is hard even for a racist to determine; Brazilian Mormons faced the challenge of determining precisely which of their ancestors were eligible for proxy ordination to the priesthood (Embry 1994: 27). In this cultural climate the Mormon Church began to retreat from a doctrinaire position on priesthood. The reason for the ban on African-Caribbeans was argued to be a divine mystery; Mormons hoped that God would act to lift the ban once the time was ripe. Some Mormons even argued that the exclusion of black men from the priesthood was more a matter of cultural practice than of revealed faith, a practice shaped, moreover, by the Church's unfortunate exposure to racist ideology in the antebellum South. In 1978, after earnestly praying for guidance, the president of the Church, Spencer W. Kimball, received a revelation from God that the ban on blacks entering the priesthood had been lifted. As with its abandonment of polygamy, openness to divine revelation provided the Mormon Church with a theological basis for a timely reversal of doctrine and practice.

Although many Mormon beliefs are the same as or similar to the teachings of mainstream Christian churches, there are some striking departures that mark Mormon belief and practice as 'deviant'. An obvious instance is the status of the Book of Mormon as a sacred text alongside the Bible. Only Mormons and Mormon splinter groups treat it as sacred; other faiths either ignore or dismiss it. Baptism performed vicariously for deceased ancestors is a uniquely Mormon rite. A further departure from the Christian mainstream is the teaching that God is not an immaterial spirit but a being with a physical male body of flesh and bone. One consequence is the belief that Jesus was conceived in a physical union between God and Mary. There is also a widespread belief among Mormons – though it appears to fall short of an official doctrine – that we have a 'Mother in Heaven', implying that God is married (Heeren et al. 1984). Mormons also believe – and there are parallels here with Eastern Orthodox spirituality – that righteous human beings can attain the status of godhead in the celestial kingdom, though without ever becoming equal with God himself.

Significantly, church members do not draw attention to these more deviant beliefs and practices in their initial contacts with potential converts. Unlike mainstream Christian churches, the Church of Jesus Christ of Latter-day Saints is reticent about various details of its doctrine and temple worship, reserving their disclosure to people who are already members. One example is the 'temple garment', an item of underclothing covering the chest and part of the lower body, and modelled on a revelation by the angel Moroni to Joseph Smith. Latter-day Saints are urged not to display it to non-Mormons (D. J. Davies, 2003: 217), which has inevitably provoked prurient speculation about its appearance. It is, as befits the church, a modest and somewhat clumsy garment, symbolizing wholesomeness rather than allure. Among Mormons, it has been popularly endowed with magical properties, including protecting the wearer against fire, accidents and sexual temptation.

In carefully cultivating such secrets, the church resembles Freemasonry: the secrets of the craft are revealed gradually, and only after a man has been initiated into the brotherhood. Joseph Smith based Mormon ritual on Masonry, into which he was initiated as a young man, and which he came to see as a degenerate version of the early church rites that he was restoring (O'Dea 1957: 57).

If Mormonism maintains beliefs and practices that give it a distinct identity, it also displays a significant degree of continuity with the concepts, beliefs, values, mores, symbols and rituals of the dominant religious tradition of the host society. Individual converts can retain most of their cultural capital, which they simply transfer to their new faith; they are not starting totally from scratch (Stark 1998: 39–40). The Church regards itself not as a new religion, but as a restoration of the early Church as it was in the time of the apostles in the first century. Christians who convert to Mormonism do not have to recast most of what they once believed and practised – which they would have to do if they joined, say, Hare Krishna. Mormons read the Christian Old and New Testaments, adding to them new revelations in the Book of Mormon, the *Doctrine and Covenants*, and the *Pearl of Great Price*. Since all these sacred volumes are written in the language of the King James Bible (the 'Authorized Version'), they have a familiar ring and an overall coherence (D. J. Davies, 2003: 43–4).

Mormonism has much in common with core values of conservative Christianity in the USA. Mormons uphold family life, a conventional gender division of labour, obedience of children to parents, and marital fidelity. They oppose abortion, gambling, pre-marital sex, pornography and homosexuality. They require members to dress 'modestly'. They advocate the virtues of the Puritan ethic, including hard work, thrift and deferred gratification. They virtuously extend the Puritan prohibition of alcohol and tobacco to all beverages containing caffeine, including tea, coffee and cola drinks – an apparently trivial proscription, but one with a deep cultural significance (C. Davies 1996). Like the Jewish dietary laws, it has a boundary-maintenance function, setting Mormons apart as a peculiar people and making sharing a meal with 'Gentiles' more difficult – a factor that is especially important in the socialization of Mormon children. Unlike in the Jewish case, it is also an aid to proselytism: it signals that Mormons are even more clean-living than conservative Protestants, and it resonates with contemporary preoccupations with a healthy diet. It is a telling instance of the potent combination of cultural difference and cultural continuity.

As Wilson says (1970: 200), Mormons' adherence to the Puritan work ethic is 'dissociated from the tensions of Puritan asceticism'. Worldly achievement is not a problem to them. The value of education as an engine of success was decisively symbolized by the foundation of Brigham Young Academy in 1875, which in 1903 became Brigham Young University. Personal advancement does not end with death, but continues in the afterlife. The Mormon Church teaches that there are three heavenly kingdoms, characteristically arranged in a hierarchy. The *celestial kingdom* is reserved for the righteous, who will dwell with God. They will live with their spouse and their children, with whom they have been sealed for eternity, and in the company of ancestors who have accepted the baptism performed for them by their descendants. Couples in the celestial state will continue to propagate children (these will be spirits). Second in the heavenly hierarchy is the *terrestrial kingdom*, which is visited by Jesus but not by God, and in which people will be single rather than married. Mormons who have married outside the faith will reside here, separated from their former partner. Below this stands the *telestial kingdom*, reserved for people who have led unclean lives. They will receive the Holy Spirit and be ministered to by members of the terrestrial kingdom, but are for ever banned from the presence of God and Christ. Although transfer from one kingdom to another is not available, it is possible to improve one's position within a kingdom by good works. Opportunities for upward mobility never cease.

Jehovah's Witnesses: overcoming the failure of prophecy

Jehovah's Witnesses have enjoyed an exceptionally high rate of growth, averaging approximately 5 per cent annually, which means that they double their membership about every fifteen years. In 2005 there were more than six and a half million Jehovah's Witnesses worldwide. In some ways, their growth is even more spectacular than that of the Mormons. Witnesses count only active 'publishers' as members, which means that they exclude from their statistics almost everyone under the age of sixteen.

The Watch Tower Bible and Tract Society mobilizes the services of millions of unpaid, dedicated lay volunteers ('publishers') who, despite all the insults they endure, persist in knocking on strangers' doors to bring them the good news and a chance to come into the truth. Every Witness is a missionary, leaving no role for anyone who wishes simply to tag along as a free-rider (Iannaccone 1997: 35–6). Kingdom Halls are businesslike places where members are prepared for the challenge of spreading a demanding faith to a frequently hostile public. Sociability is not valued as an end in itself (Beckford 1975: 86).

Tension has periodically been extremely high. Witnesses were sent to concentration camps in Nazi Germany. They were severely persecuted under Communism. In Muslim societies they are in a precarious situation, given that it is a crime to persuade anyone to apostatize from Islam. In some Catholic countries, such as Spain and Italy, it has been illegal until quite recently for Witnesses to function, and they continue to experience problems in Greece. In the United States, the Watch Tower Society fought a long battle to enable its members to opt out of saluting the Flag and saying the Pledge of Allegiance. Their constitutional rights were eventually upheld by a Supreme Court ruling in 1943. During the Second World War, Witnesses throughout the West were imprisoned for refusal to enlist in the war effort. Their treatment by the authorities was typically harsher than that experienced by more respectable conscientious objectors such as Quakers – which is not to minimize the hardship that Quakers suffered.

For Jehovah's Witnesses, then, the problem has been to keep tension with the wider society in check. That said, it is also probably true, as Stark and Iannaccone comment (1997: 145–6), that in their everyday life most Witnesses are not too uncomfortable with the wider culture. Above all, they are not a 'peculiar people' who display oddities that set them apart. They drink alcohol (though not to excess), they do not eat a special diet, they use cosmetics to look smart, they do not wear unusual dress or any uniform, they have no obvious peculiarities of speech, and they take part in popular social activities such as spectating at sports events, going to the theatre and cinema, and watching television (though they are careful to avoid sex and violence). Except when they are on the doorsteps, they are not visible as Witnesses. Stark and Iannaccone (1997: 146) suggest the hypothesis that 'visibility may, in fact, be the crucial factor for identifying when groups impose too much tension or strictness'.

The movement's roots, like those of other millenarians such as Seventh-day Adventists, lie in the 'Great Disappointment' – the failure of William Miller's prediction that the world would end in 1843 or 1844 (Bainbridge 1997: 89–96). For many years the Watch Tower Society taught that the present world order would come to an end in 1975. Although the movement now denies that it was officially predicted by the society, there is no doubt that the vast majority of Witnesses were expecting momentous events before 1975 was out. Yet nothing happened. How then did the movement survive?

A classic study by Festinger, Riecken and Schachter (1956), *When Prophecy Fails*, has often been read as demonstrating that, paradoxically, movements are strengthened by the failure of prophecy. The argument draws on the social-psychological theory of *cognitive dissonance*. According to this theory, people find it stressful to hold dissonant cognitions – that is, contradictory beliefs, opinions, attitudes or self-perceptions. Because dissonance is unpleasant, people try to resolve it by changing their cognitions to make them consistent with one another. Festinger et al. used cognitive dissonance theory to explain the behaviour of members of a flying saucer cult. They believed that their leader was in touch with a spiritual being called Sananda, the personification of Jesus Christ. Sananda warned that large areas of the United States would be destroyed on 21 December 1954, but promised that his followers would be rescued by spaceship. The due date arrived, and passed without incident. The crucial point, Festinger et al. claim, is that far from abandoning their beliefs, the cult members redoubled their efforts to proselytize at the very moment when their prediction had been disproved. Bringing more people into the movement would reduce the dissonance between the leaders' prophecy and the failure of either the cataclysm or the spaceships to appear. If more and more people are persuaded to join, a belief system becomes psychologically more plausible. Festinger et al. speculate that a similar mechanism may have been at work after Jesus's messiahship ended in crucifixion, the most agonizing and humiliating death that the Roman Empire could devise.

There are many reasons to doubt that this interpretation stands up, as Bainbridge (1997: 134–8) has pointed out. The flying saucer cult had a tiny membership, and Festinger's research team appear to have contributed unintentionally to the group's vitality and sense of its own importance. The news media were also pressing for a statement from the cult about the failure of its prophecy. There is no evidence of sustained proselytizing endeavour by cult members. Far from it: after a period of turmoil, the movement soon fizzled out. The evidence points the opposite way to the conventional interpretation. A catastrophically failed prophecy caused the movement to fold after a brief posture of defiance.

Other studies have failed to confirm this thesis of cognitive dissonance theory. The point, surely, is that a failed prophecy is a serious problem that has to be overcome. Failed prophecies cause people to leave movements, not join them. When prophecy fails, the movement has to devote considerable cultural work to repairing the damage. For this reason, Stark has added the following proposition to his theory of religious growth: 'New religious movements are likely to succeed to the extent that their doctrines are non-empirical' (Stark and Iannaccone 1997: 143).

On a rational calculation of organizational benefit, there is no need for a religious movement to predict exactly when the world will end. In religious terms a prophecy does not have to entail a prediction. Prophets are not necessarily seers or clairvoyants. The essence of prophecy is that the prophet calls down God's judgement on the world. The prophet's core activity is to forth-tell God's will, not foretell the future. One of the ways in which religious movements cope with failed predictions is to emphasize their prophetic element. So, even though 1975 was not the end, it remains obvious to Jehovah's Witnesses that we are living in the last days. A few minutes watching the news on TV is all it takes to prove this.

The failure of the 1975 prophecy set the movement back (Stark and Iannaccone 1997: 142–4). Some members were demotivated, some defected, the movement's growth rate slowed down, and there was a crisis among the leadership over the failed prophecy (Penton 1985).

Only with considerable effort did the movement re-establish its rate of growth. It appears that the society is unlikely to set a new date for Armageddon. The conclusion is the converse of the one conventionally drawn from Festinger et al.'s study. It is not that failed prophecies stimulate religious growth, but that strong movements can survive failed prophecies.

A crucial consequence of its high growth rate is that at any given time a significant proportion of the society's members are relatively recent converts. Probably more than 60 per cent of today's Jehovah's Witnesses joined the movement after 1975. The society has less need to explain to them why prophecy failed. Typing '1975' into the search engine on the society's official website yields no references to the failed prophecy. In the spiritual autobiography of Jehovah's Witnesses it is pre-history. High rates of growth help movements to live down past problems.

However successful they are in winning recruits, Jehovah's Witnesses and the LDS Church are likely to remain voluntary religious movements. They are not politically motivated to seize command of the state's instruments of power. Although they are international in scope, they have had only a weak impact on the societies in which they operate. They have reached an accommodation with their host societies. Despite their spectacular growth, Jehovah's Witnesses and Latter-day Saints lack the capacity or even the will to transform the world. These epistemologically authoritarian movements, according to secularization theorists, should be seen not as agents of social change but simply as the form of religion best adapted to survival in a secular world.

The new paradigm and the rise of the megachurches

Donald Miller (1997) argues that we are witnessing a Third Great Awakening, or even a second Reformation, manifested in the growth of a new form of Christian community. These 'new paradigm' churches have succeeded in responding to the therapeutic, individualistic and anti-establishment themes of contemporary culture, but without falling into the trap of narcissism. Their teachings are conservative – they value conventional family formations and gender roles, oppose abortion, and condemn homosexuality – but this is not a 'fundamentalist', backward-looking rejection of modernity. Their golden age is not a fictionalized small-town America but a vision of first-century Christianity, when the fledgling Church was filled with the Holy Spirit.

'New paradigm' churches developed from the mid-1960s onward, attracting people who were born after 1945 – the 'baby boom' generation.

Their main constituency is white middle-class families, well educated and consumer-oriented. Worship is contemporary, generates physical and emotional involvement, and is infused with the spirit of joy and celebration. Preaching is firmly rooted in the Bible, but does not take the form of stern admonitions and fear of hell-fire. Clergy are approachable, while displaying strong leadership qualities. Many clergy have not undergone official training, and are therefore unfettered by outdated seminary prescriptions on how to run a church. Lay people are actively engaged in leadership roles.

New paradigm churches have kept in touch with the values of the baby boom generation. Baby boomers, in Miller's analysis, lack brand loyalty, and do not cherish denominational traditions. Their orientation is to their local situation, not to a hierarchy located in some remote headquarters. Although they respect ministers of religion, they also expect to be involved in running church affairs. These churches are, in Miller's words (1997: 1), 'democratizing access to the sacred by radicalizing the Protestant principle of the priesthood of all believers'.

One example of the new paradigm are small-scale gatherings of young people who share particular ethnic identities or lifestyle choices (Flory and Miller 2000). These communities reject received understandings of religion, formal denominational boundaries, traditional authority structures, and conventionally ascribed status positions. They revel in fluidity, indeterminacy, and flouting convention. Hence such transgressive combinations as clean-cut surfer punks, evangelical Christians sporting tattoos, and skinheads opposed to racism. Their quest is not for community as conventionally understood, but for a looser neo-tribal association, a community without commitment, in which aesthetic preferences, particularly tastes in music, are a vital source of individual and cultural identity. Contrary to the stereotype of idleness, drifting, cynicism and malcontent, the participants in these gatherings include dynamic spiritual entrepreneurs who do not simply consume religion, but produce it.

Of all the various manifestations of the new paradigm, so-called megachurches have attracted the most attention. This is Protestantism revamped, and on a big scale. As their name implies, megachurches are defined by their size; astonishingly, they attract at least 2,000 worshippers each week. By contrast, the median size of a congregation in the USA is seventy-five regular participants (Chaves 2004).

Megachurches have enjoyed explosive growth since the 1980s. Although their heartland is the sunbelt states of California, Texas, Florida and Georgia, they are now spreading north, and have also established a presence in Latin America, the UK, Australia and Singapore.

Their favoured location is in the suburbs of sprawling cities, where they are easily accessible by car and where extensive parking can be provided. If the future is suburban, megachurches may have a permanent place among the religious formations that are well adapted to the modern world.

The size of the megachurches has a number of crucial consequences (Thumma 1998). Sheer size is attractive to anyone who believes that big is beautiful and a sign of God's blessing. Megachurches are affluent, and they lavish resources on well-appointed buildings and facilities and professionally presented worship. Their celebration of success and prosperity is unabashed. Size brings choice: these huge communities can cater for all manner of spiritual and recreational tastes. The superabundance of services they offer replicates the consumer experience of shopping in a hypermarket or mall. Size also reduces the free-rider problem. Free-riders may be less of a financial drain on a large organization than on a small one. More importantly, even if free-riders are not making a full contribution, their mere presence is beneficial, since it swells the numbers and adds to the image of a massively successful community.

The megachurch phenomenon is not without problems. Church leaders may adopt an informal manner, but this does not negate the degree of charismatic authority they wield, which lends itself to problems of authoritarianism, corruption, and the potential for a succession crisis. Size also brings the challenge of creating a sense of intimacy and fellowship among a congregation numbered in thousands – although many megachurches address this problem by providing small group meetings in addition to the main worship (Wuthnow 1996).

Megachurches relate to the Christian mainstream in various ways, as Thumma points out. At one pole are the non-traditional churches, which aim to appeal to seekers and the unchurched, and which are purposely remaking tradition by discarding many of the negative symbols of organized religion. At the other pole, the conventional megachurches retain and emphasize symbols traditionally found in church. Whatever their type, the majority of megachurches are not affiliated with, or have only very loose ties to, any denomination. This, one might say, is the principle of denominationalism carried to its logical conclusion.

The Pentecostals

On a worldwide scale, probably the most startling growth has been achieved by churches and church groupings, including megachurches, that can be broadly termed Pentecostal and neo-Pentecostal/charismatic. According to Martin's conservative estimate, they amount to a quarter of a billion people, which is one in eight of the world's Christians and one in twenty-five of the global population (Martin 2002: 1).

Pentecostalism has outgrown its origins in Methodism and the late nineteenth-century Holiness Movement that arose from it. It now appeals to a wide constituency, from the respectable poor of Latin America to the new middle classes of West Africa and South-East Asia. As state and church monopolies begin to crumble, so Pentecostalism is freed from constraints, enabling it to offer, as it has done in Brazil, a 'substitute society' which 'cares largely for its own, by way of schools, orphanages, homes for the elderly and informal employment exchanges' (Martin 1990: 258). Its operations may be local, but its vision is global. Bruce (2003: 93) points to its successful blend of 'a highly abstract imagined international community with a local voluntary association of self-selecting like-minded believers'.

Not only has Pentecostalism challenged the supremacy of the Catholic Church in Latin America, it has also appealed to a growing number of Hispanic migrants to the United States. The statistics are contested, but it is undeniable that some inroads into Catholicism have been made. Pentecostal and other Protestant churches typically offer a warmer welcome, a more informal and exuberant style of worship, and closer and less hierarchical relations with people in ministerial roles (Christiano et al. 2002: 222–3). Since the values promoted by Pentecostal churches are conducive to economic advancement and social respectability, conversion may facilitate assimilation.

Most Pentecostal churches have moved away from the sectarian forms of community that were widespread 100 years ago. The label 'fundamentalist' is often applied to them, but as Martin observes (2002: 1–2), it is seriously misleading. True, Pentecostal churches are theologically conservative and emphasize the binding authority of the Bible. Thus the Assemblies of God, the largest and by no means the most conservative of the Pentecostal churches, unequivocally proclaims that 'The Scriptures, both the Old and New Testaments, are verbally inspired of God and are the revelation of God to man, the infallible, authoritative rule of faith and conduct.' Its teachings on controversial issues such as women's ministry, homosexuality and abortion are all framed in terms of scriptural authority.

Even so, Pentecostalism is radically different from the fundamentalism depicted in Ammerman's *Bible Believers* (1987), as discussed in the next chapter. Pentecostalism emphasizes not the rationalistic defence of an inerrant Bible, but the empowerment of the individual through experiencing the gifts of the Holy Spirit. Its worship is enthusiastic and emotionally charged. Far from seeking to keep apart from the world, as strict fundamentalist do, Pentecostal churches are keen to compete in the spiritual market-place. For all their conservatism, they are less a protest against modernity than a vehicle and a celebration of it.

Pentecostal and charismatic Christianity are the leading examples of what Woodhead and Heelas (2000) call 'experiential religions of difference'. Traditional 'religions of difference' emphasize the gulf between God and humanity, locating ultimate truth, goodness and authority in a realm that transcends the domains of nature and culture. Pentecostalism and charismatic Christianity retain this emphasis on the transcendent, but add to it a vital role for personal experience and spirituality. They have succeeded in combining three elements: doctrinal certainties, intense personal spirituality, and a vibrant community of faith. Drawing on the classical sociological theories discussed in chapter 4, it can be said that they provide what Durkheim saw as essential, a moral community, while also building something that was vital to Simmel's analysis of the crisis of modernity – a bridge between the objective content of religious doctrines and the subjective reality of spiritual experiences.

6

Fundamentalism

The choice between authority and uncertainty is one of the 'tribulations of the self' identified by Giddens (1991: 181–208) as existential dilemmas that confront us all. In a detraditionalized culture, there are no final authorities. Radical doubt is always with us, insinuating itself into every corner of the life-world. Fundamentalism, so-called, is a possible haven, though a precarious one. Pursuing a theme developed by Berger, Giddens argues that reflexivity affects even fundamentalism: it is hard to escape the uneasy acknowledgement that fundamentalism is itself a cultural choice from a range of options. Fundamentalism's strident denunciation of its opponents is thus a sign of its weakness. For Giddens, as for Berger, dogmatic authoritarianism is a pathological mutation of faith.

Any serious discussion of 'fundamentalism' must address the objection that the concept is useless for the analysis of the ideologies and social movements to which it points. Fundamentalism has arguably become such an ambiguous, misleading and derogatory term that its use may serve not to challenge prejudice and stereotypes but to perpetuate them.

Acknowledging these reservations about fundamentalism, Bruce (2000) maintains that academics fuss too much about linguistic problems. Since all key concepts are contested, it would be foolish to expect complete consensus on their meaning. In any case, he says, fundamentalism is now so entrenched in discourses about religion that trying to dislodge it would be hopeless. Even so, debates about fundamentalism typically reveal at least as much about 'us' as about the fundamentalist 'others'.

Bible believers

Although fundamentalism in common usage has come to imply ignorance, bigotry and fanaticism, it originated as a positive assertion of Christian faith. Protestant fundamentalists in the United States claimed their name from a series of tracts entitled *The Fundamentals*, which were written by leading American, Canadian and British conservative theologians. Financed by two Californian oil tycoons and published between 1910 and 1915, more than three and a half million copies of the tracts were distributed in North America and the United Kingdom (Ruthven 2004: 10–15).

The Fundamentals called for a return to what were claimed to be the core doctrines of the Christian faith as clearly expounded in the Bible. The essays aim to rebut the methodology and findings of the 'Higher Criticism', in which the sources and literary methods used by biblical authors are subjected to sophisticated critical scrutiny, yielding results that called into question many of the traditional understandings of biblical authorship and authority. Fundamentalists insist that the Bible is without error, and its truths valid for all eternity. Fundamentalism requires believing literally in the biblical account of Creation, the Virgin Birth of Jesus Christ, his deity, the biblical miracles, including his bodily resurrection, and in his imminent Second Coming.

These beliefs are used as *shibboleths*, acid tests to distinguish between true believers and 'nominal' Christians – the 'liberals'. The doctrine of the Virgin Birth is a key instance of how this works. From a rational point of view, the Virgin Birth is hard to accept. It has all the qualities of a myth, a suspicion confirmed by anthropological evidence of myths of virginal conceptions worldwide (Leach 1969). If it were not in the Bible, who would believe it? Here, then, is an ideal test for smoking out the liberals. For Protestant fundamentalists, that is precisely the function of the Virgin Birth (Barr 1977; Aldridge 1992). Ironically, Mary has only a minor role in the Virgin Birth. All that matters about her is that she was submissive to God's will and her hymen was unbroken. She is not an object of devotion, and plays no part in the spiritual life of fundamentalist Protestants. The culture of fundamentalism is assertively masculine, subordinating women and abhorring homosexuals.

Although they share a commitment to conservative theology, fundamentalists tend to distinguish themselves from evangelicals. Nancy Ammerman underlines four criteria by which the distinction is made.

First, fundamentalists insist on their distinct identity, their sharp separation from the modern world. '*Compromise* and *accommodation*' are, she points out, 'among the most dreaded words in the Fundamentalist vocabulary' (Ammerman 1987: 4). Fundamentalist churches are steadfastly independent. Church and the home are the fundamentalists' two great refuges in a world careering towards its doom.

Second, fundamentalists hold fast to the inerrancy of the Bible, usually cleaving to the King James (or Authorized) Version. Evangelical faith is also steeped in the Bible, but does not insist on its complete lack of factual 'error'.

Third, fundamentalists are typically committed to dispensational pre-millenarianism. This view, expounded in the nineteenth century by John Nelson Derby and popularized in the twentieth through the influential Scofield Reference Bible, sees history as unfolding through a series of distinct eras. Each era is characterized by a different dispensation: that is to say, by the changing relationship between God and humanity. History begins with the dispensation of innocence in the Garden of Eden, and ends in the millennial kingdom that is to come after the current dispensation, the Church Age, is swept away. Before the millennium arrives, humanity will witness a succession of crises: the resurrection of the faithful dead and the Rapture of the faithful living, all of whom will be suddenly transported to heaven; the Tribulation and the rule of Antichrist, a seven-year reign of terror inflicted on the unfaithful who are left behind on earth; and the eventual defeat of Antichrist and Satan in the War of Armageddon.

Fourth, their commitment to dispensational pre-millenarianism means that fundamentalists are preoccupied with proclaiming the relevance of Biblical prophecies to contemporary events. In doing so, they strive to distinguish themselves from other religious movements, such as Jehovah's Witnesses, who have similar expectations of the millennium based on their understanding of biblical prophecy. To fundamentalists, 'similar' is not good enough: if doctrines are merely similar to the truth, they are not the truth, and are therefore falsehood.

Although it presents itself as preaching the plain truth of the Bible that was there from the beginning, fundamentalism is a modern phenomenon. It depends upon the modern world for its *raison d'être*: in Ammerman's words (1987: 8), 'Only where traditional orthodoxy must defend itself against modernity does Fundamentalism truly emerge.'

Fundamentalism and monotheism

Given that fundamentalism has its origins in Christianity, does it exist in other religions?

One line of argument, pursued by Bruce, is that fundamentalism is to be found only in monotheistic faiths. Because they believe in one God and a holy scripture that is without error, fundamentalists are 'dogmatic', 'doctrinaire' and 'fanatical'. It is not surprising, he says, that 'fanaticism' is more common in Christianity, Judaism and Islam than in Hinduism and Buddhism. Believing in a variety of gods, or in the variety of forms that the divine can take, creates 'a climate of tolerance' (Bruce 2000: 5). If fundamentalism is characteristic of monotheistic faiths, it nevertheless takes different forms within them.

The distinctive feature of the revival of Orthodoxy in Judaism, which sets it apart from conservative revivals within Christianity and Islam, is that it is aimed entirely at fellow Jews, and has no mission to proselytize outside the Jewish community.

In the 1970s a strong current in Jewish culture called for *teshuvah*, a repentant 'return to Judaism' and to observance of the *halakah*, the Jewish law. Assimilation is the enemy. As the chosen people, Jews should insulate themselves against Gentile culture. To the Orthodox, Jewishness must not become simply an ethnic identity or an emotional attachment to a set of folkways. Instead, the essence of Judaism is unblinking acceptance of dogma and strict observance of the *mitsvot*, the 613 injunctions listed in the Torah, comprising 248 prescriptions and 365 prohibitions which regulate the whole of life. This is at variance with Reform Judaism, which sees the *halakah* as in need of revision to accommodate contemporary values and lifestyles.

The primary objective of Jews calling for *teshuvah* is to resist assimilation and combat Enlightenment universalism. A specific object of scorn is the *Haskalah*, the Jewish Enlightenment of the eighteenth century, which aimed to enrich Jewish culture by opening it to secular influences. The ultra-Orthodox groups – the *haredim*, meaning those who 'tremble' at God's word – base their communities around strict observance of the *mitsvot*. The *haredim* are a minority within a minority, representing some 30 per cent of Orthodox Jewry, which itself is only 15 per cent of the 12 million Jews worldwide. *Haredim* see themselves as the true Jews, standing in an unbroken line from Abraham to the present day. Heilman and Friedman (1991) describe them as 'contra-acculturative activists'; Sharot (1992) prefers 'neotraditionalists'. The essential point is the same: the *haredim* are self-consciously committed to a vision of the past, specifically an idealized image of life in Central and Eastern Europe before the Holocaust. They actively resist anything which is inimical to the reaffirmation of this tradition. A sharp division exists between their world and the *chukos ha goyim*, the ways of the Gentiles. Interestingly, *haredi* groups are typically dependent on guidance from their *rebbe*, who wields far more power than the rabbis of the rest of the Jewish world, since a *rebbe* acts as an authoritative interpreter of the sacred tradition. Sharot argues that the traditions of the *haredim* are invented traditions, and that the role of the *rebbe* is to reinvent the tradition in the light of contemporary cultural change.

One prominent group of *haredim*, the Lubavitch, have their own demanding system of dietary prohibitions, the *glat-kosher*, which sets them apart from other Jews. They make strenuous efforts to socialize their children into Orthodox belief and practice. In Lubavitch primary schools in France, the only non-religious subjects taught are French and mathematics. As Kepel remarks (1994: 200), 'Cultural interaction with the non-Jewish world is reduced to its most basic terms: you learn to read and add up. Here we see the communal phenomenon at work in its most absolute expression.'

Since it is aimed at persuading Jews to return to their 'true' path, not at converting Gentiles or attacking non-Jewish states, the revival of Jewish ultra-Orthodoxy has failed to excite as much attention as Christian and Islamic forms of fundamentalism. Bruce's book (2000) reflects this, concentrating on the comparison between Christianity and Islam. In his view, they differ in several important ways. Christian fundamentalism is individualist, whereas Islamic fundamentalism is communal. Christianity emphasizes orthodoxy, true belief; whereas Islam emphasizes orthopraxis, correct practice. Christian fundamentalists withdraw from the world, whereas Muslim fundamentalists struggle against the world. Christian fundamentalism tends to pacifism, Islamic fundamentalism to militancy.

Bruce explicitly disclaims any idea that Christianity is essentially pacifist and Islam essentially warlike, reminding us of the Crusades, the European Wars of Religion, and the Spanish Inquisition. He does claim, however, that 'we could describe the communal fundamentalism of Islam as pre-modern and the individualistic Protestant fundamentalism as modern' (Bruce 2000: 10). Communal fundamentalism, with its intimate links between religion, ethnicity and nationalism, is part of the Christian West's past, but the Islamic world's present.

Christian fundamentalism formulates lines of division between the righteous and the unrighteous principally in terms of what they believe. Christian history can be written as a series of schisms over correct belief, and as the triumph of self-proclaimed orthodoxy over heresy. When we turn to assertive forms of Judaism and Islam, they differ from Christianity in the priority they give to everyday practice. Key symbols here are what you eat and how you dress. To the faithful and their opponents, these are not the trivial matters that they may seem to the rationalist. They are the basis of identity. The sartorial style of ultra-Orthodox Jewish men – long black Lithuanian-style coat, black fedora, uncut beard and earlocks – is liable to inspire admiration or provoke contempt. The same is true of traditional Islamic dress, particularly for women. *Khimaar*, the headscarf; *niqab*, the face veil; *chador*, a long black cloak and veil; and the *burqa*, a voluminous garment which swathes the body, leaving simply a lattice to enable the woman to see out – all are potent symbols of gender and sexuality.

A key problem in applying the term 'fundamentalism' outside a Christian context is the nature of the Christian Scriptures. To fundamentalists, the Bible was inspired by God, and therefore contains no errors. If the Bible says that Noah took all the animals into the ark two by two, then that is exactly what he did. This is not a flippant example, since taking these events literally is essential to fundamentalist belief. Abandon belief in Noah's ark, and the whole edifice of fundamentalism collapses with it: it is all or nothing. The Bible is read as an exact record of historical events. Of course it contains other elements such as poetry, prophecy and visions. But for fundamentalists the historical record is the core; and prophecy is read as history, the history of the near future.

There are many other ways of reading the Bible. Brief passages may be chosen as food for meditation, as in contemplative religious orders. Some people read the Bible straight through from beginning to end, others dip into favourite passages as the mood takes them. Jehovah's Witnesses read the Bible through the lens of the society's literature; it is a reference work. Some Christians have used the Bible as an oracle, opening it at random and reading a passage as a guide to decision making – the practice of bibliomancy, a Christian version of the *sortes Virgilianae*, the oracles of Virgil, where the educated classes used the works of the Latin poet to the same end. The churches have their lectionaries – extracts from the Scriptures to be read out in public worship on a regular cycle throughout the year. Although fundamentalists claim to be letting the Bible speak for itself, theirs is simply one system of interpretation alongside others.

The contrast with Islam is particularly marked. If one insists on trying to use the term 'fundamentalism' in the Christian sense, then all Islam has to be labelled fundamentalist, despite the wealth of cultural variety within Islam worldwide. The case for saying that Islam is inherently fundamentalist is this. The Qur'an is not simply the Muslims' Bible. Muslims believe that the Qur'an is uncreated and coexistent with God. Qur'an means recitation, and the text is the word of God delivered to the Prophet Muhammad by the Angel Jibreel (Gabriel). Strictly,

it is untranslatable from Arabic. In Christian terms, the Qur'an functions less as the Bible than as Christ. It is an object of reverence in ways
that the Bible usually is not, even to Christian fundamentalists. The
Qur'an is not primarily a historical narrative, and it is not arranged in
chronological sequence. Disagreements about the seaworthiness of
Noah's ark, and reports that it has been discovered in Turkey, have no
parallel here. In the case of the Qur'an, it is not possible to distinguish
between liberal and conservative interpretations in the Christian sense
of the terms.

Islam, like Judaism, puts great emphasis on the religious law, much
of which lies outside the Qur'an itself. In Islam, as in Judaism, the law
began as an oral tradition that was later codified and set down in
writing. This means that Islam and Judaism are inherently less scrip-
turalist than Protestantism (Sharot 1992: 28–30), so that divisions
within them do not turn on the interpretation of the sacred texts. Within
Christianity itself, much the same could be said of Catholicism. Even
the reactionary Catholic traditionalism of Archbishop Lefebvre was
not fundamentalist.

The example of *Hindutva*, meaning 'Hinduness', would appear to
contradict Bruce's thesis that 'fundamentalism' is characteristic of
monotheistic religions. In his own terms, it fits the definition of fundamentalist movements as ones 'that respond to problems created by
modernization by advocating society-wide obedience to some authentic and inerrant text or tradition and by seeking the political power to
impose the revitalized tradition' (Bruce 2000: 94). *Hindutva* has another
feature that is said to typify fundamentalism: belief in a golden age
whose glory can be restored. For Hindu 'fundamentalists', that golden
age is Aryavarta, the Kingdom of Ayodhya, ruled by Lord Rama, the
seventh avatar of Vishnu. In 1992, a mob of Hindu activists destroyed
the Babri Masjid, the mosque built at Ayodhya in 1528 by the Moghul
conqueror Babur. They claimed that the mosque had been an act of sacrilege, provocatively erected on the ruins of an eleventh-century Hindu
temple sited at Rama's mythological birthplace (Corbridge and Harriss
2000).

Writers who are willing to use the term 'fundamentalism' have seen
no difficulty in applying it to such militant expressions of Hinduism.
Bruce contends that they are wrong to do so. He gives three reasons why
Hindu nationalist movements should not be classified as fundamentalist: 'First, they have been provoked more by the threat of Islam than by
a decline in the religious observance of Hindus. Secondly, they are
directed more to expelling or subordinating "foreigners" (as they see
most Muslims) than to revitalizing and purifying the Hindu faithful.

There is no decline in orthodoxy to redress because there is no orthodoxy. Thirdly, they are only tangentially a reaction to secularization'
(Bruce 2000: 97).

The problem with this is that it appears designed to rescue the thesis
of a link between fundamentalism and monotheism. If the term 'fundamentalism' is to be applied outside the Christian context, refusing to
accept that it can apply to Hinduism is more a matter of definition than
a finding.

Islamophobia

The Runnymede Trust, a voluntary organization whose mission is to
promote a successful multi-ethnic Britain, defines 'Islamophobia' as an
'unfounded hostility towards Islam, and therefore fear or dislike of all
or most Muslims' (Runnymede Trust 1997: 4). Although they were not
the first to use the term, their definition has been widely discussed.
'Islamophobia', like all key concepts, is controversial.

Halliday (1999) argues that the concept of Islamophobia unwittingly
plays into the hands of extremists. By implying that Islam is an
undifferentiated cultural phenomenon, it sets the stage for a struggle
between extremists who hate Muslims and radical Islamists who desire
to impose Islamic culture and shari'a law. Both parties construct Islam
as an essence; in their hands, culturally variable and invented traditions
are transformed into the eternal truths of the Qur'an and the life and
teaching of the Prophet. Islamophobia lends credence to the contention
that there is a deep-seated and inevitable conflict between Christian and
Islamic civilization. The concept of Islamophobia, Halliday argues, distracts attention from the enormous cultural diversity within and
between Islamic communities, and from the social and cultural currents
of change that have swept through them. Islamophobia misrepresents
the target of hostility, which is not the faith that is Islam but the people
who are Muslims. Halliday therefore proposes, by analogy with anti-
Semitism, the term 'anti-Muslimism' – a term which has not, however,
gained wide currency.

The comparison with anti-Semitism raises the issue of new forms of
racism that emphasize culture rather than biology. The biological
concept of 'race' has lost both respectability and credibility, but this
does not mean the dawn of a society that has abandoned racial
prejudice and discrimination. Instead, racism has transformed itself.
The new racism sets itself apart from the old through the use of sani-
tized, coded language that deploys liberal rhetoric for illiberal ends.

Indignantly denying racial prejudice and racist aims, the new racists shift the focus from supposed biological inequalities to the preservation of cultural and national identity – *our* 'way of life' (Ansell 2000: 30).

The concept of 'cultural racism', Modood (1997) argues, captures the social realities that 'Islamophobia' allows to escape. Racists use phenotypes (physical characteristics such as skin colour and physiognomy) as markers that indicate a genotype (a 'racial' group). They proceed to impute inferiority to 'races' other than their own. Unlike the Nazis, however, cultural racists do not see racial inferiority as biologically determined; instead, it is the product of the racial group's culture, as expressed in its history, traditions, values, norms of conduct, and most acutely in its religion. In the wake of the Holocaust, people in the West tend to conceive of racism as necessarily based on biology. Modood contends that nineteenth- and twentieth-century biological racism is the exception; cultural racism has been far more prevalent, manifesting itself specifically in anti-Semitism and hostility towards Muslims, and more generally in ideologies that construct the 'problem' of assimilating 'backward' colonial peoples into the refined civilizations of the West.

Despite the power of cultural racism, it is perhaps premature, as Mason points out (2000: 10), to pronounce the demise of racism based on biology. One might add that, to a racist, biology and culture are intimately linked, since cultural inferiority is caused by the innate intellectual and moral inferiority of the 'race' which produced it.

The debate about terminology is significant; it points to the intersection and overlapping of a family of key concepts – religion, ethnicity, 'race' and nation. While Halliday is right to say that religion is not the only thing of significance, it should not be discounted. What becomes crucial, then, are the implications of the way in which Islamophobia has been measured and assessed.

The Runnymede Trust Report identified four aspects of Islamophobia: *prejudice*, institutionalized in the mass media and pervasive in everyday social interaction; *discrimination* in employment practices and in the provision of services such as education and health; *exclusion* from employment, from management and positions of responsibility, and from politics and government; and *violence*, whether in the form of physical assaults, vandalizing of property, or verbal abuse.

The Report is most famous for its identification of Islamophobia as a 'closed' rather than an 'open' view of Islam. It is 'closed' in eight respects:

- Islam is seen as monolithic and static. It is intolerant of internal diversity and debate, and unreceptive to new cultural and scientific developments.
- Islam is perceived as entirely 'other'. It has little in common with other cultures, refuses to be affected by them, and therefore exerts little influence upon them.
- Islam is seen as inferior to Western faiths and philosophies. It is unenlightened: primitive, barbaric, oppressive, irrational and sexist.
- Islam is seen as a violent, aggressive religion that lends comfort, support and legitimacy to terrorists. It poses a grave threat to our values and way of life. We are parties to a 'clash of civilisations', in which Islamic states are not partners but enemies.
- Islam is not a genuine faith sincerely practised by its followers, but a political ideology manipulated by autocratic regimes for political and military advantage.
- Islamic criticisms of the West have no validity and are dismissed as worthless.
- Hostility towards Islam serves as justification for discrimination against Muslims and their social exclusion from mainstream society.
- Anti-Muslim and anti-Islamic ideas and practices are accepted as natural and normal.

This closed view constructs Islam in essentialist terms, and opposes it to an equally essentialized and mythologized Britishness, Americanness, Frenchness and so on, indiscriminately compounded of culture, history, ethnicity, 'race' and religion. The opposition constructs Islam as an enemy, and Muslims as potential traitors to the countries in which they reside. Muslims are said to have their primary loyalty to the *umma*, the worldwide Muslim community, not to the nation-state; they are supposedly taught to see the world as divided between *dar al-Islam*, the house of Islam and governed by shari'a law, and *dar al-harb*, the house of war; they are allegedly bound by a sacred obligation to wage *jihad* or holy war in defence of Islam, irrespective of the national interests of the host society; and – a view given colour by the attacks of September 11, 2001 – they venerate martyrdom in the cause of Islam, even if it involves carnage and self-immolation. In Ansari's words (2004: 8), 'The West has constructed and stigmatised an Islam with little resemblance to anything that is of value in ordinary Muslim lives.'

Islamophobia has deep historical roots. Medieval Christianity had a complex relationship with Islam, a love–hate affair manifesting both deep insights and gross distortions – mostly the latter. Islam was seen as an implacable enemy, a warrior religion bent on conquest. Christian polemics attacked Muhammad as an illiterate impostor, or a lascivious hypocrite, or a dangerous madman. The Qur'an was, correspondingly, an ignorant farrago, a wicked fabrication, or an insane fantasy.

Against this background, secular writers such as Adam Smith, Karl Marx and Friedrich Engels, and Max Weber contrasted the economically dynamic and politically liberal-bourgeois West to the economically static and politically autocratic Orient. The contribution of Islam to scientific knowledge was either ignored or written off as no more than a restatement of the discoveries of classical Greece (B. S. Turner 1991: 33–5).

Weber's scattered and incomplete comments on Islam paint it as the opposite of Western Puritanism (B. S. Turner 1974: 7–21). Islam, for Weber, expresses a hedonistic philosophy of life, not least in its view of women, luxuries and property. At an early stage, the Prophet's message was embraced and recast by a tribal warrior society; Islam allegedly became, in the stereotypical phrase, 'a religion of the sword'.

One feature of Islamophobia, identified above, is its portrayal of Islam as a violent religion that justifies terrorism under the rubric of *jihad*, holy war. Atrocities perpetrated in the name of Islam and praised by Islamist extremists are invoked as evidence of the propensity to violence inherent in Islamic fundamentalism. In considering this proposition, it is important to note that every one of the world's major faiths has been used to justify acts of terrorism (Juergensmeyer 2003: 14). Given the capacity of religion to supply the ultimate justification of human acts, this should not be surprising. Martyrdom for the faith is universally recognized as praiseworthy; in the words of the early Christian writer Tertullian, 'the blood of the martyrs is the seed of the church'. Contemporary terrorists present themselves as martyrs in cosmic battles on behalf of their faith community. Their targets are not so much military as symbolic, and their stage has a global audience. The carnage they wreak creates an impression of power, but they are the product of impotence. Kepel (2002: 375) argues that September 11, 2001, should be seen as 'a desperate symbol of the isolation, fragmentation, and decline of the Islamist movement, not a sign of its strength and irrepressible might'.

The First Gulf War (1990–1), the carnage of September 11, 2001, Western intervention in Afghanistan in 2001 to oust the Taliban regime, and the invasion of Iraq in 2003, did not create Islamophobia; but they have undoubtedly intensified it. They appear to have strengthened xenophobia and racism, creating a climate of fear and hatred which neo-Nazi and other extremist groups have sought to exploit. This has given a public platform to some of the most radical Islamist leaders, to

142

the alarm of most of the Muslims for whom they claim to speak. An accumulating body of evidence shows that minority Muslim communities feel more vulnerable to prejudice, discrimination, exclusion and violence than any other social group. These fears have been experienced throughout Europe (Allen and Nielsen 2002). Muslims have been increasingly subjected to verbal abuse, harassment and aggression. Women wearing *hijab* have been particular targets, as have men wearing turbans, most of whom are in fact Sikhs. Mosques have suffered graffiti and vandalism, as well as arson and bomb attacks. Visual identifiers of Islamic 'otherness' are a focus of abuse; where these are not apparent, Muslims have been relatively free from harassment. An example of this is Finland's long-established Tatar community: Muslims of Turkish descent who are well integrated into Finnish society, and who display few if any visual markers that they are Muslim. The Tatars have escaped abuses to which other Muslims in Finland have been subjected.

For all the doubts raised about it, 'Islamophobia' persists as a term that is widely used, not least by Muslims who feel themselves to be its targets. The term has the merit of signalling that religion is a salient badge of identity and source of social discrimination and hostility in a society that is frequently taken to be secular.

7

Civil Religion and Political Ritual

Ritual and social integration: the legacy of Durkheim

Ritual, as Durkheim argued, is an essential dimension of religion. It is through rituals that we are brought into contact with the sacred. Ritual also has a cognitive function. The social world is represented to us through the symbols used in ritual action; or, putting the same point more sharply, we understand the social world through symbols. We create, dramatize and reinforce social realities through ritual action. Rituals play a vital part in social integration, literally holding society together. Without them, nation building is undermined, and society risks disintegration. Durkheim thought that his own society was in an unhealthy pathological state, and one cause, symptom and effect of this, he believed, was its lack of public rituals.

Many sociologists have argued that Durkheim underestimated the continued vitality of ritual in contemporary societies. They share his emphasis on the role played by ritual in expressing and reinforcing consensus on ultimate values, a consensus which they take to be essential to social integration. Thus for Shils and Young (1953) the coronation of Queen Elizabeth II in 1953 was 'a great act of national communion' through which ordinary citizens were able to experience contact with the monarchy as the repository of the sacred values of British society. This is a clear restatement of Durkheim's theory that religion is 'society worshipping itself'. The grief and mourning that followed the assassination of President Kennedy is similarly treated by Verba (1965) as a set of rituals which re-dedicated the American people to allegiance to their political community. Blumler et al. (1971) saw in the investiture of

Charles Windsor as Prince of Wales a ceremony through which fundamental values of family solidarity and national pride were symbolically
enacted and reaffirmed. Similarly, Warner's famous studies of 'Yankee
City' (W. L. Warner 1959, 1962) interpreted Memorial Day as a modern
cult of the dead, specifically those who fell in the Civil War – a cult that
unifies people into a sacred community, the nation. Most influentially
of all, Bellah (1967) used the inauguration of US Presidents as a vehicle
for analysing what he called 'civil religion' – a religious dimension that
puts citizens in touch with the sacred. Bellah's work is examined more
fully below.

These authors tend to overstate the role played by value consensus in
holding societies together (Lukes 1975). They play down coercion,
political manipulation and pragmatic compliance, selecting for analysis
those rituals where the argument for value consensus is at its most plausible. But surely there are rituals that express and reinforce social divisions? What of such rituals as Orange parades and Republican funerals
in Northern Ireland, neo-Nazi marches displaying the symbols of the
Nazi era; burning the American flag in anti-Vietnam War protests, or
the burning by Muslims of Salman Rushdie's *The Satanic Verses*? These
rituals reinforce social solidarity among the subcultures that support
and participate in them, but they are deeply divisive at the level of the
nation-state.

Rituals do not just arise spontaneously; they are created, and can be
mobilized for political and ideological purposes. To treat rituals as
beyond time is to accede to their own mythology.

'In God We Trust': civil religion in the United States

Bellah's seminal article on civil religion in America drew explicitly on
Durkheim's theories of religion and ritual. The term 'civil religion' was
taken from Rousseau's classic text of political philosophy, *The Social
Contract*, first published in 1762. Rousseau argues that the social integration of any healthy society depends on a set of basic religious
dogmas. These are belief in God, belief in a life after death, and the conviction that virtue will be rewarded and vice punished. The good society
also commits itself to the practice of religious tolerance.

Civil religion as Rousseau conceived it is a set of beliefs deliberately
created by the state and imposed on citizens for the benefit of social
order. In applying the concept of civil religion to the contemporary
United States, Bellah turns Rousseau's analysis on its head. Instead of
being dictated from the top, civil religion emerges from the grassroots

(Demerath 2003: 354) as a pervasive religious dimension of American political life existing independently of the churches. All American citizens are expected to take part in civil religion. Paradoxically, this does not violate the right to freedom of religious worship and assembly guaranteed by the First Amendment to the Constitution. American citizens enjoy religious liberty in their private devotion and in their voluntary activity. Civil religion applies to the public sphere, manifesting itself in calendrical festivals such as Thanksgiving and the Fourth of July, in rituals such as reciting the Pledge of Allegiance, and in ceremonies such as Presidential inaugurations. Freedom of religion does not lead to social disintegration, thanks to the socially integrative role played by civil religion. Civil religion provides a unifying set of symbols that integrate a geographically, ethnically and religiously diverse society.

In Durkheimian fashion, Bellah argues that American civil religion is made manifest in the great rituals of public life. He takes Presidential inaugural addresses as a case study. For example, the address to the nation by President Kennedy after his inauguration in 1961 referred to God three times. Importantly, although Kennedy was a Catholic, he made no allusion to Catholic symbolism: no Our Lady, no Mass, no prayers for the dead. Civil religion embraces Protestants as well as Catholics as part of its integrative function. The constitutional separation of church and state means that civil religion cannot be a vehicle for religious divisions, but must transcend them.

American civil religion goes further, embracing not just Christianity but also Judaism. Hence the God that is invoked is the God of the Hebrew Scriptures. Presidential inaugurals do not normally include specifically Christian references. If they do, as in President Reagan's first inaugural in 1981, an equivalent Jewish reference must also be supplied. Thus Reagan referred to 'Arlington National Cemetery, with its row upon row of simple white markers with crosses and Stars of David, adding up to only a tiny fraction of the price that has been paid for our freedom'.

Presidential inaugural addresses draw on and play into the complex set of symbols that make up American civil religion. The symbols include sacred texts such as the Declaration of Independence and the Gettysburg Address; sacred heroes such as Washington, Jefferson and Lincoln; sacred places, such as the Lincoln Memorial; and sacred historical events, such as the War of Independence and the Civil War.

American civil religion accords a unique role to the United States. The American nation has a special historic mission to liberate the whole of humanity from bondage – a belief which Britain held of itself in its imperial heyday, but which is now confined to extremist right-wing groups in the UK (Lane 1981: 258–9). The USA is the new Zion, God's chosen people. Washington was a Moses leading the people out of captivity into the promised land. Lincoln is a Christ-like figure, sacrificed for us all. Like biblical Israel, the USA plays a crucial role in God's redemptive plan for the human race. This theme was particularly prominent in Ronald Reagan's 1981 inaugural, at the height of the Cold War against what Reagan called the 'evil empire' of the USSR. Asserting that Americans enjoy more liberty than any other people, Reagan said: 'We are a nation that has a government – not the other way around. And this makes us special among the nations of the Earth.' The quasi-biblical nature of this last phrase was of course entirely fitting as an expression of civil religion.

It might be thought that civil religion is simply a mechanism for providing the state with religious legitimation. Bellah argues, however, that it is also a cultural resource on which citizens can draw to call down God's judgement on the nation. There is, then, a *priestly* role for civil religion in celebrating national achievements, and a *prophetic* role in calling the nation to account for breaking its covenant with the Almighty (McGuire 1992: 180–1). At the height of the anti-Vietnam War protests, Bellah sharply criticized the way in which the military dictatorship in South Vietnam became sacralized in civil religious discourse as 'the free people of South Vietnam and their government'. Senator William Fulbright, in Bellah's view, was a prophet calling the nation to judgement. So too were Martin Luther King and other civil rights activists, who drew on American civil religion to point up the contrast between the nation's self-image and its actual achievement.

The tension between the priestly and the prophetic shows, according to Wuthnow (1988), that there is a deep divide between conservative and liberal versions of civil religion. The conservative view can be said to emphasize the 'one Nation under God' aspect of the Pledge of Allegiance. The founders of the American republic and the framers of the Constitution were God-fearing, far-sighted individuals who knew exactly what they were doing: forging a society in accordance with the will of the Almighty. The USA is a specially chosen nation, uniquely destined to spread the Christian gospel throughout the world – a gospel whose secular aspect is the capitalist free enterprise system and the liberal-democratic political order. In contrast, the liberal version of American civil religion rests on the Pledge's commitment to 'liberty and justice for all'. Instead of resting on the uniqueness of the Judaeo-Christian tradition, the liberal view speaks of human rights and our common humanity. Liberals tend to see themselves as like the biblical prophets, fighting for peace and justice against almost overwhelming odds.

American civil religion transcends the state and secular institutions. In so far as it legitimizes them, it does so only conditionally. If we apply the Durkheimian formula that religion is society worshipping itself, the American case shows, according to Bellah, that the object of worship is not necessarily the society as it exists, but may be 'a higher reality which upholds the standards that the republic attempts to embody' (Bellah 1990: 418). The prophetic role may take precedence over the priestly. In a deregulated religious economy, civil religion is a resource available to prophets. Although this can find its supreme expression in great endeavours such as the campaign for civil rights, it can also result in witch-hunts against ordinary citizens for 'un-American activities', as in the McCarthyite era of the 1950s, or even against the powerful, as in the claim that President Clinton's covert sexual affairs amounted to 'high crimes and misdemeanours' requiring his impeachment.

American civil religion may be inclusive, but it still has boundaries. Movements judged to be sects or cults have never been an acceptable part of American civil religion even when, as in the case of the Moonies, they long to be included (Robbins et al. 1976).

In Bellah's classic article, civil religion embraces mainstream Protestantism, Catholicism and Judaism. It connects to the concept of Judaeo-Christian civilization, which came to prominence in the 1930s as a repudiation of the Fascists and Nazis whose anti-Semitism was legitimized by an often cynical appeal to Christian culture (Silk 1984). In the 1960s, the concept of Judaeo-Christian civilization was used by civil rights campaigners to oppose suspicion and hostility between black Americans and Jews.

The idea of Judaeo-Christian civilization has also been useful to conservatives, who have deployed it in two directions: outward, in the Cold War against 'godless Communism', and inward, against the values of 'secular humanism' and the vision of a 'multicultural' America. Atheism is not a popular option; according to the American Religious Identification Survey 2001 (Kosmin et al. 2001), only about 1 per cent of adult Americans identify themselves as 'atheist' or 'agnostic'. Atheism serves as a symbol of the rejection, by morally vacuous self-interested individuals, of cultural membership in American society (Edgell et al. 2006). Edgell and her colleagues found that 'out of a long list of ethnic and cultural minorities, Americans are less willing to accept intermarriage with atheists than with any other group, and less likely to imagine that atheists share their vision of American society' (2006: 216). Tolerance of religious diversity is not unbounded; atheism is a symbol of its limits.

Whether used to support liberal or conservative causes, the concept of Judaeo-Christian civilization has tended to be used in a positive sense (Hartmann et al. 2005). Recently, however, the growth of religious pluralism in the United States, and specifically the status of Islam, has caused some rethinking. Because the US Census does not include questions about religious identity or affiliation, it is hard to be precise about comparative membership figures. What is clear is that the Muslim population is small, but growing. The American Religious Identification Survey found that self-identified Muslims made up 0.5 per cent of the adult population; the General Social Survey gives the figure as 0.45 per cent (T. Smith, 2002). It is not just a question of numbers; culturally, Muslims are claiming a place in the mainstream. In the wake of September 11, 2001, a tendency to identify the Judaeo-Christian tradition with 'the West', and to imply a cultural clash with Islam, has led to suggestions that the phrase Judaeo-Christian should be replaced by Judaeo-Christian-Islamic, or Abrahamic. The three faiths have common roots: all are monotheistic; Muslims revere Jesus (Iesa) as a prophet and respect his mother, Mary. In his first inaugural address in January 2001, President George W. Bush was deliberately inclusive: 'Church and charity, synagogue and mosque lend our communities their humanity, and they have an honored place in our plans and in our laws.' In the context of the 'war against terror', it is likely that strenuous efforts will be made to incorporate Islam into American civil religion.

A failure of civil religion: Canada

The religious history of Canada has been marked by the institutional and cultural dominance of 'the big three': the Roman Catholic Church, the United Church of Canada (a union of Presbyterians, Methodists and Congregationalists), and the Anglican Church of Canada (O'Toole 1996). In recent decades, however, their power and influence have declined, membership and active participation have fallen, and the Catholic Church, although now by far the biggest of the three, faces a crisis over the lack of men coming forward with a vocation to the priesthood.

The 2001 Canadian Census found that 72 per cent of the population gave their religion as Roman Catholic or Protestant – a significant fall from 1991, when the corresponding figure was 80 per cent. The defection of younger people is a particular concern for these churches. Evangelical churches have gained members, but, unlike their counterparts in the United States, they lack political influence, not least because

Canadian culture is arguably becoming more secular. In 2001, 16 per cent of Canadians said that they had no religion, whereas before 1971 the figure had been less than 1 per cent.

Canada is an interesting case of a modern democratic society that has no overarching civil religion expressing social, cultural and political unity. In Kim's (1993) analysis, the absence of a pan-Canadian civil religion is attributed to regionalism and biculturalism.

Taking Canadian regionalism first, Kim sees it as a product of three sets of factors. Geographically, Canada is a vast country with a sparse population concentrated in cities hundreds and even thousands of miles apart. Historically, Canada's regions were settled by different migrant ethnic groups at different times in the nation's history. Politically, extensive powers have been devolved to the provinces from the relatively weak federal government in Ottawa.

Canada has been historically a bicultural society, divided between Anglo and French Canada, two non-native founding cultures struggling for supremacy. Biculturalism is multidimensional, manifesting itself in language, schooling, religion, cuisine and the media. The 'third force' of Canadians from ethnic backgrounds other than these two has not successfully organized as a serious challenge to the two dominant cultures. Even so, Canada is becoming more multicultural. New patterns of migration have led to rapid growth in the numbers of Muslims, Hindus, Sikhs and Buddhists, alongside the country's long-standing Jewish community.

Symbolism inherited from Britain, including the link to the British monarchy, reminds French Canadians of their colonial defeat by the British. Despite the fact of a national flag depicting the maple leaf, at public ceremonies in Quebec it is common to see only the Quebec flag flying. More remarkably still, the national anthem, 'O Canada', achieved official status only in 1980, 100 years after its composition.

The Canadian landscape plays a prominent part in the nation's self-image. The beaver and the maple leaf are evocative, as is the imagery of a ruggedly beautiful northern country. These images and symbols have not been fully sacralized. They have remained closely tied to the natural realm, and have not acquired a transcendent significance. They do not point beyond themselves to abstract qualities that define national history, character and identity. The Canadian beaver is not invested with the deep symbolic meaning of the American bald eagle, the Russian bear, or the British bulldog.

Canadian national identity contains some powerfully negative elements, including 'defeat, division, the difficult ecological challenge, and an uneventful or uninteresting history' (Kim 1993: 269). The heroic strand that is so prominent in the civil religions of the USA and former imperialist countries such as the UK is absent from Canadian culture.

Symbols of nationhood in Canada are divisive and deeply contested. Not only is there a lack of shared sacred symbols of national identity, there is also disagreement on how to characterize the essence of Canada as a nation-state. Is it one Canada? Is it a dual culture? Is it a cultural mosaic? Is it a multicultural society? Fundamentally, Kim argues, the absence of pan-Canadian civil religion intensifies the threat of Quebec separatism and signals a failure of nation building.

Symbolic division in society: Northern Ireland

'The Northern Ireland conflict is a religious conflict' (Bruce 1986: 249). Explanations that try to reduce the conflict in Northern Ireland to something other than religion – for example, to class conflict, in Marxist fashion – are unconvincing.

This does not mean that the conflict is purely religious, since religion as a social phenomenon is never 'pure'. In Northern Ireland, the religious divide coincides with and reinforces social divisions based on education, occupation, neighbourhood, social clubs, sport, newspapers and political parties (McGuire 1992: 197). These divisions are actively maintained. On the one hand, the Catholic Church hierarchy supports the continuation of separate schooling for Catholic children, to insulate them from Protestant as well as from secular culture. On the other hand, the Protestant majority has discriminated against Catholics in housing, employment and the police service. Discrimination has been reinforced by political gerrymandering to weaken the democratic impact of the Catholic vote. The Protestant working class struggles to maintain its dominant position in skilled manual occupations. In 1974, a hardline Unionist organization, the Ulster Workers' Council, used intimidation by loyalist paramilitaries to cause what was referred to as a 'strike' by Protestant workers against the British government's attempt to give more political power to Catholics. This brought the province to a virtual standstill and killed off the new power-sharing Northern Ireland Executive.

The conflict between Catholics and Protestants is not primarily over doctrine or theology. Most people are not, and do not want to be, theologians. The conflict is not between theologians or church leaders, who have little power to control it. Rather, it is a conflict of civil religions (McGuire 1992: 205–9).

Catholic civil religion in Northern Ireland – or, in its own terms, the North of Ireland – is Irish, Republican and Nationalist. It opposes

British colonialism, and celebrates the heroes and martyrs, and the sacred myths and symbols, of Irish rebellion against British rule. It is not anti-Protestant, however.

Protestant civil religion, by contrast, is explicitly anti-Catholic. This is particularly marked in the Free Presbyterian Church led by the Reverend Dr Ian Paisley (Bruce 1986). In Paisleyite ideology, Roman Catholicism is not merely in error but deeply evil. The papacy is the Antichrist. Free Presbyterians share with Jehovah's Witnesses and other fundamentalist Protestant groups the belief that the Roman Catholic Church is described in the Bible, most graphically in chapter 17 of the Book of Revelation, as 'the great whore' and 'the mother of harlots and abominations of the earth'.

Free Presbyterianism embraces a conspiracy theory in which the Roman Catholic Church is both devious and highly effective. Rome has worked consistently to persecute true Christians and to subvert democratic institutions that owe their existence to the Protestant faith. For example, the Vatican promotes the ecumenical movement as a means of sapping the vitality of Protestantism. The same is true of European Union. The Pope has voiced his longing for a united Europe. The 'Schuman plan' which established the European Coal and Steel Community in 1951 was drafted by Konrad Adenauer, Jean Monnet and Robert Schuman – all Catholics. The founding charter of European union was the 1957 Treaty of Rome – where else? The UK's membership of this crypto-Catholic organization is one among many threats to the democratic rights of the Protestant people of Northern Ireland.

Northern Ireland is the stage for a conflict of civil religions. Crucially, this conflict is asymmetrical. In Bruce's words (1986: 258), 'The conflict in Northern Ireland involves a nation on the one hand and an ethnic group on the other.' Irish Republicanism is nationalist. Most Catholics in the North see themselves as part of the Irish nation. Committed Ulster Protestants, in contrast, are not straightforwardly British. Though 'Loyalist', their loyalty is strictly conditional on the British government's delivering them what they want. Their loyalty is to the sacred symbols of the Crown, not to the secular politics of the government in Westminster. The Britain revered by Loyalists is an idealized nation that disappeared in the nineteenth century, if indeed it ever existed. The contemporary British mainland is offensively liberal, permissive and irreligious. Most Ulster Protestants would prefer provincial self-determination within Britain to complete integration with the British mainland (Bruce 1986: 251–3).

Ulster Protestants, in Bruce's analysis, are members of an ethnic group. Their culture embraces a shared history, traditions, values, beliefs, lifestyles and symbols. It is characteristic of ethnic groups that they foster what Weber called 'ethnic honour', including an abiding sense of the superiority of their culture and the inferiority of alien cultures. Ulster Protestantism constitutes itself by a set of virtues recognizably embodying the Weberian Protestant ethic: 'respectability, uprightness, honesty, order, respect for authority, work ethic, cleanliness and tidiness, modesty and informality in social relations, social and political conformity' (Ruane and Todd 1996: 182). These virtuous traits contrast with the vices attributed to Catholics, such as fecklessness, dishonesty, subservience and disloyalty. Furthermore, the Protestant virtues can be presented to employers as valid grounds for preferring Protestant to Catholic workers, and to the security forces as an entitlement to be treated with respect as a good citizen.

Their Protestant faith is the one secure basis of their cultural identity as an ethnic group. Evangelical Protestantism is 'the only identity that can make sense of their history and that justifies their separation from the South' (Bruce 1986: 262). They increasingly feel embattled. They suspect that the British government sees Northern Ireland, politically and economically, as a liability, rather than an asset. Demography is also a concern. The 1991 Census shows Catholics at 43 per cent of the population, a significant increase over the decade since the previous Census. This is accounted for by the higher birth rate among Catholics and by higher rates of emigration among Protestants (Davie 1994: 99).

A key characteristic of public ritual in Northern Ireland are the Loyalist and Republican parades. Jarman (1997) provides a richly detailed analysis of these. Each year there are approximately 3,500 parades, most of them passing without violence. Parading was once widespread in Europe and North America, but gradually died out as these societies became industrialized and urbanized. In maintaining a vigorous tradition of parading, Northern Ireland is self-consciously anachronistic.

Loyalist and Republican parades differ both quantitatively and qualitatively. Each year there are more than 2,500 Loyalist parades, compared to a little over 300 Republican ones; the remaining parades are not linked to either cause. There are revealing differences between them. Loyalist parades draw heavily on militaristic symbolism. Spectators are strictly segregated from participants: a parade marches past its spectators. Participants are male. They are divided into independent quasi-regimental units. The parades are a triumphalist assertion of Loyalist culture, of the civil rights of the Loyalist community, including the right to 'walk', and of Protestant military defeat of Catholics. The intense emotion invested in and generated by Loyalist parades reflects the Protestant community's sense of being under siege.

Republican parades, in contrast, are less formal, less structured, and open to anyone to take part, including women. They are far less militaristic. Unlike Loyalist parades, they may include American-style marching bands. They also draw on the tradition of funeral processions – a tradition which, as Jarman points out (1997: 153–5), feeds into IRA funerals. In 1981, an estimated 100,000 people lined the route of the funeral procession of Bobby Sands, who led the hunger strikers in the H blocks of Belfast's Maze Prison and was the first to die. The emphasis is on honouring fallen heroes.

This theme of martyrdom is powerfully expressed in the Republican Easter parades (Jarman 1997: 153–5). In Easter 1916, a group of Nationalists and Republicans took control of key buildings in Dublin and proclaimed the formation of an Independent Irish Republic. After heavy bombardment by the British army, the rebels were forced to surrender. Fourteen of their leaders were executed. These events are celebrated by Republicans as the Rising: a clear symbolic echo of Christ's Resurrection. The parallel is further reinforced by their relocation in the calendar. The 1916 Rising took place on 24 April, which was Easter Monday, but the events are commemorated on Easter Sunday, the day of the Resurrection.

To Protestant Loyalists, the Easter Rising of 1916 was a treacherous stab in the back to Britain at a crucial moment in the First World War. Protestants respond by commemorating the Battle of the Somme, which took place in July 1916 and in which the Ulster Division suffered terrible casualties. Commemorating the Somme stands in symbolic opposition to the Rising as a powerful statement of loyalty and sacrifice to the Crown.

Parades do not merely reflect community identity, they re-enact and re-create it. In Northern Ireland, these rituals are 'a cultural medium for constructing the collective Other' (Jarman 1997: 261). They reinforce the sense of difference between the communities, obliterating the memory and recognition of things they have in common.

Political religion in an atheist society: the Soviet Union

An elaborate system of public ritual flourished in the former Soviet Union from its foundation in 1917 to its collapse in 1991 (Lane 1981; Binns 1979, 1980). The Soviet state invested heavily in its ritual system as a conscious political policy. Here was a situation full of ironies. Soviet political ideology emphasized rationality, materialism, atheism, and the triumph of science over religion. In the Russian context, this meant specifically attacking the Orthodox Church, which the Soviet regime saw as doctrinaire, obscurantist and backward-looking. The Orthodox Church was seen to have collaborated all too willingly with the reactionary policies of the autocratic Tsarist regime.

Relations between Russian intellectuals and the Orthodox Church were deeply antagonistic throughout the nineteenth century (McLellan 1987: 90–2). This fed into Lenin's writings, which were contemptuous of religion. Religion and the clerics who profited from it were to be the target of revolutionary political action. Lenin equated religion with superstition and ignorance. Religion is 'spiritual booze' – a cheap intoxicant cynically doled out to the masses by the clerical lackeys of the ruling class. In a significant coarsening of Marx's famous epigram, Lenin called religion an opium not *of* but *for* the people.

The Soviet ritual system was partly designed in order to provide substitutes for religious rituals. The system had a number of dimensions.

Calendrical festivals

The Soviet calendar was an important feature of life in the USSR. Although the calendrical reforms were far more modest than those introduced by the Jacobins after the French Revolution, they were none the less significant. The structure of days, weeks and months remained unaltered, but the Soviet authorities adopted the Gregorian calendar, which had been promulgated by Pope Gregory XIII in 1582 and which was gradually adopted throughout the West, despite Protestant qualms about its Catholic provenance (for example, it was not accepted in England until 1752). The highly traditional Orthodox Church retained the Julian calendar, as devised by Julius Caesar in an earlier effort at rationalization. This meant that church rituals were often out of step with secular ones. The pre-Revolutionary use of the Julian calendar explains why the Orthodox celebrate Christmas in January, and also why the anniversary of the October Revolution falls in November.

Some Soviet rituals were in direct competition with Christian equivalents. For example, from the 1960s onwards there were new Soviet holidays contending with Easter and Pentecost. However, direct competition on the same day ran a high risk that people would opt for the religious celebration in preference to its Soviet rival. What the regime therefore tried to do was to strip out all the popular folk elements from religious rituals and transfer them to the Soviet equivalents. A good example of this was the celebration of the Soviet New Year (Lane 1981: 137–9). This involved the lighting of a 'Christmas' tree, giving gifts to children, exchange of greetings cards, alcohol-assisted revelling, and the revival of traditional festive figures such as Grandfather Frost and the Snow Maiden.

Built into the Soviet calendar were days celebrating the work of key groups, such as border guards, which had an ideologically central role in safeguarding the Soviet way of life.

Rites of passage

The various initiation ceremonies sponsored by the Soviet regime had a mixed reception (Lane 1981: 243–8). Some were relatively late introductions – for example, initiation into the working class, into the peasantry and into the armed forces – and so had little time to establish themselves. As for the family-oriented rites of passage, the wedding rite appeared to be the most popular. The rite of Solemn Registration of the New-Born Child gained some acceptance, but the funeral rite was far more problematic. This may be evidence of the regime's problems in providing answers to the ultimate questions of meaning in human life.

Mass parades

In the euphoria that followed the October Revolution, grassroots community gatherings were often spontaneous expressions of popular enthusiasm (Binns 1979). People had a good time. However, in the politically troubled years after Lenin's death, with the gradual ascendancy of Stalin, mass events lost their freshness and spontaneity, and came under the control of the state apparatus. Permanent raised tribunes were built in every city, so that political leaders could harangue the masses and review parades of Soviet organizations, troops and military equipment. The most famous of these was the May Day parade in Moscow, a reminder to the world of Soviet military capability.

A leadership cult

In his own lifetime, Lenin was concerned about the personality cult that was already beginning to develop around him. After his death in 1924 a number of crucial decisions were taken that reinforced this cult (Binns 1979). St Petersburg had already become Petrograd during the

First World War; it was renamed Leningrad. The date of Lenin's death, 21 January, became a day of national mourning. Monuments to Lenin were erected in all the major cities of the Soviet Union. His body was embalmed and placed in a mausoleum constructed under the Kremlin wall among the graves of the fallen warriors of the October Revolution. His collected works were published – a New Testament to match the Old Testament scriptures of Marx and Engels, which together formed the sacred canon of Marxism-Leninism.

Places of pilgrimage

The principal site of pilgrimage in the Soviet Union was Lenin's mausoleum. It was open to the public, and entry was free. A quasi-religious devotional atmosphere was preserved in this sacred place. Visitors were required to move in respectful silence around the corpse. Reverence was enforced by the security guards, who prevented all talking – even rational expositions of Lenin's scientific socialism were forbidden. This place of pilgrimage has been so successful that when the Vietnamese leader Ho Chi Minh died, his body was also embalmed, with the aid of Soviet experts, and displayed in a similar mausoleum in Hanoi.

Study of Soviet ritual is a means to strip aside political ideology in order to uncover the social reality which the ideology in part conceals. In contrast to the revolutionary rhetoric of the Soviet regime, what Soviet rituals displayed was a profoundly conservative symbol system. Soviet ritual sacralized the Soviet world – the supposedly good society in operation, or 'actually existing socialism', as it was known officially. The ritual system did not cultivate Marx's vision that the state would 'wither away' once communism was fully achieved. Rituals idealized labour productivity, not the liberation of workers from the dull compulsion of alienated labour. The cult of the leader, seen not only in the central cult of Lenin and the subsequent cult of Stalin, but also in minor cults of successive leaders such as Khrushchev and Brezhnev, was a conservative force that deviated from the progressive rationalistic ideology of Marxism-Leninism.

A final key feature of Soviet ritual was that it was literally that: *Soviet* ritual, not for export to other countries, not even to the former Communist societies of Eastern and Central Europe. Communism's internationalist rhetoric contrasted with Soviet ritual, which was profoundly nationalistic, patriotic and militaristic. Thus Soviet ritual was deployed to legitimize the Stalinist policy of 'Socialism in One Country'. The capital had been moved east from St Petersburg, the country's most cosmopolitan city, to Moscow, architecturally and culturally a more distinctively Russian city. Lenin's mummified body became a further symbol of the nationalization of Marxism (Binns 1979). A popular belief in the Orthodox tradition is that the body of a saint will not putrefy. By scientifically embalming Lenin, the Soviet authorities had made a symbolic gesture against this popular superstition, while paradoxically elevating Lenin to the status of a saint.

This was not the only irony in the Soviet ritual system. The 1960s saw a flourishing of new rituals, particularly ones designed to channel family life and leisure pursuits in politically desired directions. This appears to have been a conscious effort by the state to shore up a political religion in decline. By the 1960s, the October Revolution was a distant memory, and even the heroic defence of the motherland in what Russians call 'The Great Patriotic War' against Hitler's invasion in 1941 had lost its immediacy as a symbolic resource for the regime. Young people were beginning to look more knowledgeably to the West for images of the good society. They saw the attractions of consumerism. The new Soviet rituals of the 1960s were probably counter-productive. Despite the political objectives of the regime, the rituals tended to reinforce individualism and consumerism. Filtering out the official propaganda, as Soviet citizens could skilfully do, people took advantage of unofficial aspects of the rituals such as meeting friends and joining in the festivities (Binns 1980). These gratifications contrasted with and underlined the greyness of everyday life in the USSR.

Lane (1981) argues that the ritual system of the former Soviet Union should be seen not as civil religion, but as political religion. Civil religion represents transcendent categorical truths on which people and interest groups can draw not only to support existing political institutions but also to protest against them, evoking religious legitimation for their protest. In Western liberal-democratic societies, civil religion is also constrained by norms of tolerance: the civil rights and liberties of people of all faiths are to be respected.

This was not the case in the USSR. Political religion was consciously planned and rationally administered by the regime as a system of symbols and rituals sacralizing Soviet society and the Soviet state. It fused political ideology and religion into an indissoluble entity – hence the term 'political religion'. The Soviet state held a monopoly on sacred values: dissidents were tantamount to heretics, and crimes against the state were sacrilege. The ritual system was a vehicle of top-down 'cultural management'. In Geertz's terms (1968: 7), rituals were 'models for', rather than 'models of', social relationships: they did not arise organically out of social relationships, but were ideologically driven models of what those relationships should be, and therefore designed to mould society in the desired direction.

The collapse of the Communist regime in 1991 led to a rapid abandonment of most of the symbols of the Soviet era. In 2004, the public holiday celebrating the October Revolution was finally abolished. Even the cult of Lenin was profoundly affected. Many of the statues of Lenin were dismantled, discreditable facts about his life were publicly aired, and Leningrad reverted to its former Tsarist name St Petersburg. Even so, Lenin's corpse still rests in its mausoleum. The former President, Boris Yeltsin, indicated that he would like to see Lenin buried literally as well as figuratively, but there is still widespread political and popular opposition to what would be the ultimate act of anti-Soviet sacrilege.

Political religion and charismatic leadership: Nazi Germany

A huge torchlight procession celebrated Hitler's appointment as Chancellor in 1933. This was no routine change of government; the symbolism heralded the dawn of a new era. Although Hitler's thousand-year Third Reich lasted less than thirteen years, it produced an abundance of sacred symbols and rituals, including rites of passage, calendrical festivals and mass rallies.

There are many parallels between political religion in the former Soviet Union and Nazi Germany (Lane 1981: 273–9). Both regimes celebrated the following: the seasons, infusing popular holidays with pagan associations; familial life-cycle rites; the incorporation of young people into social and political organizations such as the Komsomol and the Hitler Youth; labour and the individual's contribution to the economy; the anniversary of the foundation of the new political order; a sacred history of fallen heroes; and a cult of the leader.

Despite these common features in the ritual systems, there were also marked dissimilarities, reflecting profound ideological differences between the two regimes. Whereas the Soviet Union was committed to rational (though inefficient) planning, Nazi Germany was profoundly irrational (though bureaucratic). Lane's analysis suggests that whereas the Soviet regime found ritual *politically useful*, in the case of National Socialism it was *culturally essential*.

The irrationality of Nazism manifested itself in many ways, not least in the cult of the Führer, which far from being antithetical to the regime was of its very essence. Hitler carefully cultivated his public image, making sure that he did not display any emotional or physical weaknesses. Although, ironically, neither Hitler himself nor most of his associates resembled the physical ideal of the 'Aryan' male, the cult of the leader emphasized his physical appearance and prowess – linked to the key Nazi symbols of blood and 'race'. One reason why so many observers failed to see the threat posed by the rise of Nazism was that they underestimated the power of its personality cult (Kershaw 1989: 29).

In contrast to Stalin, Hitler was impatient with bureaucratic procedures (even though his regime spawned a huge bureaucracy). He tended not to issue detailed commands; instead, he set forth a vision, which his followers were eager to translate into practical measures that would please the Führer. Even when the regime faced setbacks, criticism focused not on Hitler, but on the officials who had supposedly let him down. Nazism demonstrated the truth of Weber's observation that charismatic movements need to demonstrate continual success to the faithful. Hitler had apparently rescued Germany from economic collapse, and had restored a form of social 'order'; he enjoyed considerable successes in foreign policy; and in the first two years of the War, the strategy of *Blitzkrieg* appeared to prove that he was a military genius.

The year 1936 marked a watershed: after Germany's unchallenged reoccupation of the Rhineland, Hitler openly embraced his own myth, proclaiming himself a man in mystical union with the German people and infallibly guided by Providence (Kershaw 1989: 82). All manner of mystical powers were attributed to him. For example, it was popularly believed (Grunberger 1991: 121) that if a house was destroyed in an Allied bombing raid, one wall would remain standing: the wall bearing Hitler's portrait.

The treatment of organized religion in the Soviet Union and in Nazi Germany was different. In the Soviet case, repression and persecution alternated with periods during which the state simply waited for religion to wither away of its own accord. Nazi Germany, on the other hand, had a deeply ambivalent relationship with Christianity and the Christian churches. For some members of the Catholic hierarchy in the occupied countries, anti-Semitism and hostility to communism united to dispose them to collaborate with the National Socialist programme. Some German Protestants, the Deutsche Christen (German Christians), co-operated in fusing Nazi and Christian symbols into a new religious system – a 'positive Christianity' (Steigmann-Gall 2003). To Nazi ideologists, Christianity had become a religion for slaves, emphasizing meekness, humility and care for the weak. These were not National Socialist virtues. Similarly, Christ as a crucified saviour, a suffering servant and, moreover, a Jewish man, was not a suitable symbol for Nazi heroes. The solution arrived at by positive Christians was to claim that Jesus was not a Jew but an anti-Semitic Aryan.

In the Soviet case, there were very few rituals surrounding the Communist Party itself. Since party members were ideologically mature, they were thought not to need rituals. Rituals were devised and administered by the party for the masses – ironically, a Marxist-Leninist opium for the people. It was quite otherwise in Nazi Germany, where the party itself was saturated with symbolism and surrounded with ritual.

Stalin repeatedly and ruthlessly purged the Communist Party of potential rivals; Hitler's instinct was to remain loyal to his close colleagues, particularly those who had been with him in the early days of the movement in the Munich of the 1920s. Their adoring support was a vital element in sustaining the mythology surrounding him. None of his associates ever posed a challenge to his leadership. He appeared to be irreplaceable; no mechanisms were ever put in place to transmit his charisma to a successor.

Character and society

Much of the analysis of civil religion has located itself in the Durkheimian approach to ritual and symbolism. Yet Bellah's own work draws its inspiration not only from Durkheim but also from the tradition stemming from Tocqueville. As discussed in chapter 5, Tocqueville saw religion as essential to any republic of free citizens. Bellah (1990: 415) echoes this, arguing that a despotism will have despotic customs and a republic republican customs – ones that are conducive to public-spiritedness and commitment to the public good.

Tocqueville's influence is explicit in the widely read study *Habits of the Heart*, which Bellah co-authored with Madsen, Sullivan, Swidler and Tipton (1996). Their aim was to explore the relationship between character and society, the private and the public sphere. Does the private sphere prepare people for participation as citizens in public life? And does public life meet people's private aspirations? Answers to these questions are seen as crucial to gauging the health of the republic. Tocqueville said that the 'tyranny of the majority', an oppressive egalitarianism, was the greatest threat to the American social order. For Bellah and his colleagues, this is no longer the case. Instead, rampant individualism is now the gravest danger, carrying with it the prospect of social disintegration. The integrity of the social order depends upon the continued vitality of the republican and biblical traditions, both of which are key components of a civil religion that transcends individualism in the name of the public good. Thus in Bellah's perspective civil religion is much more than a 'lowest common denominator', as Bruce (1986: 233) has it. The role of civil religion is to forge a connection between character and society.

8

Brainwashing, Consumer Protection and the State

Brainwashing – old and new

Minority religious movements, particularly those of the world-rejecting type, have faced persecution throughout their history. Many movements – including Mennonites, Shakers, Hutterites and Doukhobors – fled Europe to escape persecution and pogroms, seeking asylum in a New World which held out the promise of religious tolerance backed by a constitutional guarantee of freedom of worship and assembly. The New World itself gave rise to a rich diversity of home-grown movements that have had an impact internationally, including Christian Science, Seventh-day Adventism, Jehovah's Witnesses and the Church of Jesus Christ of Latter-day Saints.

Even in the United States, there is a long, though largely forgotten, history of persecution of minority religions (Bromley and Shupe 1981: 6–20). Faiths that have achieved respectability were once vilified. Persecution of religious minorities is usually legitimized by what sociologists have called 'atrocity stories'. Just as warring nations accuse one another of crimes against humanity, so religious minorities are the target of atrocity stories, both true and false.

The bloody history of confrontations between Mormons and the wider society is a dramatic example of hatred fuelled by religion. Less graphic, but no less telling, is the case of Roman Catholicism. Bromley and Shupe (1981: 11–15) identify five themes in anti-Catholic polemics in the history of the United States.

Deception and coercion   Roman Catholics were thought to be indoctrinated by priests, nuns, Jesuits and other agents of papal authority, who used Confession as a means of extracting guilty secrets to use as blackmail against the hapless victim.

The illegitimacy of Catholic beliefs   In the ultra-Protestant version of history, the Protestant Reformation of the sixteenth century restored the true Christian faith which had been betrayed by heretical Catholic beliefs and practices. Backed solely by the illegitimate doctrine of papal infallibility, these beliefs and practices had no foundation in the Bible. A prime example is the cult of the Virgin Mary, seen by ultra-Protestants as pure paganism.

Sexual perversion   The celibacy of priests and members of religious orders was portrayed as repressing natural sexual drives which would inevitably find an outlet elsewhere: using the services of prostitutes, homosexual acts, seducing young people, sexually abusing children. Convents, abbeys, monasteries, priests' houses, seminaries – all were allegedly hotbeds of perversion.

Political subversion   Catholicism was seen as a conspiracy bent on undermining democratic institutions and freedoms, replacing them with the unfettered autocratic power of the Vatican. Successive waves of migration from Catholic Europe to the New World were part of a papal design to seize power in the United States. This theme of political subversion lives on, as we have seen, among fervent Protestant Loyalists in Northern Ireland.

Financial exploitation   The Catholic Church was portrayed as extracting large donations from its members, duping them into believing that this would relieve their sufferings in this world and the next. An extreme example was the practice which grew up in the late Middle Ages of selling indulgences. At considerable cost, people could buy indulgences from professional 'pardoners'. Purchasing an indulgence would reduce the time that the sinner would have to spend in purgatory before entering heaven. The money raised was often devoted to construction projects: most notably, it contributed to the cost of building St Peter's in Rome. Eventually banned by Pope Pius V in 1567, the highly commercial activities of the pardoners, who were in effect selling salvation as a commodity, were held up by the Protestant reformers as a powerful symbol of Catholic corruption.

The five themes identified by Bromley and Shupe recur in atrocity stories told about contemporary religious movements. They are given a specifically modern inflection: cults are accused of thought reform, mind control and brainwashing.

The term 'brainwashing' was originally used to describe the experiences of US military personnel who were taken prisoner and indoctrinated by the Chinese Communists during the 1950–3 Korean War. This indoctrination, it was argued, built on and intensified techniques of persuasion which the Communists had already used successfully on their own people. American prisoners of war were subjected to a variety of techniques: inadequate and unbalanced diets; sleep deprivation and disruption; ideological indoctrination; psychotropic drugs; repeated interrogation; beatings and torture; and threats of beatings, torture and execution. This brutality was aimed at reducing prisoners to a state of physiological dysfunctioning and psychological disorientation and suggestibility, which would leave them susceptible to deep-seated attitude change. The American public was shocked to see films of prisoners of war making zealously pro-Communist statements and denouncing Western capitalism and American imperialism. How had these dramatic ideological conversions come about? An apparently convincing answer was supplied: mind control through coercive and powerful techniques of brainwashing. In a body of academic literature (Sargant 1957; Lifton 1961) published during the era of the Cold War, techniques of brainwashing were analysed as mechanisms of social control characteristic of totalitarian societies.

The achievements of Communist brainwashers were less than was once thought. Scheflin and Opton's book *The Mind Manipulators* (cited in Bromley and Shupe 1981: 99–100) showed that of the more than 3,500 Americans taken prisoner during the Korean War, only about fifty made pro-Communist statements, and only twenty-five refused repatriation to the USA when the war ended. Obviously, many of the pro-Communist statements were motivated by self-preservation rather than ideological conversion.

When the activities of world-rejecting religious movements came under scrutiny in the West from the late 1960s onwards, a parallel was drawn between their socialization practices and the techniques used on prisoners of war. Brainwashing in religious movements has been said to involve the following:

- use of deception to conceal the movement's identity and true purpose;
- sleep deprivation brought about through long, exhausting and irregular work schedules;

- an unbalanced diet, particularly one excessively high in sugar, which produces a state of euphoria known as 'sugar buzzing';
- disruption of sexual activity;
- denial of privacy;
- repetitive chanting of mantras and ideological slogans;
- participation in childish team games;
- disruption of contact with the outside world;
- intense displays of love, admiration and concern (love bombing).

Assuming that these techniques have indeed been used by minority religious movements, how effective are they? Sociological studies give a clear answer: they are remarkably ineffective and short-lived. A well-known demonstration of this is Barker's study of the Moonies (Barker 1984: 145–8). In a survey of more than a thousand people who attended a two-day workshop in the London area in 1979, she found that only one in ten actually joined the movement for more than a week. From the perspective of the Unification Church, this is a poor rate of take-up, especially since the people who attended the initial workshop were not a random cross-section of society but a highly self-selected sample of seekers – good prospects, in other words. People dropped out of the movement at regular intervals. After one year, only 7 per cent of the people who had joined were still members; after two years the figure had fallen to 5 per cent, and by the end of four years it had fallen still further to 3.5 per cent at most. This drastic rate of attrition shows that the Moonies' techniques of persuasion are ineffective, and hardly warrant the grandiose title of brainwashing. The rapid turnover of members reflects the movement's recruitment strategy, and its targeting of relatively unattached young people who can enjoy the luxury of a brief interlude of 'time out' before re-entering the mainstream of society. However, as Barker points out, both the Moonies and their opponents have a vested interest in exaggerating Moonie successes.

The power of the brainwashing metaphor

When the accusation of brainwashing is applied to religious movements, it evokes deep-seated fears and anxieties. Thus the debate about brainwashing sheds light not only on minority religions but also on the wider society. A number of closely related fears can be identified.

Fears of psychological manipulation

The debate about brainwashing taps into broader fears about the capacity of new technologies to manipulate people's thoughts, emotions and desires. This has been a common theme in science fiction and dystopian novels, as well as in critiques of consumer society.

Fears of charismatic leadership

Jim Jones of the Peoples Temple, David Koresh of the Branch Davidians at Waco, Marshall Applewhite ('Do') of Heaven's Gate, Luc Jouret of the Ordre du Temple Solaire, Asahara Shōkō of Aum Shinrikyō: all of these led their followers to disaster. The shock of the mass suicide of the Peoples Temple at Jonestown in 1978 transformed public sentiment in the West. Minority religions were all subject to the suspicion that they would follow the apocalyptic example of the Peoples Temple and induce their members to commit suicide. In each of the cases cited above, a deranged charismatic leader was seen as possessing extraordinary mental powers, enabling him to take control of the mind and the will of his followers.

Fears of collectivism

It is no coincidence that allegations of brainwashing have their roots in the Cold War. The threat posed by the apocalyptic ideology of Communism, backed by the Soviet Union's formidable nuclear arsenal, and the longer-term menace of Communist China, indirectly coloured thinking about the 'new' religions of the late 1960s and the 1970s. Critiques of new religious movements often show what Robbins (1988: 73) calls an 'atomistic bias', since they assume that authentic religious experience must necessarily be deeply personal and individual. Movements in which the religious community provides a powerful mediation and reinforcement of spirituality risk being seen as manipulative and inauthentic. Individual autonomy is threatened just as much by religious collectivism as by atheistic Communism.

One illustration of anti-collectivism is the hostility displayed towards mass wedding ceremonies performed by the Unification Church. These ceremonies, involving thousands of arranged marriages in which the partners are ostensibly selected by Moon himself, strike a symbolic blow at Western individualism and its faith in romantic love. They are an expression of the Unification Church's affirmation of community service and duty, rather than individual self-realization.

Ironically, the Unification Church is fiercely anti-Communist. Early in his career Moon was imprisoned and ill-treated by the Communist authorities in North Korea. Part of the Moonie message to the West is that the United States has been the leader of the free world in a deadly struggle with godless Communism.

Fears of the alien 'other'

The explosion of new religious movements and a new religious consciousness in the West from the late 1960s onwards gave rise to a wide-ranging debate in sociology and in the media about the social significance of these apparently new phenomena. The term 'cult' became widely used to characterize the new religions and the personal relationships operative within them. Although 'cult' may have been understood neutrally by sociologists, it was certainly used negatively by journalists and other commentators. Part of what it connoted was an alien intrusion into 'our' culture. At least the sects were home-grown! For all the problems they are thought to present, Jehovah's Witnesses take their place on the far wing of extreme conservative Protestantism, just as the Mormons, despite all the doubts about the authenticity of the Book of Mormon and the justification for polygamy, are a recognizably American movement rooted in American history and suffused with conventional American values – clean living, the nuclear family, the success ethic. But Hare Krishna? The Divine Light Mission? The Moonies? What were *our* young people doing joining *them*?

What new religious movements offer their recruits

One feature of the accusation of brainwashing, as has often been pointed out, is that it takes attention away from the content of religious beliefs and practices, and focuses on the processes through which believers are brought to a state of passive dependence on the movement. In doing so, it carries the implication that these movements have nothing of value to offer their members. From a sociological point of view, however, we cannot simply dismiss out of hand the benefits which members claim to experience. Following Barker (1995: 25–31), six main types of benefit may be distinguished; as one would expect, movements usually offer more than one of these. These factors are not unique to minority religions, though many who join say that they did not find them in mainstream religion.

Success in careers   It is mainly the world-affirming religious movements which provide techniques of self-improvement promoting the achievement of worldly career goals. These movements offer their services to individuals and also to business corporations interested in improving the motivation and commitment of their personnel.

Improved health and longevity   Again, this claim is common among world-affirming movements. Health is typically viewed holistically as embracing mental, spiritual and physical well-being. Cartesian dualism, with its strict division between mind and body, is rejected.

Community   Some movements, especially the world-rejecting type, provide communal living for their devotees. Even where this is not the case, members develop affective ties of friendship and loyalty. Family imagery is very common, with fellow worshippers being called brothers and sisters, and the leaders mother and father (as in the Unification Church, where Moon and his wife are referred to as 'True Parents').

Kingdom building   World-rejecting movements often attract idealistic young people with the promise that they will be building a better world, even the Kingdom of God on earth. Fired by religiously inspired altruism, members may engage enthusiastically as unpaid volunteers in labour-intensive community projects, recruitment drives and fundraising activities. However, disillusionment can set in if the member comes to feel that recruitment and fundraising are the dominant goals, leaving the social action programmes and charitable work as little more than a public relations exercise.

Self-development   This theme is particularly strong among world-affirming movements. The distinction between secular self-advancement and spiritual development is often unclear. Some people start out with straightforwardly this-worldly success goals, but then discover as they progress in the movement that the spiritual dimension gradually takes priority. Equally, self-development is not incompatible with altruism. For example, Transcendental Meditation teaches that if a critical mass of people engage in TM, it will have positive benefits for the whole of their society. It is on this basis that the Natural Law Party, the political wing of TM, fielded candidates in general elections in the USA, Canada, New Zealand and the UK (with no success).

Religious experiences   New religious movements cultivate a variety of religious experiences, and, crucially, offer a forum in which religious experience is validated. This can be attractive to people who feel that mainstream religion is spiritually barren, or that the wider culture is hostile to spirituality (Hay 1987). Barker found that more than three-quarters of the Moonies she interviewed claimed to have had religious experiences before they joined the Unification Church (Barker 1984: 218). The majority had never told anyone about these experiences, for fear of being ridiculed or branded as a fanatic. New religious movements offer, then, an outlet for repressed spirituality.

Disengaging from new religious movements

Members of new religious movements typically cite the benefits discussed above. In evaluating their accounts, we need to recognize that they are just that – accounts, which seek to make sense of social phenomena and social processes (Beckford 1978). Like any account, they are not simply spontaneously generated: they are called forth in certain contexts, retold to certain audiences, and they are also learned. Becoming a member of a religious movement is a complex process in which the prospective convert is socialized into appropriate motivation, behaviour and discourse. For these reasons, any conversion account is in part scripted, which does not imply that it is insincere or untrue.

Precisely the same considerations apply to accounts of deconversion given by people who have left a religious movement. In the sociological literature these people are often called 'apostates' – an unfortunate term, since in religious discourse it can carry implications of defection and heresy. Apostasy in that framework is the religious equivalent of military desertion, a serious disciplinary offence. In the early Christian church, apostasy, murder and fornication were the three sins considered unpardonable if committed by a baptized Christian. Later, in Western Christianity, the term was applied more specifically to the unpermitted renunciation by monks and nuns of their lifelong vows. In Islam, apostasy is a grievous sin, potentially punishable by death in some Islamic cultures. Significantly, the freedom to change one's religion is not recognized as a human right by any Islamic state (Boyle and Sheen 1997: 8–9).

Although sociologists are supposedly using the term neutrally, much of the sociological literature, as Beckford (1985: 146) points out, tends to be dismissive of apostates' accounts of their experiences. To avoid the pejorative associations, the term 'ex-members' is preferred here.

Ex-members are prominent among those who tell atrocity stories about new religious movements. Their testimony gains credibility from being firsthand. They claim to be in a position to reveal the sordid truths which outsiders, including sociologists, have failed to uncover. Some ex-members have been active in anti-cult movements, whereas others simply recount their experiences to family and friends. A theme running through some of these stories is that the ex-member was brainwashed. Not all accounts, however, conform to the brainwashing paradigm. Beckford's work on the Moonies (1985: 149–217), based on interviews with ex-members and their families, provides telling insights into the appeal and also the drawbacks of the rhetoric of brainwashing.

The crucial point in Beckford's analysis is that when a committed member leaves the Moonies, she or he is likely to find it a harrowing experience. The Unification Church does not make it easy. From the church's perspective there is no valid reason for leaving. Seekership is not legitimate: ex-members cannot say that their spiritual quest is leading them elsewhere. There is no legitimate mode of exit; hence, the church makes no provision for the spiritual welfare of those whom it sees as apostates. People who leave the church therefore do so suddenly and unexpectedly. Even if they had been harbouring misgivings for a long time, they would have found it risky to share them with fellow Moonies for fear of rejection or betrayal. Defectors are stigmatized, and their example is held up to members as evidence of the power of Satan to seduce the faithful. The Unification Church tries to prevent ex-members from communicating with their former friends in the movement – the mirror image of its efforts to disrupt communications from members to their family and friends.

Family and friends unwittingly place additional strains on the ex-member. As Beckford points out, most ex-Moonies return to the parental home. It is a situation fraught with embarrassment, confusion and mutual suspicion on both sides. The period during which the ex-Moonie was active in the movement is likely to have caused worry and anguish to the parents, doubly so if they were themselves facing a mid-life crisis in relationships or career. Involvement in new religious movements is also widely regarded in Western culture as foolish and immature – scarcely an enhancement of anyone's curriculum vitae. In welcoming their children back, parents typically seek an account of why they joined the movement and of why they left it. In rendering an account, the ex-Moonie is not merely telling a story but restoring a balance, making reparations for a breach in the social order. The account is expected to paint a harsh picture of life in the Unification Church. Brainwashing and mind control fulfil this role, enabling blame to be attributed entirely to the church. Ex-Moonies are required to renounce their Moonie past, obliterating it from their c.v. as a condition of their relaunch into the mainstream of social life.

The rhetoric of brainwashing can offer a way forward to ex-Moonies, enabling them to discount their Moonie past as the product of brainwashing, and to re-enter social life virtually at the point where they left it. Some ex-Moonies have made a career in the anti-cult movement, offering themselves as experts on brainwashing.

Beckford's evidence shows, nevertheless, that many ex-Moonies have problems with embracing the brainwashing rhetoric whole-heartedly. Ex-members often feel guilty about leaving the church, fearing that they have let down their Moonie companions. They also typically experience a sense of failure, since they were unequal to the challenge of living the Moonie life. Despite their doubts, they may not have abandoned all hope that Moon is the promised Messiah. They may well have pleasant memories of the good times: the spiritual support, the kingdom building, the companionship of a close-knit community. These experiences, after all, were what attracted them to the movement in the first place, meeting needs that they had been unable to satisfy before they joined. Now, it seems, they are required to deny that there was anything good at all about being a Moonie. They are under pressure to make a full confession in order to be absolved, clearing the path for a fresh start. If, however, they believe that the Unification Church has betrayed the trust they showed by being spiritually 'open' when they were members, they tend to be wary of repeating that mistake. They may also feel that they are being treated as incompetent – back to childhood with a vengeance.

Disengagement from new religious movements is often a solo performance, and in that sense a taxing virtuoso act. Movements like the Unification Church provide no support, and the contribution of family and friends, however well-intentioned, is frequently counter-productive. Ex-members may lack a 'cultural script' for disengagement, unless they adopt the brainwashing account scripted by the anti-cult movement.

Consumer protection and the regulation of abuses

Robbins (1988: 164–8) has argued that, at least in the United States, controversy about new religious movements is fuelled by their status as *privileged enclaves*. Although the state is gradually extending its regulatory control into all areas of social life, transforming private troubles into public concerns, religion and religious movements enjoy legal privileges that insulate them from state interference in their affairs. This is one reason why so many social movements have been determined to claim a religious identity. What Robbins calls a 'regulatory gap' is opening up between tightly regulated secular organizations and their privileged religious counterparts.

As long as religious movements are content with a privatized role, cultivating members' inner spirituality (as in world-accommodating movements), their privileges seldom cause controversy. The regulatory gap becomes an issue only when religious movements broaden their scope to include more and more areas of social life. Scientology and the Unification Church have been at the cutting edge of church–state tension precisely because they are highly diversified organizations with a myriad of activities. They are not unlike multinational corporations. Activities listed by Robbins (1988: 166) include commercial and financial stakes in publishing, education, child care, residential establishments, nursing homes, political lobbying, healing and psychotherapy. Where the state's regulatory grip is relaxed, their status as religions is seen to give them an unfair competitive advantage over their secular rivals.

Consider two examples of intervention by the state to regulate abuse. First, the Moonies (Barker 1995: 214–16). The Unification Church owns a wide range of commercial operations. It has machine tool and ginseng businesses, a large fishing fleet, and owns the *Washington Times*. It trades under a number of names that conceal its identity. These entrepreneurial activities have attracted the attention of the authorities. Moon was imprisoned in the USA in the 1980s, having been found guilty of an entirely secular offence, conspiracy to evade taxation.

Second, the Rajneeshees (Barker 1995: 201–5; Bruce 1996: 178–9). In 1974, Bhagwan Shree Rajneesh, who changed his name to Osho towards the end of his life, founded a community at Poona in India. Thousands of pilgrims from the West travelled to the ashram in order to enter the guru's presence and receive enlightenment. From the very outset the movement was both fashionable and controversial, mainly because its techniques of meditation routinely resulted in group sex. A folk myth has become widespread that the title 'Bhagwan' means 'Master of the Vagina'. In fact, it means 'the High God'. It is indeed offensive – but as a blasphemy, not an obscenity, as the secular Western imagination supposes.

In 1981, Rajneesh abruptly left Poona and moved to the United States, where he purchased a 64,000-acre ranch in Oregon, building a community called Rajneeshpuram, which incorporated an elaborate nuclear bunker. Despite the movement's celebration of love and peace, Rajneeshpuram was run on totalitarian lines. Relations with the local community degenerated into violence and intimidation. Rajneesh's secretary, Ma Anand Sheela, was imprisoned for a variety of criminal offences. Rajneesh himself was caught trying to leave the USA, imprisoned, and then deported for violation of US immigration laws. Refused entry by a number of countries as an undesirable alien, Rajneesh returned to Poona, where he died in 1990.

The modern liberal-democratic state has extended its regulatory grip to include, in Beckford's words (1985: 284), 'virtually all aspects of commerce, manufacturing, hygiene and safety in places of work, health hazards in therapeutic practice, and the use of land and buildings'. Beckford argues that new religious movements have not been singled out for special attention because they are religions; it is simply that any movement, secular or religious, which aims to cater comprehensively for its members, revitalizing the host society in the process, is bound to come into conflict with the modern state.

State surveillance of new religious movements in Western societies is 'indirect, piecemeal, administrative, *ad hoc*, and liberal' (Beckford 1985: 288). It is not driven by a coherent underlying social policy; nor do the various state agencies act in concert to achieve clearly identified goals (except perhaps in Germany, where, after the Nazi era, the need to protect the state against any threat from totalitarianism was made a constitutional imperative).

All social systems, according to Habermas (1973), have a need for mechanisms that give them legitimacy in the sense of respect and active commitment that go beyond mere compliance. Contemporary capitalism requires extensive state intervention to regulate economic and social life. The state gains a high degree of legitimacy through its role in consumer protection. Although state intervention in a liberal-democratic society can give rise to what Habermas identifies as a 'legitimation crisis', in that the state increasingly interferes in its citizens' private lives, this intervention is rendered legitimate by the claim that its rationale is to defend the autonomous individual against abuse.

Returning to the examples discussed above of state action against the Moonies and the Rajneeshees, a crucial point is that these interventions were popular with the general public. Also significant in each case was the open humiliation of the movement's charismatic leader. If there is a legitimation crisis in the contemporary state, acting against world-rejecting minority religions and their leaders can be a cost-effective way of gaining popular support.

Cult scares and the anti-cult movement

Much of the sociological work on new religious movements has sought to defend them against critical onslaught and the legislative curbs proposed by anti-cult groups. A classic example of such a defence is Bromley and Shupe's 1981 book, *Strange Gods*. Significantly subtitled *The Great American Cult Scare*, this book was written in the aftermath of the tragedy of the Peoples Temple at Jonestown in 1978. It concludes (1981: 203–20) with a 'hard look' at the cult controversy.

Bromley and Shupe argue that new religious movements are the subject of crude stereotyping and unsubstantiated myths propagated by anti-cultists in an attempt to arouse public indignation. The agenda of debate has been dominated by an anti-cult crusade that is in many ways more dangerous, and more threatening to civil liberties, than the movements it attacks. To redress the balance, Bromley and Shupe are deliberately more critical of anti-cultists than of the new religions themselves.

Anti-cultists exaggerate the numerical significance and social impact of new religious movements, implausibly claiming that virtually anyone is at risk of falling victim to their techniques of brainwashing – whereas in fact very few people join. According to Bromley and Shupe, the abuses perpetrated by new religions are not the lurid scandals of popular imagination, but relatively minor offences – for example, street soliciting for funds while concealing the movement's true identity. Leaders of the movements are neither more nor less sincere than the leaders of mainstream churches, Bromley and Shupe assert. It is incorrectly assumed that they wield absolute power, whereas they have to deal continually with doubt, dissent and the threat of factionalism.

For anti-cultists, new religious movements have no positive features. Bromley and Shupe argue, in contrast, that new religions embody fresh sources of meaning, reflecting emergent needs and aspirations among significant sections of society. They are part of a normal cycle, in which an era of stability is followed by a period of revitalization. Instead of breaking up families, new religious movements more commonly help to resolve family and inter-generational conflicts. In the late 1960s and the 1970s, they played an important part in rescuing young people from the drug counterculture. Movements such as the International Society for Krishna Consciousness provided a bridge back into the social mainstream, reaching out where mainstream Christianity so often failed to do so. In reinvigorating society, they also challenge the mainstream churches to reassess their own evangelical and pastoral policies.

The anti-cult movement fails to see new religions in historical perspective. The danger they represent is exaggerated now as it was in the past. New religions are invariably seen as subversive – as Christianity was by the Roman Empire, and as the Protestant Reformation was by the Roman Catholic Church.

In our own times, the persecution of new religious movements is justified by unfounded allegations of brainwashing that legitimate forcible 'deprogramming'. This cure is ineffective, illegitimate, and far worse than the problem. Anti-cultists and deprogrammers constitute a greater threat to civil liberties and democratic pluralism than do the new religions. Ironically, persecution of new religious movements tends to reinforce their cohesion and sense of solidarity. Instead of trying to legislate morality, it would be better to leave new religions alone, so that those movements which do endure would gradually accommodate to the mainstream and evolve into an approximation of the denominational form.

The example of the Peoples Temple at Jonestown is treated as a unique tragedy that cannot be generalized to other movements. Bromley and Shupe's conclusion is that the alarm surrounding new religious movements in the USA is a 'scare' and even a 'hoax', in that it is an unnecessary panic generated primarily by anti-cultists. 'In the final analysis', they say, 'the campaign against the new religions is better understood as the product of the anticultists' interests rather than as a civic crusade to save the rest of us from a dark, evil conspiracy' (1981: 213).

Doomsday cults: five case studies

Since Jonestown, there has been a series of highly publicized disasters in which members of new religious movements have taken their own lives, or died by the hands of their co-religionists, or perished in the aftermath of intervention by the authorities. Concern has grown about the threat posed by these destructive and violent 'doomsday cults'. What are the characteristics of these movements? And do they confirm that writers like Bromley and Shupe have been too sanguine, whereas the anti-cultists were right all along?

The Peoples Temple at Jonestown

In November 1978, US Representative Leo Ryan led a delegation to the agricultural community known as Jonestown, which had been established four years earlier in virgin territory in the socialist republic of Guyana. Jonestown was a project of the Peoples Temple, whose leader was the Reverend Jim Jones.

Congressman Ryan's purpose in visiting Jonestown was to investigate the truth of stories circulating in the United States that members of the Peoples Temple were being kept in Jonestown against their will. A small number of people agreed to return with him to the USA. When they arrived at the airstrip for their flight home, Ryan and four other members of his party were shot dead by Peoples Temple security guards. After the news of this was broadcast in Jonestown itself, more than 900 people, 30 per cent of them children, either participated voluntarily in a mass suicide, drinking Flavor Aid laced with cyanide, or were shot dead or killed by lethal injection. Their bodies were found scattered in little huddles on the ground. They had often practised the ritual of 'revolutionary suicide' before, but this time the poison was real.

Jim Jones had a long history as a preacher and religious leader. In 1953, he established an inter-racial congregation in Indianapolis. In 1964, his church was affiliated to the Disciples of Christ, and he was ordained a minister. In 1965, Jones and some of his followers moved to California, where they built up congregations in San Francisco and Los Angeles. They also became active on the fringe of Democratic Party politics. On the one hand, their cultivation of Democratic politicians and their engagement in inter-racial community programmes earned them respectability. On the other hand, Jones faced allegations of financial misconduct, sexual impropriety and faking miraculous cures for life-threatening illnesses such as cancer.

The apocalyptic theme was established early in Jones's career as a key element in his theology. The initial move from Indiana to California was justified by the belief that Redwood Valley would survive the impending nuclear holocaust. In California, Jones became increasingly preoccupied with what he saw as the CIA's plan of genocide of black people. Relocation to socialist Guyana was a bid to escape the clutches of American capitalism. In the last days at Jonestown, Jones contemplated a further move to Cuba or the USSR.

Jonestown had a dramatic impact on the cultural mood in America. It led to a significant swing of public opinion away from support of the civil liberties of religious minorities; 'cults' were now under suspicion. Florid rumours grew that the propensity to ritualized mass suicide was a common feature of cults, leading to groundless fears about the self-destructive urges of law-abiding groups such as Jehovah's Witnesses. The anti-cult movement declared itself vindicated; they had told the world that this would happen. How else could it be explained, except by brainwashing? Instead of standing back, the state needed to intervene decisively and with all necessary force.

The catastrophe at Jonestown therefore brought about a further disaster: people became unwise after the event.

The Branch Davidians at Waco

In February 1993, US government agents of the Bureau of Alcohol, Tobacco and Firearms (ATF) launched an armed attack with helicopter support on the Branch Davidians' Mount Carmel settlement at Waco, Texas. Their objective was to arrest David Koresh for firearms violations. An exchange of gunfire resulted in the death of four ATF agents and six Branch Davidians. The FBI took over from the ATF; there followed protracted negotiations with the Branch Davidians over the course of a siege lasting fifty-one days. At the end of this period, and fearing that Koresh was planning mass suicide after the manner of Jonestown, the FBI advanced on the settlement in armed vehicles equipped with battering rams. They penetrated the walls of the compound and launched CS gas. Fires erupted, possibly set off by the Branch Davidians themselves. The separate sources of fire combined into a huge conflagration that engulfed the compound. Most of the members of the settlement perished, including Koresh.

The Branch Davidians are an extreme offshoot of the Davidian Seventh-day Adventists, who had separated themselves from the Seventh-day Adventist mainstream in 1935 (Anthony and Robbins 1997). When the Waco crisis broke, the Seventh-day Adventist Church made strenuous efforts to disown the Branch Davidians (Lawson 1997).

It was in 1981 that Vernon Howell joined the Branch Davidians. In 1987, he and his followers took control of the movement. In 1990, Vernon Howell changed his name to David Koresh: David after King David of Israel, Koresh the Hebrew name for the Persian King Cyrus, who defeated Babylon (Bainbridge 1997: 113). He identified himself as 'the Lamb' who would open the seven seals, after which Christ would return to earth, and the War of Armageddon would be unleashed, a war in which the Branch Davidians would play a key part.

The Branch Davidians had accumulated an arsenal of weapons at Waco, ostensibly for self-defence against the forces of 'Babylon'. Under Koresh, the Mount Carmel settlement at Waco was prophetically renamed 'Ranch Apocalypse', reflecting his belief that the compound would be the site at which the War of Armageddon would begin. The two attacks on the compound confirmed Koresh's prophecy that the cosmic struggle between good and evil would lead the Babylonians to mount an onslaught on the Lamb and his elect.

L'Ordre du Temple Solaire

In October 1994 the emergency services were called to a fire at a farm-house in Cheiry, Switzerland (Hall and Schuyler 1997). A total of twenty-three people were found dead. They proved to be members of the Order of the Solar Temple, an occult movement that emerged in the 1970s. Twenty-one of them had been shot, and the remaining two had died of asphyxiation. Ten of the twenty-three had plastic bags over their heads. In some cases there was evidence that a struggle had taken place. Following an investigation, the authorities concluded that three of the members had been murdered as a reprisal for allegedly betraying the movement.

At the same time, some sixty kilometres away in a complex of villas at Granges-sur-Salvan, a further twenty-five bodies were found, many of them burned beyond recognition. They included two of the movement's leaders, Joseph Di Mambro and Luc Jouret. These incidents were found to be linked to the earlier mysterious death in Morin Heights near Montreal of five people, including a three-month-old infant who had had a wooden stake impaled in his heart.

The Order of the Solar Temple was a secret society, one in a long line of esoteric movements that fancifully trace their descent to the Rosicrucians, an occult brotherhood supposedly founded in the fifteenth century, and the medieval Knights Templar, who originally guarded the routes for Christian pilgrims to Jerusalem. The Order's members were affluent, middle-class, francophone and lapsed Catholic. The movement's belief system mixed together environmentalism, homoeopathy, numerology, astrology, Christian symbols and reincarnation.

Fire was a central symbol in their belief system. They believed that the world would be consumed by fire, and that in order to move on to another world, they themselves would need to die by fire. Documents recovered from the farmhouse at Cheiry referred to 'the Transit'. Death is an illusion: those who 'died' thought they were moving to a higher plane of existence located on a planet orbiting Sirius, the Dog Star.

Aum Shinrikyō

In 1995, the lethal nerve gas sarin was released on the Tokyo under-ground (Mullins 1997). Twelve people died, and more than 5,000 were injured. This was the work of Aum Shinrikyō, a religious movement founded in the 1980s by Matsumoto Chizuo, who later adopted the 'holy name' of Asahara Shōkō. Aum Shinrikyō was one of many 'new

new religions', as the Japanese called them, that sprang up in Japan in the 1980s (Trinh and Hall 2000). The title Aum Shinrikyō is a hybrid of Japanese and Sanskrit roots, whose meaning is that the movement teaches the Supreme Truth about the creative and destructive power in the universe. In 1989, after a long legal battle in which it vigorously asserted its constitutional rights, Aum Shinrikyō was registered in Japan as a religious organization.

Initially, Aum Shinrikyō presented itself as an eclectic Buddhist movement, offering its members liberation from illness and suffering, and ultimately enlightenment. The movement's vision was to transform Japan into a utopia. As the movement developed, however, an apocalyptic strand grew more and more prominent, drawing on the prophecies of the sixteenth-century monk Nostradamus and the Book of Revelation. The vision of the utopian transformation of Japan was replaced by the need for Aum to prepare to survive an inevitable nuclear war. To learn what was in store for humanity, Asahara travelled forward in time to interview survivors of World War Three. As part of the movement's new imperative, Aum was reorganized into divisions mimicking the departments of the Japanese government, with Asahara as Supreme Leader. Here was a government ready to take power after the apocalypse.

The movement became increasingly embattled, developing a siege mentality and fearing that its activities might be investigated by the authorities. Aum's practices degenerated into criminal violence: punishment beatings of disgruntled disciples, including Asahara's wife; covering up the death of a member who collapsed after subjecting himself to extreme asceticism on Asahara's orders; murdering a disciple who threatened to reveal the cover-up and a campaigning lawyer who was investigating the movement; and stockpiling huge quantities of material for the construction of chemical and biological weapons (Reader 2002). Two days after the atrocity in Tokyo, the police raided twenty-five Aum centres across Japan. Aum protested that it was being persecuted as a religious minority, and that it was the victim, rather than the perpetrator, of gas attacks. Asahara, who had been in hiding, was arrested two months later, put on trial, and sentenced to death. He is currently appealing against this sentence. The movement finally admitted its responsibility for the atrocity, and renamed itself Aleph. Although it now claims to have renounced violence, it still looks to Asahara as a guru and clings to many of his spiritual teachings.

Reflecting on these events, Mullins refers to Ellul's emphasis (1989: 60–2) on 'the democratization of evil' in contemporary societies. Weapons of mass destruction are, potentially, more widely available than in any previous civilization. Access to instruments of random indiscriminate slaughter has in that sense become democratic.

Heaven's Gate

The movement was founded in the 1970s by Marshall Herff Applewhite and Bonnie Lu Nettles, who gave themselves a series of fanciful names beginning with Bo and Peep, before finally settling on Do and Ti, musical notes in the tonic sol-fa system. After its initial phase of development as a UFO cult – they waited in the Colorado desert for a spaceship which failed to arrive – the movement went underground, travelling around to different locations in the USA until eventually settling in a large rented property, which they called their monastery, near San Diego. Members were cut off from contact with friends and family, many of whom became deeply worried about their welfare given Applewhite's increasingly volatile and apparently deranged behaviour.

In common with many other Ufologists, the movement held that UFOs are interstellar spaceships crewed by extraterrestrial beings whose motive in visiting Earth is to bring humanity to a higher plane of existence. It is a familiar notion, one frequently explored in science fiction. Heaven's Gate combined this belief with prophecies they derived from the Book of Revelation concerning two witnesses who were killed, but subsequently revived and were taken up into the heavens. This prophecy concerning 'the Two' was interpreted as referring to Ti and Do.

The movement held to a dualistic philosophy according to which the human body is a temporary, debased container of the human spirit. The spirit could be detached from its physical vessel by a carefully timed act of suicide, through which members would attain the Kingdom Level of existence, transcending the limitations of mundane human existence.

Sexuality was a key theme in the movement: the Kingdom Level would be free from gender identity and sexual activity. Sexual relations between members were forbidden, and a number of men in the movement, at Do's prompting and following his example, agreed to be castrated. There is evidence that Applewhite, who was gay, was profoundly troubled about his own sexual orientation and had unsuccessfully sought therapy to change it.

Unlike the events at Jonestown and Waco, in which intervention by outside agencies played a part in precipitating the crisis, the end of Heaven's Gate was the outcome of a long process of 'deliberate disconnection' from society (Balch and Taylor 2002). The final trigger was not social, but astronomical: the appearance of comet Hale-Bopp in 1997 was interpreted as a sign from Ti, who had died of cancer in 1985, that the time had at last come to evacuate planet Earth and join the extra-terrestrials aboard a spaceship concealed on the far side of the comet. Thirty-nine members of the movement, including Applewhite, committed suicide. A videotape they left behind shows that they did so voluntarily, in excited expectation of their future life at a higher level of evolution.

Apocalypse and self-destruction

In a famous article, Bromley and Shupe (1980) warned of the threat posed by the Tnevnoc Cult. This movement preyed on impressionable young women. New recruits were stripped of their individual identity and their material possessions. They were given new exotic names, and were required to shave their head and wear a drab uniform. They were isolated from family and friends in an encapsulated community. Their lives were closely regulated, involving an ascetic discipline of self-denial and repetitive prayer. They were also required to undergo a ritual marriage with the cult's charismatic founder, who had been resurrected from the dead.

Tnevnoc is, perhaps somewhat obviously, convent spelled backwards. Although a spoof, Bromley and Shupe's article was deeply serious. The socialization practices that take place in Christian religious orders clearly qualify as brainwashing in anti-cult terms, yet few people in the West regard them as life-threatening or would wish to see them outlawed.

It seems unlikely that sociology will ever develop a formula or algorithm that will enable us to predict which religious movements will end in self-destruction or violent confrontation with the wider society. Certainly the anti-cult movement failed to do so. What it did instead was to launch an indiscriminate broadside attack on a multitude of religious movements, including many which were long established and whose members were upstanding citizens. Far from predicting such disasters as Jonestown or Waco, the anti-cult movement prevented a clear understanding of them, and in some cases may even have made matters worse.

There are innumerable new religious movements, only a few of which have a propensity to violence (Melton and Bromley 2002). Identifying the violent few is extremely difficult. Some movements are volatile, so that their plunge into violence can be rapid and hard to predict. Sudden changes of doctrine and practice can be precipitated by unforeseen events; for example, Bonnie Nettles's death from liver cancer left the already unstable Marshall Applewhite deprived of a beloved companion, and undermined his notion that the members of Heaven's Gate would move to the Next Level while still alive. Here was the seed of the idea that they could leave this world for the next through an act of suicide.

Such developments can be inward to religious movements, and hard for outsiders to discover. Many religious movements are secretive; some have an inner circle who keep their plans concealed from the wider membership – as was true of Aum Shinrikyō. Given that it is hard for outsiders to penetrate deeply enough to uncover a movement's secrets, it is not surprising that the testimony of ex-members carries weight; even so, their evidence needs to be treated with caution, and cannot simply be taken as unvarnished truth.

Analysis is further complicated by the fact that violence is not simply a propensity possessed by a religious movement, but something that is produced and reinforced by its interactions with the wider society (Melton and Bromley 2002). As will be argued below, intervention by outside agencies, or the perceived threat of intervention, can bring about the very thing it was meant to prevent; Jonestown and Waco are clear examples. Events have consequences: it is widely recognized that Jonestown created a climate of heightened anti-cult sentiment, but what is overlooked is that the siege at Waco was held up as a source of inspiration by Heaven's Gate and the Order of the Solar Temple.

Allowing for these difficulties, there are some critically important factors that can be discerned in the case studies of destructive cults outlined above.

Catastrophic millenarianism

A millenarian religious movement is one that expects the present world to come to an end in the immediate future, to be replaced by a new world order.

There are many versions of millenarianism. In the Christian tradition, the millennium refers to a thousand years of blessedness. Some conservative Christian movements believe that the world was created 6,000 years ago; 4004 BC was one widely canvassed date, as originally calculated from biblical data in the seventeenth century by James Ussher, Archbishop of Armagh. Dating creation at 4004 BC was popularized in the twentieth century through the Scofield Reference Bible, which became a key text for fundamentalists. To God, who created the world in six days and rested on the seventh, one day is as a thousand years. The millennium, therefore, will commence at the end of the period of 6,000 years since Creation.

Although mainstream Christian churches look for the Second Coming of Christ, in most cases this is not a belief that actively influences the lives of rank-and-file members as a lively expectation that the world is about to come to an end literally at any moment. It does, however, play that role for Jehovah's Witnesses, Christadelphians and Seventh-day Adventists. These movements are fired by a sense of urgency: we are all living at the end of time, in the last days. Their perspective on history is drastically compressed: nothing significant happened between New Testament times and their own foundation. Although they see themselves as the bearers of eternal truth, they are not oriented to tradition; their focus is, rather, on the present and the immediate future (Wilson 1981).

In conventional theological treatments, Christian millenarian movements are divided into two basic types. The post-millennialists believe that the millennium is a period during which righteousness will spread progressively throughout the world, preparing the way for Christ's Second Coming at the end of the millennium. The pre-millennialists believe that the Second Coming of Christ will be the time of the Great Tribulation, often involving a battle (the War of Armageddon) between the forces of good and evil, between Christ and Antichrist. Only after the final defeat of evil will the millennium commence. Among pre-millennialist groups there is disagreement about what will happen to righteous people during the Tribulation: will they be taken up into heaven ('raptured'), or will they have to endure it?

The theological distinction between pre- and post-millennialism, tied as it is to specifically Christian thought and practice, is poorly suited to sociological analysis of religious movements more generally. For sociologists, Wessinger (1997) has argued, a more productive distinction is between progressive millenarianism and catastrophic millenarianism. Progressive millenarians believe, optimistically, that collective salvation on earth will be achieved by humans working in accordance with the divine or transcendent plan. For example, some groups believe in a peaceful transition from the troubled Age of Pisces to the Age of Aquarius, a period of harmony and understanding. The catastrophic millenarians believe, pessimistically, that evil is so deeply entrenched in the present world order that only an impending catastrophe can destroy it. The propensity for violent destructive acts is at its greatest among catastrophic millenarian movements.

In small, charismatically led movements, the distinction between progressive and catastrophic millenarianism tends to be unstable. Such movements are often torn between a measured attempt to create heaven on earth and a conviction that a cataclysm is required to cleanse the world of evil, leaving the movement's faithful members as the justly rewarded survivors. So it is that they can oscillate unpredictably between peaceful withdrawal from the world and waging war on it.

The religious movement as agent of the apocalypse

Jehovah's Witnesses, Christadelphians and Seventh-day Adventists are all catastrophic millenarian movements. The Second Coming of Christ is a dominant article of faith that shapes members' lives. For example, it is because these are 'the last days' before the War of Armageddon that Jehovah's Witnesses are motivated to go out on their door-to-door ministry, offering people a chance to come into the truth before it is too late. Hundreds of thousands of ordinary Jehovah's Witnesses do this every week, despite the predictably contemptuous insults they incur.

This does not mean, though, that Jehovah's Witnesses, Christadelphians and Seventh-day Adventists are likely to engage in acts of violence against themselves or others. These are movements which, having survived for over a century, have become rationalized and routinized, adopting longer-term strategies for self-perpetuation, including the socialization of their own children. In Wilson's (1970, 1975) terminology, they are not revolutionaries, but *revolutionists*. It is not they, but God, who will act to bring an end to the evil world order. Until God chooses to do so, the task of the faithful is to obey his commandments, be law-abiding ('render unto Caesar the things that are Caesar's'), bring up their children in righteousness, and spread the good news to those in the world who will listen to it. Although they play a crucial role in God's plan, the success of the plan does not depend on them.

The situation is radically different when a movement comes to see itself as an agent of the apocalypse, actively bringing it about for themselves or others. The history of Aum Shinrikyō shows a movement whose initial vision of a utopia for everyone degenerated into self-interested preparations to survive World War Three, preparations which were then transformed into a plan to unleash Armageddon by the deployment of chemical and biological weapons of mass destruction.

Exemplary dualism

Anthony and Robbins (1997) argue that destructive religious movements are characterized by exemplary dualism. By this they mean that the movement divides the world and the people and organizations in it into two mutually exclusive, warring entities, good versus evil, Christ versus Antichrist, the Israelites versus Babylon. There are no shades of grey, and no compromises. The religious movement and its leaders are idealized, and its alleged enemies are demonized. Such a view readily breeds conspiracy theories; for example, Aum Shinrikyō believed that it was opposed by an evil alliance of Freemasons, Jews and the US government. If events move to the ultimate crisis, as at Jonestown, the beleaguered community may be persuaded that there is no way out, except to bring about the apocalypse. After the murder of Congressman Ryan, Jones told his followers that even the allegedly sympathetic Soviet Union would no longer offer them sanctuary. Exemplary dualism is not a philosophical abstraction, but a principle actively shaping members' lives and the policies and actions of the movement toward the wider society.

The charismatic leader

Movements with an exemplary dualist orientation are potentially volatile – even more so when they have a charismatic leader who sees himself as a saviour or messiah (for, although women have played leadership roles in many movements, the leaders of destructive movements have invariably been men) (Anthony and Robbins 1997: 276). Charismatic leadership is inherently less stable than systems of authority based either on tradition or on legal-rationality. Charismatic leadership is legitimized by the extraordinary qualities either claimed by the leader or attributed by the followers to him or her. This can be a licence for antinomianism (exemption from external moral restraint – literally, anything goes), allowing the charismatic leader to indulge in sexual, financial or violent excess.

Despite this apparent freedom, the charismatic leader lacks institutional support: if the followers lose faith, the leader's authority simply evaporates. The possibility of defection and treachery is therefore inherent in charismatically led movements; both Jim Jones and David Koresh lived in fear of betrayal by one of their own disciples. Paradoxically, a charismatic leader can come to feel trapped by his or her own followers, who may demand miracles or worldly success which the leader simply cannot deliver or regards as irrelevant to the mission. When Muhammad was asked for miracles to prove that he was the Prophet, he reportedly referred to the Qur'an as miracle enough.

As Weber said, a charismatically led movement will survive only if its members fare well. At Jonestown, the pioneering agricultural project ran into a number of difficulties and was clearly struggling. The stresses on the leader will be compounded if he or she is in declining physical or mental health (Robbins and Palmer 1997: 21). This appears to have been the case with Asahara Shōkō, Jim Jones, Marshall Applewhite, Joseph Di Mambro (whose cancer Luc Jouret was unable to cure) and David Koresh (who was painfully shot during the first gun battle at Waco).

The small encapsulated community

The destructive movements under consideration here involved an encapsulated community of believers who had cut themselves off from contact with friends and family. Core members had become highly dependent on the movement, not just for sustenance, but for their very sense of reality. They were also members of a small, face-to-face community, a *Gemeinschaft*, in which the charismatic leader was able to exercise close personal control over his disciples.

Increasingly cut off from the wider society, and convinced that the world is corrupt and the people in it doomed, members can persuade themselves that they no longer belong to this world, and therefore are not bound by its laws. As Introvigne and Mayer point out (2002), the Peoples Temple, the Order of the Solar Temple and Heaven's Gate all came to believe that their 'real home' was on another planet.

An external threat

The expectation of persecution is a time-honoured mechanism for reinforcing social cohesion in religious movements. That fact of persecution is regularly held up to members as a sign that they have the truth. It fits well with exemplary dualist views of the world.

The threat may not be real, but it is enough that it is perceived. Luc Jouret was threatened with an inquiry into firearms offences, as was David Koresh. Aum Shinrikyō was under intense suspicion that it had murdered one of the movement's critics and his family, and that it was stockpiling weaponry (both of which were true). Jim Jones was under growing pressure from allegations of a wide range of scandalous and illegal activities; the visit from Congressman Ryan, with its invitation to defect, was the final catalyst for the community to implode.

Given the critical role played by external intervention in a group's activities, there is always a danger that the authorities will unwittingly play their part in an apocalyptic doomsday script. Since Jonestown, the most vivid illustration of this has been at Waco. The initial assault on the Mount Carmel community met unexpected armed resistance, leading to injuries and deaths on both sides. In the ensuing siege, the authorities deployed a range of tactics intended to disorient the Davidians and undermine their morale; for example, the compound was illuminated by searchlights at night, and loud music was broadcast towards it. The effect of such tactics was to generate a sense of solidarity in the face of persecution, fuel the group's paranoia, and make group members even more dependent on the charismatic leader to answer the by now desperate question: what shall we do?

During the siege, there were lengthy negotiations between the authorities and the Branch Davidians. To the authorities, Koresh was a charlatan and a fanatic, a trader in illegal firearms and probably a sexual abuser of children. In so far as religious motivations were attributed to him, they were seen as deranged and dangerous. Following the tragic outcome at Jonestown, the authorities were convinced that Koresh was planning what was now seen as a common occurrence among cults: mass suicide.

Koresh meanwhile was grappling with the theological exegesis of the Book of Revelation. It is worth noting that although the movement became widely known as the Branch Davidians, the members normally called themselves 'Students of the Seven Seals'. This did not refer, as some among the FBI were reputed to have thought, to aquatic mammals. It was a reference to Revelation, chapter 5:

> And I saw in the right hand of him that sat on the throne a book written within and on the backside sealed with seven seals. And I saw a strong angel proclaiming with a loud voice, Who is worthy to open the book, and to loose the seals thereof? And no man in heaven, nor in earth, neither under the earth, was able to open the book, neither to look thereon. And I wept much, because no man was found worthy to open and to read the book, neither to look thereon. And one of the elders saith unto me, Weep not: behold, the Lion of the tribe of Judah, the Root of David, hath prevailed to open the book, and to loose the seven seals thereof. (Authorized/King James Version)

A few days before the siege ended in the catastrophic fire, Koresh received a revelation from God that he should write a description of the seven seals and then surrender with his followers to the FBI. Koresh's unfinished text was carried out of the compound on floppy disc by one of the few survivors. To the authorities, Koresh had been simply engaging in a delaying tactic. And from the standpoint of New Testament scholarship, Koresh's exegesis is worthless. It was none the less serious to him. His theology may have been warped, but it was theology, and entirely recognizable as such when seen in the context of Christian adventism. Wrestling with the mystery of the seven seals was not a crude bargaining chip, but what his movement was all about.

A role for cult watchers?

Very few minority religious movements engage in acts of violence, but those that do can present a grave threat to their own members and sometimes to the wider society. Even if the general message is one of reassurance, this cannot mean that there is never anything to worry about. Similarly, although there are cases where outside intervention has provoked the very crisis that it sought to avert – Jonestown and Waco being the most obvious – in other cases, such as Heaven's Gate, there was no threat of intervention, so to blame the authorities for the voluntary suicides would be perverse. As for Aum Shinrikyō, the Japanese authorities have been criticized for being too slow to intervene, given the mounting evidence of Asahara's descent into paranoia and clear signs that toxic material was being stockpiled. Aum had been very successful in exploiting the civil liberties guaranteed by the Japanese Constitution.

If vigilance is needed both to uphold the legitimate exercise of religion and to regulate abuse, then accurate information is needed to distinguish between them. A variety of 'cult-watching' groups compete to provide such information. Barker (2002) has divided them into five broad categories.

Two of Barker's types are hostile to 'cults'. 'Cult-awareness groups' typify the anti-cult movement, as discussed earlier in this chapter. All cults are viewed with suspicion; the testimony of disaffected ex-members is treated as accurate; cults use sophisticated techniques of brainwashing; the aim is therefore to help the cults' victims, and to have dangerous cults, of which there are many, investigated and banned. 'Countercult groups' have a different, more overtly religious agenda; their aim is to expose the heretical teachings of minority religious movements when viewed from the position of Christian orthodoxy.

At the opposite pole are 'cult-defender groups', whose mission is to defend minority religious movements against persecution by cult-awareness groups. Cult-defender groups are often front organizations. The most striking example is the Cult Awareness Network, which was probably the most influential of the anti-cult organizations. Disbanded in 1996 after being declared bankrupt following a court case in which it was found guilty of involvement in kidnapping and forcible deprogramming, it was taken over and relaunched in 1997 by a consortium headed by Scientologists, and has been active in defence of the rights of religious minorities, in particular Scientology (Barker 2002: 133).

In between these pro- and anti-cult organizations are two types of cult-watching groups that claim to be neutral: 'human rights groups' dedicated to a wider agenda in defence of civil liberties; and 'research-oriented groups' such as INFORM (Information Network Focus on Religious Movements) that aim to disseminate accurate, unbiased information about the beliefs and activities of minority religious movements, with the intention of defusing tension and resolving difficulties.

The various types of cult-watching groups exist in a state of tension with one another. In terms of their potential to influence public policy, the most important types are the cult-awareness groups, on the one hand, and the research-oriented groups and the sociologists who align with them, on the other. Mutual recriminations have ricocheted between the two. Cult-awareness groups are accused of indiscriminate, ill-informed, illiberal assaults on civil liberties; research-oriented groups and the sociologists who carry out the research are charged with being mere apologists for cults – and worse, being their paid mouthpieces.

Barker concludes that two things are necessary: cult watching and watching the cult watchers (Barker 2002: 147). Both need to be watched, one might add, because religious and anti-religious convictions have untold power, both for good and for evil.

Religious Identity and Meaning in Consumer Society

Individualism unchecked?

I believe in God. I'm not a religious fanatic. I can't remember the last time I went to Church. My faith has carried me a long way. It's Sheilaism. Just my own little voice . . . It's just try to love yourself and be gentle with yourself. You know, I guess, take care of each other. I think He would want us to take care of each other.

This testimony is taken from *Habits of the Heart*, a study of individualism and commitment in American life (Bellah et al. 1996: 221). The respondent is Sheila Larson (not her real name), a nurse who, the authors tell us, has received a good deal of therapy. Asked about her faith, she calls it 'Sheilaism'. The authors commented wryly that this opened up the logical possibility of more than 220 million religions, one for each American citizen. Such a state of affairs appears obviously absurd. Although we may not go all the way with Durkheim, who saw religion as essentially a social, rather than an individual, phenomenon, surely religion cannot be created and sustained simply on an individual basis? Must it not include shared beliefs and practices, and collective acts of worship?

Bellah and his colleagues feel sorry for Sheila, seeing her as a forlorn victim of a cult of individualism that has been taken to a grotesque extreme. Sheilaism stands as a striking validation of Hervieu-Léger's (2000) thesis that Western societies have suffered a collapse of collective memory and a crisis of cultural transmission. Cut adrift from any tradition, Sheila is trying to stitch together a faith from cultural bits and pieces. Significantly, Pope Benedict XVI took the opportunity early in his pontificate to warn Catholics of the dangers of such attempts; speaking to an audience of pilgrims, he said: 'Religion constructed on a do-it-yourself basis cannot ultimately help us. It may be comfortable but at times of crisis we are left to ourselves.'

Just as the American political system is based on checks and balances between the President, Congress, the judiciary, the press, the federal government and the states, so the cultural system demands that potentially conflicting principles be reconciled. Bellah et al. identify four fundamental value systems. The *republican tradition*, which has its roots in the classical civilization of Greece and Rome, emphasizes that citizens should value civic virtue above self-interest. Justice and the public good can be upheld only if citizens are committed to participation in public affairs. The *biblical tradition* has been carried historically by the Jewish and Christian religious communities; Islam now also has a claim to be part of this. These faiths teach us to be concerned for social justice, since we are all God's creatures. The republican and biblical traditions have tended to form an alliance, since they both recognize a social dimension to human individuality that gives a moral foundation and purpose to public life.

The remaining two cultural value systems are variants of individualism. *Utilitarian individualism* sees material self-interest as the motive of human actions, and judges social institutions in terms of their effectiveness in achieving prosperity. *Expressive individualism* gives priority to the individual's feelings and intuitions, and turns to therapies for the answers to problems of meaning.

Individualism is a core value of American culture, and Bellah et al. have no desire to see it eradicated. Nor is individualism irreconcilably opposed to the Bible or the republic; on the contrary, we can recognize individualism in both biblical and republican forms. Individualism has a sound pedigree in Protestant Christianity, which professes 'that the individual believer does not need intermediaries, that he has the primary responsibility for his own spiritual destiny, that he has the right and the duty to come to his own relationship with his God in his own way and by his own effort' (Lukes 1973b: 94). Implied in this are two further key ideas. First, from a spiritual point of view, we are all equal: we all have the light within; we are, as Martin Luther taught, justified by faith alone (not because of our good deeds, but because of our faith we are forgiven our sins); and we should reject any special category of priest in favour of the priesthood of all believers. The second key principle, as Lukes points out, is religious self-scrutiny: we are called to examine our conscience in order to find God's will, instead of relying passively on commands handed down by the Church's hierarchy.

What troubles Bellah et al. is the erosion of the republican and biblical traditions, which has allowed 'a strident and ultimately destructive
individualism' to flourish unhindered (1996: p. x). Individualism in its
rampantly utilitarian mode means an empty materialistic life expended
in personal ambition and consumerism. Individualism in its rampantly
expressive mode means a delusional quest for meaning through therapy.
Both involve a retreat into a 'private' sphere – a fatal disengagement
from social life. Many of the people who feature in *Habits of the Heart*
'were locked into a split between a public world of competitive striving
and a private world supposed to provide the meaning and love that
make competitive striving bearable' (Bellah et al. 1996: 292).

Habits of the Heart is a sophisticated defence of the idea that social
stability requires a common culture in which the vast majority of people
participate. Sheila's plight 'somehow seems a perfectly natural expression of current American religious life' (Bellah et al. 1996: 221), and
applies not just to people who seldom attend Church but to regular
churchgoers as well. People feel less constrained by religious authority
of any kind, whether of the Church, tradition or the Bible.

Nor is this a uniquely American concern. A cultural shift away from
a conception of religion as a mandatory set of beliefs and practices
incumbent upon all the faithful, towards the conviction that individuals have to choose for themselves their particular path to salvation, has
taken place not simply on the periphery (in 'the cults') but in the mainstream of Western cultures. The transmission of religion from generation to generation is becoming more fluid and less certain.

Individualism and authority: the Roman Catholic Church

The remarkable internal diversity of churches can be both a strength
and a weakness. It enables them to embrace a wide range of different
orientations to faith and practice, so that people can find an outlet for
their various dispositions and talents. Conversely, it raises problems of
internal cohesion. No religious institution displays these tensions more
sharply than the Roman Catholic Church.

Theological and doctrinal consistency had been secured during the
papacy of Leo XIII at the end of the nineteenth century. He encouraged
the revival of Thomism, the theology of St Thomas Aquinas, the
'Angelic Doctor' of the thirteenth century. Aquinas's teachings were
certainly not irrationalist, since he held that faith is not contrary to
reason. He taught, however, that reason is subordinate to faith, and philosophy to theology. This has a political implication: civil authority is

subject to the Church (McSweeney 1980: 67–74). Although human reason – the province of natural theology – enables us to arrive at fundamental truths about the world such as the existence of God, we can attain the fullness of faith only through divine revelation, of which the Church and its priesthood are the authoritative interpreters. In the wake of Leo XIII's reforms, theologians who departed from Thomist orthodoxy were purged from Catholic seminaries and universities.

Aspects of the everyday lives of the Catholic faithful reinforced the maintenance of a defensive subculture. A clear illustration of this is provided by attitudes to 'mixed marriages' (Hornsby-Smith 1987: 98–108). Roman Catholics were discouraged from marrying outside the faith, and this included Protestants. To do so risked provoking social disapproval and even ostracism by relatives. The non-Roman Catholic partner was usually required to state in writing that their children would be baptized as Catholics and brought up in the Catholic faith. The Catholic partner was expected to strive to convert the other. If the couple opted to have the marriage service in a Catholic Church, they would typically be offered a basic, stripped-down version of the ritual – without music or flowers, for example.

Another key symbol of Catholic identity was the Tridentine Mass, named after the Council of Trent (1545–63), which consolidated the Counter-Reformation against Protestantism. The Tridentine Mass was a miracle performed by the priest for the people. The priest faced away from the congregation towards the high altar, and murmured the canon of the mass (the prayer of consecration) in so hushed a tone that people often could not hear what was being said. The language they could not hear was Latin. Throughout four centuries, this was the style of worship of the Catholic Church worldwide. To its Protestant and rationalist detractors it represented the quintessence of obscurantist mumbo-jumbo – for what else could inaudible mutterings in a dead language possibly be? The answer, from its advocates, was that it conveyed a sense of mystery, of the numinous, of the presence of God, and the sanctity of the universal Church.

Up until the Second Vatican Council, which met from 1962 to 1965, Catholicism had constructed itself as a subculture – 'Fortress Rome' – deferential to the Church's authority and fearful of incorporation into the wider culture. Catholicism was not nationalistic but ultramontane, looking 'beyond the mountains' to Rome. At the apex of the Church hierarchy stood the Roman Curia and the Holy Father himself, whose formal pronouncements on matters of faith and morals had been declared infallible by the First Vatican Council of 1869–70. Although not infallible themselves, priests wielded considerable authority over the laity, and generally expected to be obeyed. Democratic participation was not on their agenda.

The Second Vatican Council (Vatican II) swept all this away. The mass is now usually said or sung in the vernacular. The altar is brought closer to the congregation, and typically the priest faces them and speaks up so that they can all hear. This is no longer a miracle performed for a public of passive spectators; it is a collective act of worship in which all the 'people of God' participate.

These liturgical reforms unleashed controversy. Traditionalism was cast as obdurate resistance to change, a benighted refusal of *aggiornamento*. The starkest expression of this was in France, where supporters of Monseigneur Marcel Lefebvre declared their rejection of the spirit and content of Vatican II. In France, ultra-traditional Catholicism is linked to neo-Fascist groups, whose anti-Semitism has expanded to include hostility to France's Muslim population. In other countries, traditionalism does not carry quite the same ideological freight, even though it does involve an authoritarian opposition to individualism and permissiveness. Traditionalists despair of the abandonment of a deposit of faith and practice which, so they had been taught, was universal and invariant. In this perspective, the Second Vatican Council has changed the unchangeable.

Catholic teaching on abortion and birth control was one area left largely untouched by the reforms of Vatican II. In 1968, to the dismay of the modernizers, Pope Paul VI issued the encyclical on human life, *Humanae Vitae*. Responsible parents, the encyclical stated, must recognize that they are not free to act as they choose in the matter of transmitting life. 'Artificial' means of contraception are forbidden, but 'recourse to infertile periods', the so-called rhythm method, is a faculty provided to married couples 'by nature'. The faithful are bound by this instruction:

> 'We are obliged once more to declare that the direct interruption of the generative process already begun and, above all, all direct abortion, even for therapeutic reasons, are to be absolutely excluded as lawful means of regulating the number of children. Equally to be condemned, as the magisterium of the Church has affirmed on many occasions, is direct sterilization, whether of the man or of the woman, whether permanent or temporary. Similarly excluded is any action which either before, at the moment of, or after sexual intercourse, is specifically intended to prevent procreation – whether as an end or as a means.'

This ruling, uncompromisingly reaffirmed during the pontificate of John Paul II, is unlikely to be overturned by his traditionalist successor, Pope Benedict XVI.

Alongside *Humanae Vitae*'s pronouncements on reproductive technology and sexual morality, the other major symbol of Catholic resistance to modernity is its refusal to allow women to be priests. Issues of sex and gender have become key boundary-defining issues for Catholic subculture as it seeks to differentiate itself from the wider culture. In the past, other issues served the same function. The *Syllabus of Errors* promulgated by Pope Pius IX in 1864 was preoccupied with Church–state relations, and the need to subordinate the latter to the former. By the beginning of the twentieth century, the attention of the Catholic hierarchy had switched to an attack on 'liberalism'. This involved repudiating relativistic 'higher biblical criticism' and, most importantly, the theory of evolution of the species. These issues have lost most of their salience for the Catholic Church today, but sex and gender persist as critical symbols of Catholic culture.

Chaves (1997) argues that in the United States there are two belief systems that legitimize resistance to women priests. One is Protestant fundamentalism, the other Catholic sacramentalism. What they have in common, despite all their differences, is the claim to a transcendental point of reference, valid for all times and places, which cannot be subject to secular influence. In the one case, this is an inerrant Bible, in the other, the sacraments. Only a transcendental appeal to an unchanging source of authority can justify the exclusion of women – and even this is under challenge. It is worth quoting the trenchant comments of Christiano et al. (2002: 223) on the contribution made by women to the Catholic Church in the United States:

Overwhelmingly, it is women who organize the liturgies, rehearse the choir, teach in the religious education program, edit the bulletins, convene myriad committees of the congregation, plan the fund-raisers, trigger the "telephone tree," handle outreach to the indigent and to youth, run the car pools, preside over child care, clean the sanctuary, launder the altar linens, sell the raffle tickets, gather donations of goods for parish bazaars, and bake the cakes that are for sale in the vestibule of the Church after services. For instrumental reasons if not out of a commitment to equality, therefore, any denomination that gives short shrift to its female members is asking for trouble.

A massive cultural shift has taken place in contemporary Catholicism, away from the notion of Catholic identity as ascribed, immutable and encapsulated in a protecting subculture. Hornsby-Smith's research in England and Wales shows that the shift is most evident among younger people, but it has occurred even among groups that might have been expected to resist it, including second-generation Irish migrants (Hornsby-Smith 2004: 48–53).

Catholics now draw distinctions between different elements of the faith. They continue to hold the basic credal beliefs, while being less committed to matters of faith and practice that are not in the creeds. The priesthood is still respected, but not as a body of men who can command unquestioning obedience to an unchanging faith. The fear of hell-fire and damnation has declined. Catholic laypeople claim the right to follow their own consciences on questions of personal morality. They feel less bound by the Church's disciplinary rules on attendance at mass, frequency of confession, and intermarriage. Few Catholics in Western countries feel compelled to observe the disciplines of the rhythm method of birth control. A Church that was once 'strongly rule-bound and guilt-ridden' (Hornsby-Smith 1992: 131) is no longer so. Official Catholicism has evolved into what he calls 'customary Catholicism': beliefs and practices which, although derived from the Church's teaching, are filtered through personal interpretations that have ceased to be under clerical control. Individualism and consumerism are inescapable elements in customary Catholicism, which is no doubt why Pope Benedict XVI and his predecessor, Pope John Paul II, so trenchantly condemned them.

One reading of the state of Catholicism in affluent societies is that it is fatally compromised. Iannaccone (1997) suggests that in the United States – and the point could surely be generalized to Western Europe at least – the Catholic Church has landed itself in the worst of all worlds. It has abandoned that which should have been retained (for example, the Latin mass), while retaining that which should have been abandoned (the ban on contraception and abortion, and the rule of priestly celibacy). It has adopted the fatal combination of general laxity and misplaced strictness.

An alternative reading is aptly characterized in the phrase, 'loyalty, but not obedience' (Christiano et al. 2002: 215). On a personal level, the Catholic tradition is not rigid and authoritarian, but richly diverse, flexible and creative. The tradition does not so much regulate personal life as symbolize a tradition with which, even in a consumer society, Catholic people continue to identify.

Sexuality and gender

An obvious but insufficiently studied feature of religions is their central concern with sex and gender. The ideology of compulsory heterosexuality prevails in most faith communities. Very few religions or religious movements would even profess to treat women and men equally. In many traditions, women are excluded from positions of authority, and are expected to adopt traditional and submissive roles, serving at best as auxiliaries to men.

Sexuality

Among the classical sociologists only Max Weber (1965: 236–42) was fully alert to the significance of the erotic. He argued that hostility toward sexuality is an essential feature of religion. It is not confined to Christianity, but is present in all the great religions of the world. This is because sexuality is the strongest irrational force in human life. Religions are bound to seek to control it. In particular, they aim to tie sexual expression to reproduction, regulating it in accordance with laws and norms governing lineage and inheritance. Non-procreative sexual acts are strongly discouraged in Roman Catholicism, and are regarded by most Muslims and conservatively minded Jews as forbidden. Hence the abhorrence of homosexuality found in most religions, the Roman Catholic opposition to artificial methods of birth control, and the Hebrew Scriptures' curse on the sin of Onan – which was in fact *coitus interruptus*, not masturbation, as commonly thought.

Religious control of sexuality takes many forms, ranging from ascetic renunciation, as in vows of celibacy made by religious virtuosi, through strictly confining sexuality to reproduction in the monogamous marriage, to the apparently unbridled but actually carefully controlled and ritualized sexual expression found among the devotees of the late Bhagwan Shree Rajneesh.

Women's sexuality is typically presented as a threat to men. As McGuire (1992: 115) puts it, in creation myths 'women's presumed characteristics of sexual allure, curiosity, gullibility, and insatiable desires are often blamed for both the problems of humankind and for women's inferior role'. So in the Jewish and Christian traditions it is Eve's seductive influence that leads Adam to disobey God's command not to eat the apple from the tree of knowledge. Evil temptresses are counterbalanced by women of supreme virtue, such the Virgin Mary. Arguably, the former should not, and the latter cannot, be imitated as role-models.

Within conservative Christian movements, heterosexuality is normative for everyone. Homosexuality is branded by evangelical Christianity as a deviant 'lifestyle choice', often the fault of a dysfunctional upbringing, that must be overcome through prayer, counselling and sheer effort of will. As well as drawing on their own resources to channel sexuality in the desired direction, Christian communities can refer people to inter-denominational organizations such as Exodus International, whose mission is 'Freedom from homosexuality through the power of Jesus Christ'. Being 'born again' takes on a particular meaning for people whose orientation is not heterosexual (Christiano et al. 2002: 204–6).

Lesbian, gay, bisexual and transgender (LGBT) Christians can feel torn between two parallel but conflicting demands: that they be 'born again' and that they 'come out'. Evangelical Christians demand the first, secular LGBTs the second. Given that homophobia is widespread, many people wonder why LGBTs stay within Christian communities. Not all do stay, of course; some leave, but often they do so not to become atheists but to preserve their faith (Yip 2000).

Western LGBT Muslims are more vulnerable than their Christian counterparts (Yip 2005: 50). Muslims have fewer theological resources and support networks on which they might draw to affirm their sexuality. Muslims are a minority within Western societies, and are targets of abuse and persecution; hence Islamic culture is more defensive, and asserts more control over its members. Homosexuality is depicted as a white Western disease, the product of a degenerate culture, whereas Muslims are proclaimed to be naturally heterosexual.

Many of the more liberal Christian denominations have been riven with conflict and ambivalence over homosexuality. A typical response is to draw a distinction between a homosexual orientation, which is tolerated, and homosexual practices, which are condemned. Being openly gay becomes problematic; hence the irony that gay couples in a stable loving relationship may be subjected, as 'practising homosexuals', to homophobic reactions that single people can evade. Even more exposed to condemnation are Christians who are bisexual. Bisexuality is taken to imply promiscuity. Since they are attracted to the opposite sex, their same-sex activities are represented as a sinful choice.

LGBTs who remain within Christian denominations draw on a range of defensive, offensive and creative strategies (Yip 2005) to address homophobia. Alternative textual interpretations are issued as a challenge to traditional readings of the Bible; for example, Sodom and Gomorrah were destroyed by God because of their inhospitality to strangers, not because of 'sodomy'. Biblical passages that do appear to condemn homosexuality have to be seen in their cultural context; they are not propounding universal truths. Other biblical passages are creatively reinterpreted, so that, for example, the love between David and Jonathan, and that between Naomi and Ruth, are seen as validating same-sex relationships. Christian LGBTs attack religious authorities for a 'selective fundamentalism' that is obsessed with sexuality at the expense of social justice, human rights, liberty, personal integrity and the value of cultural diversity. In opposition to officially sponsored homophobia, LBGTs assert the validity of theology grounded in the spirituality of individual believers.

One reason why LGBTs stay in their religious communities is that they often experience solidarity and affirmation from rank-and-file heterosexual Christians. Heterosexuals, too, have grounds for rejecting official pronouncements. The turn to spirituality provides common ground and, crucially, does not mean repudiating the body. Spirituality and sexuality are inseparable (Yip 2007). As Wilcox (2002) argues, a faith that assures people that God created them lesbian, gay, bisexual or transsexual (or heterosexual) can be more affirming than secular perspectives that regard sexuality as a social construct or as no more than an accident of birth.

Gender-blind religion? Quakers, Unitarians and Baha'is

Few religions would aspire to the reversal of traditional gender roles accomplished by the Brahma Kumaris (Barker 1995: 168–70) – Kumari means unmarried woman. Their founder was the wealthy diamond merchant Dada Lekh Raj, known to his followers as Brahma Baba. After a series of revelations, he set up a managing committee of eight young women in 1937 and handed over all his assets to a trust administered by them. Most of the positions of authority within the movement are held by women.

Exceptional cases for whom a claim of gender equality might appear plausible are the Religious Society of Friends (Quakers), the Unitarians (and the Universalists, with whom they have in effect merged) and the Baha'is. Other possible cases might be Christian Science, the Salvation Army and some spiritualist movements.

Quakers and Unitarians have a good deal in common, including their commitment to equality of men and women (Punshon 1984; Chryssides 1998). In Wilson's terms they are *reformist* movements. They encourage people to act out their faith through participating with others in movements for social reform such as the Campaign for Nuclear Disarmament, Amnesty International and environmental campaigns. Most members count themselves pacifists. Quakers and Unitarians are opposed to creeds and dogma, leaving it to the conscience and reason of individuals to find their own path to the truth. Science and education are

allies in this quest. Neither movement believes in sacraments, and miracles are viewed sceptically. Rites of passage are de-sacralized and tai-
lored to the needs of the individual. These movements do not have a
priesthood or academic theologians, though Unitarians have a trained
ministry. Although Unitarianism lacks formal rituals, services are
usually well planned by the ministers; similarly, Quaker worship, even
when it is at its most informed, is governed by a set of unspoken norms
regulating what is acceptable as Quakerly conduct. They are not actively
conversionist movements, preferring instead to make themselves and
their publications available to anyone who enquires. They are constituted democratically, giving considerable freedom to individual congregations, but combining this with a bureaucratic structure at national and
international levels, thereby retaining organizational coherence. The
concept of membership is attenuated, so that it is unremarkable for
Quakers and Unitarians to take part in services and activities organized
by other denominations provided they are liberal and tolerant.
Although rooted in Christianity, they are uncomfortable with assertions
that any one faith possesses a monopoly of the truth.

Women have played leading roles in the history of the Society of
Friends and the Unitarian Church, and this is important to the movements' self-image. Perhaps the most celebrated Quaker of all was the
great nineteenth-century campaigner for penal reform, Elizabeth Fry.
And arguably the greatest of all feminist tracts is *A Vindication of the
Rights of Woman*, published in 1792 by Mary Wollstonecraft, a
Unitarian. Quakers and Unitarians were prominent supporters of the
women's suffragist movement. Unitarians began ordaining women to
the ministry before the end of the nineteenth century; at the close of the
twentieth, women make up approximately half the Unitarian ministers
in the USA and one-third in the UK (Chryssides 1998: 112). Quakers,
who have no professional ministry, are committed to equality of opportunity within the Society.

The implication of all this is that both these religious movements
have been pledged to the same objectives as the 'first wave' feminists of
the suffragist movement. Suffragists campaigned not just for votes for
women, but for full citizenship, equality before the law, and equal
opportunities in public life. What is less clear, however, is how well
attuned either the Religious Society of Friends or the Unitarian Church
could be to the demands of 'second wave' feminists, the so-called
Women's Liberation Movement, which launched a broadside attack on
patriarchy as institutionalized gender inequality endemic to culture and
social structure (Whelehan 1995). Contemporary trends in feminism,
centred on the politics of lifestyle and the deliberate transgression of

conventional cultural boundaries, are likewise problematic for movements that have not shed their Puritan origins. Issues of lesbian and gay rights remain deeply divisive, as they are in mainstream Churches torn between Christian love, liberal tolerance and moral condemnation. Yet Quakers and Unitarians are not bound by dogma. It is therefore an open question how far they can accommodate themselves to contemporary cultural change.

The Baha'i faith, which arose in an Islamic context, shows some similarities to these two Christian movements. Baha'is advocate equality of women and men, although women are not permitted to be members of the Universal House of Justice, the faith's supreme authority. They embrace science and education. They lack a professional priesthood and formal rituals. They are pacifists. Like Muslims, they are averse to other-worldly asceticism, and specifically forbid the monastic life. They give responsibility to local congregations within a worldwide administrative framework. They are opposed to racism, prejudice and superstition, and claim to be undogmatic.

Despite their progressive credentials, it is even less clear than in the case of Quakers and Unitarians that Baha'is can respond to all the challenges brought by feminism. Although the Baha'i faith presents itself as non-doctrinaire, it is shaped by divine revelation and divinely inspired authoritative scriptures. It has an authoritarian vein that makes Western liberal members deeply uneasy (MacEoin 1997). It is, at root, a conversionist faith, one which engages in rationally planned missionary programmes in pursuit of its vision of a universalist religion uniting all humanity. It does not tolerate plural membership, and does not take part in rainbow alliances with campaigning pressure groups. Its scriptures prescribe monogamous heterosexual marriage and emphasize the duty to bear children. Baha'i couples require the consent of all their living natural parents before they can marry. The faith opposes divorce. It also takes a conservative stance on abortion and euthanasia. Crucially, it has little warrant to amend these principles. As society changes, the Baha'is risk being left behind in a posture that will seem less and less progressive. In this respect it is probably not gender roles, but sexuality, that poses the sharper challenge to Baha'i culture.

Gender roles and the symbolic subordination of women

The sacred scriptures, rituals and traditional practices of the world's great religions provide abundant evidence of women's subordination to men. Controversy has focused on a number of symbolic cases: the exclusion of women from the priesthood in Catholic and Orthodox Christianity, and the opening of the priesthood to women in the Anglican Communion; the veiling of women in some Islamic cultures; the strict gender division of ritual labour in Orthodox and Conservative Judaism; the strong preference for sons over daughters in Hinduism, the financially punitive dowry system that underpins it, the practice of *sati* (self-immolation by a virtuous Hindu widow on her husband's funeral pyre), and the crime of wife burning in domestic 'accidents' arranged by men intent on marrying again to acquire another dowry.

Conflicts over these practices are marked by a dialectic between the three Weberian principles of legitimate domination: charismatic, traditional and legal-rational authority. In religious disputes, legal-rational arguments are rarely sufficient by themselves, because they are essentially secular. Hence the parties to any given dispute will try to harness charismatic and traditional authority in support of their position.

Consider the debate within the Church of England over the ordination of women to the priesthood (Aldridge 1992). The exclusion of women from the priesthood prevented the Church from drawing on a pool of talented women who, in secular terms, could obviously do the job at least as well as, and often better than, men. As the number of men coming forward with a vocation to priesthood declined, the Church faced a manpower crisis that had an obvious solution – a situation now facing the Catholic Church. However, as a sacred institution, the Church needed to legitimize any change in non-secular terms. Hence the theological cast to the debate. Opponents of the ordination of women included among their arguments the following. Jesus chose men to be his twelve apostles, and this is a sign that priesthood is open only to men. St Paul taught that women should remain silent in Church, and that wives are subordinate to the authority of their husband. In sacramental functions the priest is an icon of Christ, and so has to be male, since Jesus in his human aspect was a man. The Western Catholic and Eastern Orthodox Churches have excluded women from the priesthood following the sacred ordinance of God; the Church of England, as one minor branch of Christianity, has no warrant to act unilaterally on a fundamental principle of doctrine and practice.

These propositions were countered by arguments that sought to contextualize the historic exclusion of women from the priesthood. It was pointed out that mainstream Christianity incorporates a doctrine of progressive revelation. The Church's traditional practices are not fixed for all time, but dynamic: the Holy Spirit acts in the world to bring the Church to a realization of the fullness of faith. Abolition of slavery is an obvious precedent. The ministry of Jesus and the teachings of Paul have to be seen in their cultural context, and are not to be taken as signs valid for all eternity. Jesus did not carry his ministry to the Gentiles, even making the disturbing remark that this would be casting pearls before swine. The Christian Church clearly cannot be bound by this. So too the symbolism of gender has changed, as has our scientific understanding of sexuality and reproduction. We know, as scholars in the Middle Ages did not, that in reproduction the woman is more than merely a passive breeding-ground for the man's 'seed'. As for Catholicism and Orthodoxy, perhaps Anglicanism's *raison d'être* is to give them a lead?

This debate between what might be called *traditionalists* and *modernizers* has many parallels in faiths other than Christianity. In each of these the core issue is the same. Traditionalists define culture as something separate from religion or faith. The faith as they present it is divinely ordained, unalterable and not to be contaminated by culture, which is a human creation. So Christian advocates of the ordination of women to the priesthood, and Muslim opponents of the veiling of women, are accused of 'feminism' – a secular contagion. Modernizers, on the other hand, insist on the interpenetration of religion and culture: there is no such thing as a culture-free religion. In all the major religions of the world, practices vary enormously from one country and one historical period to another. Modernizers argue that much of what passes as tradition is in fact recently invented. They also point out that traditionalists are highly selective in their account of the tradition, insisting on some points while overlooking others. For example, slavery and concubinage are permitted under Islamic shari'a law but have virtually disappeared in Muslim societies, and certainly do not serve as a shibboleth of Islamic life in the way that the veiling of women has come to do (Ruthven 1997: 93–4). Modernizers within Islam often emphasize that some traditional practices, such as the genital mutilation of young girls performed in some Muslim communities, have no justification in the Qur'an.

Given that for modernizers there is no such thing as culture-free religion, it follows that they hold the spirit of the law to be more important than its letter. In the case of Islam, a good deal of attention has focused on the legal rights and disadvantages of women. In the Qur'an, women are legally inferior to men. A woman's testimony in some court proceedings carries half the weight of a man's. Under Qur'anic laws of inheritance, women receive half as much as their brothers. A man may marry up to four wives, provided he can support them and treat them equally. He may marry a Christian, a Jew or a slave, whereas a Muslim woman cannot have more than one husband, and he must be a Muslim.

A man may beat his wife if all other methods of discipline have failed, but she must never strike him. Divorce is discouraged, but is far easier for a man to initiate.

Traditionalists argue that the Qur'an, and also the sayings and conduct of Muhammad himself, were more protective of women and gave them far greater legal rights than they had previously under the *jahilyya*, the pre-Islamic age of ignorance, or in other cultures of the period. They sometimes add that Christians should examine their own practice more critically. Against this, modernizers argue that the fact that the Qur'an and the Prophet were caring towards women shows that the same underlying principle should be applied in the changed conditions of the modern world. Their problem is to justify altering the letter of an unalterable law.

A surprisingly neglected question is this: given that most religions and religious communities are patriarchal, why do so many women participate in them? Why, in particular, are women so prominent and active among the rank and file of the faithful? As Walter and Davie (1998: 640) point out in their analysis of the available literature, 'In Western societies, women are more religious than men on every measure of religiosity,' whether we consider churchgoing, or private prayer, or belief. The gender imbalance is greatest in the case of private devotion, which suggests that men withdraw from participation when there is less social pressure to conform. It also suggests, conversely, that women's commitment is voluntary.

The significance of women's religiosity is central to one controversial critique of the secularization thesis. Secularization is not, according to Brown (2001), a long-term trend caused by modernization. Taking Britain as his case study, he argues that popular religion flourished throughout the period of industrialization and urbanization between the 1750s and the 1950s. Although it had a male leadership, Christian culture was predominantly a woman's world. The death of this culture in Britain occurred suddenly, during the 1960s. Gender roles were redefined, femininity was divested of its links with piety, and women 'cancelled their mass subscription to the discursive domain of Christianity' (Brown 2001: 195). Women continue to outnumber men in British Churches, but, ominously, young women and girls are absent.

In any religious movement, the official hierarchy is rarely the most salient issue for ordinary members. Even though the organization may be patriarchal, everyday congregational life can be open and participative. It is the congregation that matters: 'for many people', as Walter and Davie say (1998: 645), ' "the church" is the social life built up by the (largely female) congregation over decades'.

Patriarchy is a reality, but it may be mitigated by some benefits for women. Patriarchal communities provide a haven for women who yearn for the comfort and security of traditional gender roles. Davidman's (1991) study of two Jewish settings, an Orthodox synagogue in Manhattan and a Lubavitcher Hasidic community in St Paul, Minnesota, shows that both communities justified patriarchy in terms of the exalted status they accorded to women. Women converts welcomed the prospect of meeting men who valued family life and who promised to be caring and responsible fathers.

The case of Latin American men who have joined Pentecostal Churches is a graphic illustration of the power of conversion. Becoming a Pentecostal requires and enables men to break free from the culture of *machismo* and its hyper-masculine cult of gambling, smoking, drinking and promiscuity. Converts tend to become more caring and responsible as bread-winners, husbands and fathers (Brusco 1995).

The same is probably true, Walter and Davie add, of all-male evangelical groups such as the Promise Keepers, a movement founded in 1990 by Bill McCartney, a former University of Colorado football coach known to PK members as 'Coach Mac'. Promise Keepers are urged to 'reclaim' their masculinity and their rightful leadership roles in public and domestic life. They encourage male bonding in what they call 'a masculine context'.

The movement has echoes of nineteenth-century 'muscular Christianity', which originated in Britain in the 1850s (Hall 1994) and rapidly spread to the United States (Putney 2001). Muscular Christianity glorified the manly virtues of patriotism, courage, hard work, self-control, physical strength and athleticism. Jesus was a role model – but specifically a Jesus who was strong, fit and decisive. The social vision and religious certainties of muscular Christians inspired the foundation of the YMCA, the Boys' Brigade, and the Scouting and Guiding movements. Their stress on manliness betrayed a somewhat anxious rejection of the alleged 'feminization' of Christianity and an abhorrence of 'effeminacy'.

The Promise Keepers' leaders present themselves as success stories of corporate America, but rank-and-file members are all too often its casualties. Susan Faludi (2000: 232–3) points out the contrast between Bill McCartney, who abandoned his prestigious and lucrative career as a football coach, and ordinary PK members who are afraid 'that their families would junk *them* because they *didn't* have high-paying, flourishing careers'.

The ideology of PK leaders is explicitly patriarchal. For example, in a much-quoted passage, Timothy Evans gave this advice to PK members:

'The first thing you do is sit down with your wife and say something like this: "Honey, I've made a terrible mistake. I've given you my role. I gave up leading this family, and I forced you to take my place. Now I must reclaim that role." Don't misunderstand what I'm saying here. I'm not suggesting that you *ask* for your role back, I'm urging you to *take it back*' (cited by Faludi 2000: 229). The patriarchalism is unashamed, but it is partly rhetorical bravado; not all PK members have such conversations with their wives. If we discount the bombast, we can recognize, as Williams observes (2000: 9), that the movement 'is overwhelmingly made up of ordinary men trying to figure out their place in a changing society, where work roles, family relations, and personal identity are all in flux'. The PK mission statement gives a clue to this, with its reference to 'a world of negotiable values, confused identities, and distorted priorities'. Hence the importance of personal counselling within the movement (Lockhart 2000). The quest for practical solutions to its members' family and marital problems implies, as Lockhart points out, an element of compromise with mainstream cultural norms.

The Promise Keepers give a contemporary inflection to the cult of manliness: men are encouraged to get in touch with and express their emotions. There is a tension within the movement between the celebration of 'instrumental masculinity', conceived of as men's natural authority over women, and acknowledgement that men need to embrace in themselves the 'expressive feminine' qualities of sensitivity, insight and compassion (Bartowski 2000).

Even in overtly patriarchal movements, men's authority over women is not straightforward. Ammerman's classic study of fundamentalists speaks of 'a delicate balance of submission and influence', epitomized in this observation by one of her respondents: 'If I honor his opinion after I've given him mine, and then if I go along with him, the Lord will make it right, and Joe will come around' (Ammerman 1987: 140).

As Brasher (1998) found in her study of two congregations in southern California, Christian fundamentalism typically erects 'a sacred gender wall' that partitions the community into two symbolic worlds. Men are in charge of overall congregational life, but there is a parallel symbolic world composed of and led solely by women. Despite the patriarchal ideology and practice, women are far from being passively dependent on men. Women organize a wide range of activities, including Bible studies and retreats, social and recreational events, community outreach ministries, and counselling and victim support programmes. These activities are designed to attract new members, and are a powerful reason why fundamentalist congregations can appeal to women.

The persistent overrepresentation of women in faith communities suggests that a deep cause is at work. Perhaps, as Walter and Davie speculate, women are more exposed to the vicissitudes of life, biologically through the experience of childbirth and culturally through their traditional roles as professional and informal carers. Women are made more immediately aware of the vulnerability of human life. When men are put in a similar position – on the battlefield, for example – they too turn to prayer.

Reclaiming the symbols of subordination

In *Alone of All Her Sex*, a historical and cross-cultural survey of the cult of the Virgin Mary from a feminist perspective, Marina Warner (1978) argues that the cult is pathological. It holds up to women a manifestly unattainable ideal, a Virgin Mother who, unlike the rest of humanity, was conceived immaculately – that is, conceived without the taint of original sin. Following the teaching of St Augustine, the medieval Church held that original sin was transmitted through the sex act, which inescapably involves sexual desire. Although it is no longer tied to this particular interpretation of original sin, Catholic thinking remains preoccupied with the conditions of conception. This is reflected not only in its prohibition of artificial contraception but also in its official hostility to *in vitro* fertilization, an 'unnatural' technique that necessarily requires masturbation.

The impact of the Mary cult, Warner argues, is to induce in women a hopeless yearning and an ineradicable sense of inferiority to men. The myth reinforces itself, creating the very desires, fears and anxieties it purports to assuage. Brought up as a Catholic herself, Warner testifies that for years after she had abandoned her faith she had to fight against 'that old love's enduring power to move me' (M. Warner 1978: p. xxi).

Despite emphasizing the impact of the cult of the Virgin Mary on the psyche of the devout, Warner offers a sociological, rather than a psychological, analysis of it. She has little time for Freudian interpretations, dismissing them as crudely reductionist, but she devotes some space to Jungian analyses. To Jungians, the Virgin is not pathological, but a healthy expression of an archetype. An archetype involves a tendency for certain qualities and attributes to cluster together in the individual and collective unconscious. The Virgin expresses the mother archetype. Other examples of this archetype are the Hindu goddess Kali, the Greek goddess Demeter, the wicked witch and the stepmother. The mother archetype is composed of positive and negative attributes. Positively, the mother connotes femininity, magical power, caring, wisdom, helpfulness, fertility and sympathy. Negatively, the mother connotes secretiveness, darkness, seduction and devouring.

Warner argues that a Jungian approach to the cult of the Virgin Mary colludes with the objectives of the Church's hierarchy. The Vatican, says Warner, proclaims that the concept of the Virgin Mother of God always existed, and Jungians proclaim that all men need a symbolic Virgin Mother. Perhaps the most striking illustration of the Jungian approach is Jung's own view of the Assumption. In 1950, the Pope proclaimed as an official doctrine of the Catholic Church what many Catholics had believed for centuries: that after her earthly life the Blessed Virgin Mary was assumed body and soul into heavenly glory. To Jung this was a momentous development. People had a deep psychological longing that Mary, as intercessor and mediator, should take her place as Queen of Heaven alongside God the Father, the Son and the Holy Spirit. The Trinity came to fulfilment as a Quaternity, as God in four persons – a wildly unorthodox view theologically, but one which for Jung expressed a profound psychological truth. If we take into account popular beliefs as well as official teachings about the Virgin, it is remarkable how many parallels there are between her sacred story and that of Jesus. Jesus's Virgin Birth is paralleled by Mary's Immaculate Conception; Jesus was Son of God, Mary has the title Mother of God; Jesus's Ascension is matched by Mary's Assumption; there is a tradition that Mary's tomb was empty, and early apocryphal texts attested that she too rose on the third day; the cult of Mary as Jesus's mother has its counterpart in the cult of Mary's mother, St Anne, which has been popular in Brittany; the Stations of the Cross are paralleled by the Rosary, and the Man of Sorrows has a *Mater Dolorosa*.

The collusion that Warner detects between Jungians and the Vatican goes deeper than Jung's idiosyncratic endorsement of popular elements of Mariology. Warner's fundamental point is that the cult of the Virgin collapses history into myth, nature into culture. A cult that has been shaped by the interests of the Church's hierarchy is turned into something supposedly natural and eternal. Following Roland Barthes's (1972) theory of mythology, Warner argues that this is the basic transmutation wrought by ideology. In becoming natural, the cult of the Virgin is stripped of the interests that shaped and changed it over time. Through the operation of mythology, nothing seems more natural than 'this icon of feminine perfection, built on the equivalence between goodness, motherhood, purity, gentleness, and submission' (M. Warner 1978: 335).

Warner believes that the cult of Mary is a spent force, incompatible with contemporary conditions. It will cease to be an active myth and become instead a sentimental legend like Robin Hood – an outcome that she would clearly welcome. Other feminists, such as Rosemary Radford Ruether (1979), have been concerned to 'reclaim' the historical Mary from the Church hierarchy. Ruether agrees with Warner that the dominant view of Mary, within Protestantism as well as Catholicism, sees her as the passive recipient of the grace of a male God and his earthly representatives, the clergy. However, Ruether and other Christian feminists believe it possible to assert a different Mary, emphasizing her courage, her struggles and her radical credentials – her song of praise, the Magnificat, speaks of God's elevation of the poor and humbling of the mighty. The aim is to reclaim the woman Mary as a sister, freeing her from centuries of oppressive Mariology, much as in the nineteenth century there was a theological quest for the historical Jesus, the real man concealed under the weight of theologically sophisticated Christology. Here is another parallel between the careers of Jesus and his mother.

This same dilemma – to reject a symbol as oppressive or to reclaim it – presents itself to women in many faiths. The Mormon concept of a Mother in Heaven is one example (Heeren et al. 1984). The LDS Church interprets it in a conservative way to legitimize patriarchy. The Mother in Heaven is an idealized symbol of womanhood and motherhood, and she is subordinate to the Father. Mormon feminists have sought to use the concept to boost women's self-respect, to vindicate the rights of Mormon women, and to open up a space within Mormonism for feminist theology.

The veiling of women in Islamic cultures has been interpreted as a powerful symbol of patriarchy. To many Westerners it is an icon of the Otherness of Islam, as the *affaire des foulards* in France, the headscarf affair discussed in chapter 1, makes very clear. The Taliban forces in Afghanistan rigorously enforced the most stringent dress codes on women as one component of their policy to exclude women from public life and encapsulate them in the domestic sphere.

Traditional Muslim dress, as so often with tradition, is a modern invention. It is legitimized as the dress worn by the Prophet's wives to conceal their hair, their body and most of their face. The implication is that women's bodies are a strong temptation to men, and thus potentially disruptive to the social order. As Ruthven says (1997: 112–13), *hijab* has become a shibboleth, a symbol through which a Muslim woman displays her religious and political allegiance. Its supporters say that it is liberating, since it frees the woman from the voyeuristic gaze of male *flâneurs*. Western feminists, in contrast, see the veil as an inherently oppressive symbol that nullifies the individual and renders women invisible.

To speak of 'the veil' is in fact a gross oversimplification, as Watson

(1994) points out. There is a continuum of veiling, from state-regulated voluminous garments, through colourful peasant attire, to fashionable designer scarves worn by affluent women. Underlying each of these is the symbolic aim not only of preserving the woman's modesty, but of maintaining the cosmologically significant boundary between the sexes.

From religion to spirituality?

Weber's pupil and colleague, the theologian Ernst Troeltsch, foresaw that the rise of mysticism would be a potent force in the modern world. The key to mysticism is its 'radical religious individualism' (Troeltsch 1931: 377), an individualism that is not self-seeking but spiritual, aesthetic and idealistic. Rejecting the religious formalism and dogmatic rigidity of churches and sects, it shifts the emphasis away from doctrine and worship toward personal experience. Although it repudiates materialism, rationalism and pragmatism, it remains compatible with other currents in contemporary culture, above all, the ascendancy of individualism and the collapse of deference to traditional authorities. Mysticism's capacity to absorb cultural elements from traditions other than Christianity gives it an evolutionary advantage over churchly and sectarian religion, which are closed and rigid. For Troeltsch, mysticism flourishes in urban societies, appealing particularly to the educated middle and professional classes. In all this, Campbell (1999) argues, Troeltsch accurately foresaw a major dimension of contemporary religious sensibility. We see it today in the growth of mystically oriented cults, the revival of Romanticism, and the emergence of New Age spirituality.

In *The Invisible Religion*, a classic work that anticipated much later writing on the subject, Luckmann (1967: 117) writes of the decline of church-oriented religion and its replacement by 'a radically subjective form of "religiosity" characterized by a weakly coherent and nonobligatory sacred cosmos and by a low degree of "transcendence" in comparison to traditional modes of religion'. He identifies the major sacred themes of contemporary culture as 'individual "autonomy," self-expression, self-realization, the mobility ethos, sexuality and familism' (1967: 113). The sacred cosmos, once a transcendental fount of absolute authority, has become privatized and subjective.

This privatized religion was 'invisible' in a conventional sociological perspective, which in practice and sometimes in theory concentrated on traditional religious organizations. Narrow substantive definitions of their subject matter led sociologists to look for religion only in churches, chapels, synagogues, mosques, temples and gurdwaras. They overlooked the religious aspect of culture as a lived experience.

Heelas and Woodhead's study of Kendal, Cumbria, a market town in the north-west of England, found evidence of a marked cultural shift from religion to spirituality. They report a discernible trend 'away from life lived in terms of external or "objective" roles, duties and obligations, and a turn towards life lived by reference to one's own subjective experiences' (Heelas and Woodhead 2005: 2). It is 'a spiritual quest culture' (Roof 1999: 295), in which identity is less a matter of belonging to a social group than of seeking personal meaning as an individual. *Seeking* takes precedence over *dwelling* (Wuthnow 1998).

The trend away from religion toward spirituality is part of a wider 'subjective turn' (Taylor 1991), as a society based on agriculture and industry gives way to one oriented to services. Social stability and personal security are less valued than social dynamism and personal flexibility. Social institutions such as political parties, trade unions and traditional women's organizations are losing their appeal, mainly because they offer hierarchically organized predefined roles into which members are expected to fit.

The decline of the older style of women's organization points to the importance of gender in the shift from religion to spirituality. Religion is associated with conventional gender roles, women's subordination to men, the sanctity of marriage, prurience about recreational sex, and abhorrence of homosexuality, lesbianism and bisexuality. All of these have come under increasing challenge in the wider society and within religious organizations themselves. A notable feature of movements that cultivate spirituality is the prominence of women within them. This was true in the nineteenth century, as shown by the examples of Mary Baker Eddy, the founder of Christian Science; Helena Petrovna Blavatsky, founder of Theosophy, and her successor Annie Besant; and Margaret and Kate Fox, who achieved fame and notoriety as spirit mediums.

The subjective turn does not imply an inevitable descent into selfishness and self-absorption. Heelas and Woodhead argue that it is frequently a matter of cultivating social relationships, and therefore is not necessarily individualistic. Nor is it necessarily amoral. The subjective turn is linked to a heightened moral seriousness about the natural environment, rejecting arrogant notions that humans have dominion over it. Another outcome of the subjective turn is its emphasis on compassion. We can hear this in Sheila Larson's comments, quoted at the beginning of this chapter: 'It's just try to love yourself and be gentle with yourself. You know, I guess, take care of each other. I think He would want us to take care of each other.'

Heelas and Woodhead detect a difference of orientation between men and women. In a conventionally masculine perspective, the subjective turn appears self-absorbed, narcissistic and disturbingly 'touchy-feely'. For many women, however, the culture of subjectivism is entirely congruent with women's professional and informal roles as carers. The subjective turn implies a feminization of culture.

It also implies, according to Campbell, a process of Easternization. Core elements of Western religion are being displaced, he claims, by Eastern alternatives. The church as a disciplined community of true believers is conceding ground to looser associations of spiritual seekers, and salvation is yielding to spiritual advancement as the goal of the religious quest. The trend is not new – it is traceable to nineteenth-century precursors such as Theosophy – but it accelerated in the closing decades of the twentieth century.

To account for the trend, Campbell argues that Easternization compensates for the impact of the rise of science, which 'served to undermine people's faith in traditional religion, only, second, for the optimism which had been attached to science and technology to be itself undermined' (1999: 44). Because it does not set itself up for a contest with science, the Eastern paradigm is less vulnerable to the onslaught of scientific rationality.

The thesis of Easternization is suggestive, but it raises several problems. Campbell's conclusion may be premature; the turn to the East is far from widespread or complete, and has not offset the decline in traditional religious activity. Campbell acknowledges the limits of the thesis: 'A true shift away from a Western paradigm would require a turning towards a more resigned, if not fatalistic, attitude towards the world on the part of individuals' (1999: 45). This has not happened. Even though people have less faith than they once had in technologically driven economic growth, the dominant orientation to the world is actively world-affirming rather than fatalistically world-denying. Eastern religions that have flourished in the West – such as Sōka Gakkai, a lay religious movement within Nichiren Buddhism – adapt themselves to Western lifestyles and values (Wilson and Dobbelaere 1994). Easternization should not be taken too literally; it is more a metaphor for the cultural turn than a fact of cultural invasion.

A New Age?

Another metaphor is that of the 'New Age', which implies rejecting the old and embracing the new. Among the things rejected are the unquestioned authority of science; organized religion as authoritarian, moralistic and lifeless; arrogant claims to professional expertise; presumed mastery over the environment; Cartesian mind–body dualism; materialism; bureaucracy; and masculine domination. These rejections imply things to be affirmed: seekership as open to anyone, not just to religious virtuosi; the legitimacy of moving between traditions and practices; the desirability of combining traditions and practices; perennial truths that have lain hidden in the world's faiths; respect for and nurturing of the environment; feminine imagery and principles; holistic therapies that embrace mind, body and spirit; and spirituality as a quality that unites us as human beings.

Until the 1970s, the term 'New Age' was widely used by people who believed in an imminent apocalypse, the end of the strife-torn Age of Pisces and the dawning of the harmonious Age of Aquarius. This apocalyptic vision of a new world was abandoned in the 1970s in favour of an emphasis on self-realization in the present. As a consequence, 'New Age' lost its resonance among spiritual seekers. It became more and more an *etic* term: an outsider's phrase perceived *emically* by insiders as misleading and pejorative. A telling demonstration of this is the Findhorn Community on the Moray Firth in the north-east of Scotland. Founded in 1962 by Peter and Eileen Caddy and Dorothy Maclean, Findhorn was formerly an international icon of the New Age but is now increasingly reluctant to deploy the term, preferring instead to describe itself as 'a spiritual community' (Sutcliffe 2003: 150–73).

Viewed as a social movement, the New Age has serious problems, since it lacks most of the key features that determine success, including 'a distinctive corporate body, a legislative mechanism, historical consciousness, organisational infrastructure, boundaries, and other indices of membership and belonging, and, crucially, unambiguous self-identity and concrete goals' (Sutcliffe 2003: 198).

The degree of engagement in the New Age obviously varies between people. Heelas (1996: 117–19) distinguishes three levels of commitment. The most deeply committed are those he calls *fully engaged*, people who have given over their lives to the spiritual quest. Some of them have abandoned conventional lifestyles in favour of the counterculture. They are often practitioners providing services to clients, or organizers of New Age events. A lesser degree of commitment is found among the *serious part-timers*. Their New Age spirituality is compartmentalized as a part of their life, and does not prevent them from living conventional lives and pursuing conventional careers. The lowest level of commitment is found among the *casual part-timers*. These are the consumers. They are interested in exotic and esoteric things, but are wary of getting deeply involved. The New Age is fun, 'time out' from the stresses of humdrum living. Other aspects of their lives are typically more important than the New Age.

Although statistical data are impossible to obtain, it seems clear from Heelas's extensive research that the fully engaged are a small minority. The New Age is largely peopled by serious and casual part-timers. It is this last group, and the consumerist values it embodies, which threatens the New Age from within. For Heelas, the authority of the consumer is incompatible with the authority of the transcendent. Religion cannot be consumed; if it is, it is no longer religion.

Despite the apparent conflict between New Age thinking and Western rationality, the continuity between the two is at least as significant as the divergence. This is shown in the growth of interest in alternative therapies and complementary medicine. Orthodox medical practitioners and their professional associations are losing the capacity to stigmatize alternative therapies as unscientific 'quackery'. Levels of reported satisfaction with alternative therapies are typically high. Consumer organizations increasingly treat them seriously. Some forms of alternative practice are deeply rooted in and legitimized by minority ethnic communities – for example, Ayurvedic medicine, which serves the Asian community. In these cases it is not possible to separate out the 'religious' element in the therapy, even if religion is defined narrowly – which is difficult to do when dealing with Hinduism. Faith healing is an important element in alternative practice; integral to Pentecostalism, it has become more respectable in the Christian mainstream as a result of charismatic renewal. The growth of alternative medicine and its relocation in the cultural mainstream call into question narrow definitions of religion and science and sharp distinctions between them (Saks 1998).

If New Age is a category 'we' need to construct 'them' as an Other, then religion is a term 'they' throw at 'us'. As Roof says (1999: 177), 'the word *spiritual* is a basis of unity, invoked positively as a basis of self-identity, whereas the term *religious* is used often as a counter-identity for clarifying who they are not'.

This binary opposition between 'religion' and 'spirituality' denies the overlap and compatibility between them, yet seekership culture is not alien to institutional religion. On the contrary, evidence from the USA suggests that seekership is more prevalent and stronger inside faith communities than outside them; 'seekers' tend to be 'religious' (Marler and Hadaway 2002). The notion that spirituality is necessarily suppressed by organized religion shows a failure to understand the complexity of religions and their capacity to respond creatively to social and cultural change. What the spiritual turn has accomplished is less a repudiation of religion than a democratization of practices that might once have been thought to be the preserve of an elite.

Religion and spirituality online

'Red Alert – HALE-BOPP Brings Closure to: Heaven's Gate.' This apocalyptic message was displayed on the website of the Heaven's Gate movement in the days before its thirty-nine core members committed suicide. They believed that they would be transported to a spaceship crewed by extraterrestrial beings and concealed behind the tail of comet Hale-Bopp (see pp. 180–1). Their website invited others to join them in this last chance to escape to the 'Kingdom Level Above Human' before planet Earth was 'recycled' and its human 'weeds' were 'spaded under'.

Heaven's Gate stands as a chilling instance of a lethal cult's attempt to use the internet to win converts to its self-destructive ideology. Yet no one appears to have answered their call for people to join them in suicide. Religious conversion is almost always achieved through face-to-face encounters and networks of personal relationships. The evidence suggests that the internet is not by itself an effective vehicle for recruitment to minority religious movements (Dawson and Hennebry 2004).

Discussions of the significance of religion on the internet tended initially to polarize. Pessimists portrayed the internet as a realm of dangerous fantasy, peopled by casual spiritual shoppers, isolated individuals adrift in cyberspace, dangerous cults, anti-cult propagandists (Mayer 2000; Introvigne 2005) and religiously motivated terrorists. Optimists argued that cyberspace had the potential to be a virtual community free from the constraints of hierarchy and conformism, in which the commodification of religious culture could be resisted (Brasher 2001) and new forms of spirituality explored. What pessimists and optimists have in common is a tendency to generalize boldly, despite the lack of hard evidence.

An interesting distinction has been drawn between religion-online and online-religion (Helland 2000). *Religion online* refers to the use of the internet by religious institutions to communicate information to their members and other interested parties. Only officially approved positions are allowed, feedback is not sought, and there is no dialogue between providers and users. *Online religion* is a new form of communication that exploits the interactive potential of the internet. The aim is to promote unstructured, open, and non-hierarchical interaction. It is a virtual form of what the anthropologist Victor Turner (1995) calls *communitas*: an intense feeling of sharing, spontaneity and togetherness, free from inequality, convention and status distinctions. Virtual *communitas* offers the possibility of 'a unique public space for individual and personal spiritual exploration without the restraints of traditional organization and community' (Helland 2000: 219).

Contrasted in this way, religion-online and online-religion appear to be mutually exclusive. If religious hierarchies are concerned with control, they will scarcely welcome virtual *communitas*; conversely, surfers in cyberspace are rarely looking to submit themselves to dogmatic systems. The reality, however, is more complex: the boundaries between top-down communication and free-flowing interaction have become blurred (Dawson and Cowan 2004: 7). Authoritarian sects may still count as examples of conventional religion online, but mainstream Churches have learned to embrace innovative online religion.

A large-scale US survey (Hoover et al. 2004) found that 64 per cent of people with access to the internet have used it to pursue religious or spiritual interests. One important finding of the study is that faith-related activity online is not treated as a substitute for offline religious life. People typically use the internet both to augment their congregational life and to enrich their personal spiritual quest. Going online is not a fringe activity monopolized by spiritual seekers and shoppers, but is popular among mainstream believers, the vast majority of whom would describe themselves as both religious and spiritual.

Consuming religion

'Humanity today is living in a large brothel! One has only to glance at its press, films, fashion shows, beauty contests, ballrooms, wine bars, and broadcasting stations! Or observe its mad lust for naked flesh, provocative postures, and sick, suggestive statements in literature, the arts and the mass media!' So wrote the extreme Islamist Sayyid Qutb from his prison cell in Egypt, where he was executed in 1966 (cited by Ruthven 2004: 37). Qutb's writings have been a key source of justification for terrorist atrocities. The decadent consumer culture of the West, exported to the rest of world by the might of capitalist corporations, is presented as a legitimate target, not least because it has infected Muslim societies, perverting them from the true path of Islam into a state of *jahiliyya* – the pagan condition of ignorance that prevailed before the Qur'an was revealed to the Prophet Muhammad.

Qutb's attack on Western consumer culture comes from the outside. Other critiques emerge from the margins of Western society itself, from its 'fundamentalists'. As an example, consider the *Left Behind* series of novels and films. Expressing the theological position known as pre-millenarian dispensationalism, these works begin with the Rapture, when Christ secretly comes to Earth and, in an instant, takes all the faithful Christians with him to Heaven. Those who remain on the planet face seven years of Tribulation, during which they must endure the unremitting horror of torture, terrorism, war, famine, pestilence and plagues. An evil figure will arise, the Antichrist, who will demand total obedience; most people will submit to him, and only a few will turn to Christ. After seven years, Christ will come again, defeat the Antichrist and reign in glory.

In her study of the ways in which followers of the *Left Behind* series respond to and interpret it, Frykholm found that two key events spoke powerfully to her respondents. The first of these is the moment of Rapture itself, when people disappear, leaving their possessions behind. Contact lenses, stockings, wedding rings: such items lie scattered on the ground, 'useless, unanimated, and lifeless' – a 'picture of consumer culture undone' (Frykholm 2004: 122). The second iconic moment is when the Antichrist commands that everyone bear his brand on their forehead – the 'Mark of the Beast' referred to in the Book of Revelation and usually interpreted as the number 666. No God-fearing person can accept the mark, since it indicates allegiance to Satan; yet, without the mark, people are forced out of society into an undercover struggle for survival. 'In the image of the Mark of the Beast', Frykholm suggests (2004: 123), 'concerns about consumer culture come vividly alive. Those who take the mark conform to the world. They become zombielike followers of the Antichrist and can no longer think for themselves. They are slaves to an evil economy.'

Although, in one sense, the critique of consumerism implicit in the *Left Behind* series comes from the cultural margins, it is also a product of the American mainstream. People who read the *Left Behind* books or watch the films are not fundamentalists encapsulated in a sub-culture of pre-millenarian dispensationalism; their fascination with the Apocalypse may clash with the beliefs and values of the liberal denominations, but it resonates with a broader evangelical constituency.

It would be a serious mistake, therefore, to overlook the critiques of consumer culture that emerge from within that culture itself. 'Consumerism' often refers to sad pathologies or wilful vices: self-indulgence, obsessive pleasure seeking, individualism, possessiveness, materialism, narcissism. Shopping functions as a symbol we evoke to deplore the ethos of our decadent times (D. Miller 1998). Consumption is equated with excess, and consumer society is condemned as shallow and materialistic. No wonder that Pope John Paul II identified consumerism as the gravest threat to faith following the collapse of Communism. His successor, Benedict XVI, emphasized the potentially corrosive effects of consumerism, notably on the celebration of Christmas.

The 'consumer attitude', Bauman says (1990: 204), is prevalent in Western culture. Life is experienced as a series of problems that demand solutions. Solutions are available for purchase; we have to decide rationally which of these solutions to buy. The art of living has narrowed down to the skills of making successful purchases. In a degenerate mutation of Puritanism, consumption has become a duty.

Viewed in this perspective, religion and consumption are incompatible; the consumer and the Almighty cannot both be sovereign. As Heelas (1994: 102) succinctly puts it, 'Religion would appear to be the very last thing that can be consumed.' Religion in the United States is cited by commentators such as Wilson (1966: 86–102) and Bruce (1996: 129–168; 2002: 204–228) as evidence of the detrimental effect of consumerism. By accommodating itself to the values of consumer society, organized religion has undermined its own foundations, a process evident in the liberal denominations that have pushed such accommodation to the extreme.

The 'death of God', if secularization theorists are correct, has been caused by consumer apathy, a force more lethal than the rational arguments of militant atheists. Self-consciously irreligious atheism implies caring about religion, whereas the prevailing mood in secular societies is, Bruce suggests (2002: 41–3), one of widespread and growing indifference to religious ideas and practices. 'Most people', he claims, 'did not give up being committed Christians because they became convinced that religion was false. It simply ceased to be of any great importance to them; they became indifferent' (Bruce 2002: 235). As religious communities have decayed, faith has shrunk, at least in Western Europe, to merely 'a vague willingness to suppose that "there's something out there"' (Voas and Crockett 2005: 24). This feeble remnant of religious faith is personally and culturally negligible; nobody lives or dies by a creed that is so intellectually and emotionally impoverished.

So why, in a highly individualized consumer society, would anyone turn to religion? The evidence suggests that there is something wrong with the question. Neither religion nor consumer society have been correctly understood. Consumers might be expected to choose religions that offer easy benefits at low cost; yet it is the more demanding forms of religion that appear to prosper, at least in terms of membership figures and profits. Consumers often choose to be challenged, because the rewards can exceed the costs.

Equally suspect is the assumption that consumerism is a form of self-absorption, as in the stereotypical image of shopping. The bulk of the purchases we make are not simply for ourselves; they are on behalf of a wider group or network. Miller's (1998) ethnographic work on shopping has shown that far from being self-indulgent, it is a labour of love. It is predominantly women's work directed at the welfare of other members of the household. The very fact that it is socially constructed as women's work is a reason why it is persistently misunderstood and devalued. Despite the mythology, shopping is not selfish, but altruistic. It is not the epitome of hedonistic ungodliness, but a devotional ritual serving the cult of domesticity. Religion is not threatened by it.

Indifference and apathy do not accurately describe the ways in which societies respond to religion. Societies recognize the power of religion, and seek to regulate and harness it. That is why the 'rule-and-exemption' approach, discussed in chapter 1, is so common: societies pass laws, but grant exemptions on grounds of religion. To hard-line political liberals, such exemptions are unjustified concessions; to militant secularists, they are a craven pandering to irrationality. Atheistic regimes have, however, had little success in their attempts to eliminate religion altogether. Most societies try to distinguish good manifestations of religion from bad, so that the former can be supported, or at least tolerated, and the latter suppressed.

Religious movements have faced a wide variety of accusations. Some have been seen as little more than blatant money-making enterprises. For example, during the years of his controversial mission to the West, Bhagwan Shree Rajneesh, founder of what became the Osho movement, was notorious for owning a fleet of ninety-two Rolls Royce limousines. To his devotees, this was a fitting tribute to their guru; to most outsiders, it appeared to be a manic and perhaps deranged act of grotesque self-indulgence. Scientology is another movement vilified as money grubbing. Its courses in self-improvement are famously expensive. Worse, it is widely alleged by the movement's critics that its founder, Lafayette Ron Hubbard, deliberately invented Scientology as a means of escape from the poverty of his faltering career as an author of pulp science fiction.

Even more telling are accusations of sexual abuses. Numerous charismatic leaders stand accused of sexually exploiting their followers. Self-righteous television evangelists have been caught in sexual acts that they were hot in condemning; for example, Jim Bakker, who was exposed as having committed adultery, and Jimmy Swaggart, whose denunciations of Bakker proved to have been hypocritical, since he himself was found to be availing himself of the services of a prostitute. The movement formerly known as the Children of God, now The Family, was notorious for its practice of 'flirty fishing': young women in the movement offering their sexual services to powerful men, with the aim of gaining political or financial support for the movement. Even the mainstream Christian churches have been embarrassed by repeated revelations of sexual abuse perpetrated by their priests and ministers (Shupe et al. 2000).

So far, we have been examining cases where the allegation is one of deliberate acts of fakery, extortion and abuse. Equally if not more troubling, are cases where the mental stability of religious leaders is at issue. Examples were discussed in chapter 8, including David Koresh, leader of the Branch Davidians, whose compound at Waco, Texas, was engulfed in flames during a confrontation with the federal authorities; Marshall Applewhite ('Do') of Heaven's Gate, whose members committed suicide; Luc Jouret and Joseph Di Mambro of the Order of the Solar Temple, and Jim Jones of the Peoples Temple, whose members either committed suicide or were shot; and Asahara Shōkō, leader of Aum Shinrikyō, a movement that unleashed lethal sarin gas on the Tokyo underground.

Recurrent moral panics over brainwashing and mind control in so-called cults, and the persistent undertow of fears about fundamentalism, scarcely demonstrate a relaxed indifference. The end of the Cold War has led to the re-emergence of fault lines caused by conflicts in which religion is important. Even in the supposedly secularized countries of Western Europe, religion remains a primary concern. After the carnage of September 11, 2001, the focus is on terrorists who carry out atrocities on innocent victims in the name of religion.

Nor is it easy to reconcile the thesis of indifference and apathy with the evidence of the continuing significance of religion in the lives of individuals and communities: the intimate ties that exist between religion and other sources of identity, above all nationality and ethnicity; the role of religious world-views in shaping the policies adopted by political leaders; the turn to spirituality in the heartlands of the supposedly secular West; and religious responses to the dislocating effects of globalization, both on people socially excluded from its rewards and on those who appear superficially to be its beneficiaries.

'The one inevitable fact of life in the 2000s', argue Elliott and Lemert (2006: 176) in their analysis of the new individualism, 'is that everyone must think – and think about themselves, deeply and seriously.' Globalization exposes us to a form of individualism that carries high emotional costs – 'a unique cultural constellation of anguish, anxiety, fear, disappointment and dread' (Elliott and Lemert 2006: 9). This enforced privatization of identities does not mean the death of collective ideals or the public sphere, though it may require their reconstruction. If so, the future of religion is assured, and the advent of secular society should be postponed indefinitely.

Afterword: dialogues in a post-secular world

In January 2004, Jürgen Habermas engaged in a dialogue with Cardinal Joseph Ratzinger, the future Pope Benedict XVI. Many of his admirers found it hard to see why the great secular sociologist and philosopher would want to debate religion with a prelate who had earned a reputation as a theological conservative, and who from 1981 to 2005 was head of the Congregation for the Doctrine of the Faith (historically, the Inquisition).

Until recently, Habermas took the view that religion was inescapably dogmatic (see pp. 93–5). He now believes it vital that religious and secular believers engage in constructive dialogue (Habermas 2006). To do so, all participants must be prepared to observe certain fundamental principles. People with a religious faith must recognize the integrity of other religions; they must not use dogma as a weapon to question the legitimate authority of science; they must be willing to submit their beliefs to critical scrutiny; and they must strive to translate their faith-based convictions into terms that can be rationally debated. Conversely, people of no religious faith, such as atheists, agnostics and humanists, have to concede that religion is not necessarily irrational. People with a religious faith, who enter into dialogue in the manner Habermas proposes, are entitled to have their opinions and their identity treated with respect. Secularists who treat all religion as nonsense are simply refusing to enter into a rational discussion.

An example of what Habermas has in mind when he speaks of narrow secularism is the work of the distinguished biologist Richard Dawkins. To Dawkins, contemporary secular societies display an astonishing and unwarranted respect for religion. Religions are granted all manner of unjustified exemptions from the law, exemptions that would not be conceded on any other ground; religions have 'a weirdly privileged status' (Dawkins 2006: 338). The problem is not fundamentalist extremism, but religion itself. Religion is by its very nature 'an especially potent silencer of rational calculation'; unquestioned faith, the very antithesis of scientific enquiry and rational debate, is regarded as desirable. All religion, however moderate it may profess to be, is an invitation to extremism. What is really pernicious, Dawkins contends (2006: 307–8), 'is the practice of teaching children that faith itself is a virtue. Faith is an evil precisely because it requires no justification and brooks no argument.' Dawkins implies that the chief culprits in this indoctrination are the professional ministers and theologians of the world's religions; but, if we were to accept his argument, we should also have to

blame the millions of 'gullible' parents who bring up their children in their faith.

To understand religion in the contemporary world, we would do well to follow the route sketched out philosophically by Habermas. A militantly secularist agenda is not attuned to dialogue. Repudiating stereotypes, ideologies and prejudice, sociological studies of religion investigate the complex dynamics of religious institutions and religious movements, and the rich spiritual experiences and religious identities of 'ordinary' people. That is sociology's contribution to mature discussion of the continuing significance of religion in post-secular societies.

Bibliography

Aldridge, A. E. 1992: Discourse on women in the clerical profession: the diaconate and language-games in the Church of England. *Sociology*, 26 (1), 45–57.

Allen, C. and Nielsen, J. S. 2002: *Summary Report on Islamophobia in the EU after 11 September 2001*. Vienna: European Monitoring Centre on Racism and Xenophobia. <http://eumc.eu.int>

Ammerman, N. T. 1987: *Bible Believers: fundamentalists in the modern world*. New Brunswick, NJ: Rutgers University Press.

Ammerman, N. T. 1997: *Congregation and Community*. New Brunswick, NJ: Rutgers University Press.

Andreski, S. 1974: *The Essential Comte*. London: Croom Helm.

Ansari, H. 2004: *'The Infidel Within': Muslims in Britain since 1800*. London: Hurst.

Ansell, A. E. 2000: The new face of racism: the metamorphosis of racism in the post-civil rights era United States. In P. Kivisto and G. Rundblad (eds), *Multiculturalism in the United States: current issues, contemporary voices*. Thousand Oaks, Calif.: Pine Forge Press, 29–42.

Anthony, D. and Robbins, T. 1997: Religious totalism, exemplary dualism, and the Waco tragedy. In T. Robbins and S. J. Palmer (eds), *Millennium, Messiahs, and Mayhem: contemporary apocalyptic movements*. New York: Routledge, 261–84.

Aron, R. 1968: *Main Currents in Sociological Thought*, vol. 1, trans. Richard Howard and Helen Weaver. Harmondsworth: Penguin.

Aron, R. 1970: *Main Currents in Sociological Thought*, vol. 2, trans. Richard Howard and Helen Weaver. Harmondsworth: Penguin.

Baert, P. 2001: Jürgen Habermas. In A. Elliott and B. S. Turner (eds), *Profiles in Contemporary Sociological Theory*. London: Sage, 84–93.

Bainbridge, W. S. 1997: *The Sociology of Social Movements*. New York: Routledge.

Bainbridge, W. S. and Stark, R. 1980: Scientology: to be perfectly clear. *Sociological Analysis*, 41 (2), 128–36.

Balch, R. W. and Taylor, D. 2002: Making sense of the Heaven's Gate suicides. In D. G. Bromley and J. G. Melton (eds), *Cults, Religion and Violence*. Cambridge: Cambridge University Press, 209–28.

Barker, E. 1984: *The Making of a Moonie: brainwashing or choice?* Oxford: Blackwell.

Barker, E. 1993: Charismatization: the social production of 'an ethos propitious to the mobilization of sentiments'. In E. Barker, J. A. Beckford and K. Dobbelaere (eds), *Secularization, Rationalism and Sectarianism: essays in honour of Bryan R. Wilson*. Oxford: Clarendon Press, 181–201.

Barker, E. 1995: *New Religious Movements: a practical introduction*. London: HMSO.

Barker, E. 2002: Watching for violence: a comparative analysis of the roles of five types of cult-watching groups. In D. G. Bromley and J. G. Melton (eds), *Cults, Religion and Violence*. Cambridge: Cambridge University Press, 123–48.

Barr, J. 1977: *Fundamentalism*. London: SCM.

Barry, B. 2001: *Culture and Equality: an egalitarian critique of multiculturalism*. Cambridge, Mass.: Harvard University Press.

Barthes, R. 1972: *Mythologies*. London: Cape.

Bartowski, J. P. 2000: Breaking walls, raising fences: masculinity, intimacy, and accountability among the Promise Keepers. *Sociology of Religion*, 61 (1), 33–53.

Bauman, Z. 1990: *Thinking Sociologically*. Oxford: Blackwell.

Baumann, G. 2004: Grammars of Identity/Alterity: a structural approach. In G. Baumann and A. Gingrich (eds), *Grammars of Identity/Alterity: a structural approach*. New York and Oxford: Berghahn, 18–50.

Beckford, J. A. 1975: *The Trumpet of Prophecy: a sociological study of Jehovah's Witnesses*. Oxford: Blackwell.

Beckford, J. A. 1978: Accounting for conversion. *British Journal of Sociology*, 29 (2), 249–62.

Beckford, J. A. 1985: *Cult Controversies: the societal response to new religious movements*. London: Tavistock.

Beckford, J. A. 1989: *Religion and Advanced Industrial Society*. London: Unwin Hyman.

Beckford, J. A. 1996: Postmodernity, high modernity and new modernity: three concepts in search of religion. In K. Flanagan and P. C. Jupp (eds), *Postmodernity, Sociology and Religion*. London: Routledge, 30–47.

Beckford, J. A. 2003: *Social Theory and Religion*. Cambridge: Cambridge University Press.

Bell, D. 1979: *The Cultural Contradictions of Capitalism*, 2nd edn. London: Heinemann.

Bellah, R. N. 1967: Civil religion in America. *Daedalus*, 96 (1), 1–21.

Bellah, R. N. 1990: Religion and legitimation in the American republic. In T. Robbins and D. Anthony (eds), *In Gods We Trust*. New Brunswick, NJ: Transaction Publishers, 411–26.

Bellah, R. N., Madsen, R., Sullivan, W. M., Swidler, A. and Tipton, S. M. 1996: *Habits of the Heart: individualism and commitment in American life*. Berkeley: University of California Press.

Bendix, R. and Roth, G. 1971: *Scholarship and Partisanship: essays on Max Weber*. Berkeley: University of California Press.

Berger, P. L. 1967: *The Sacred Canopy: elements of a sociological theory of religion*. New York: Doubleday.

Berger, P. L. 1999: The desecularization of the world: a global overview. In P. L. Berger (ed.), *The Desecularization of the World: resurgent religion and world politics*. Washington, DC: Ethics and Public Policy Center, 1–18.

Binns, C. A. P. 1979: The changing face of power: revolution and accommodation in the development of the Soviet ceremonial system, part 1. *Man*, 14, 585–606.

Binns, C. A. P. 1980: The changing face of power: revolution and accommodation in the development of the Soviet ceremonial system, part 2. *Man*, 15, 170–87.

Blake, M. 2005: Stations of the Cross: how evangelical Christians are creating an alternative universe of faith-based news. *Columbia Journalism Review*, 3. <www.cjr.org/issues/2005/3>

Blumler, J. G., Brown, J. R., Ewbank, A. J. and Nossiter, T. J. 1971: Attitudes to the monarchy: their structure and development during a ceremonial occasion. *Political Studies*, 19 (2), 149–71.

Boyle, K. and Sheen, J. 1997: *Freedom of Religion and Belief: a world report*. London: Routledge.

Brasher, B. E. 1998: *Godly Women: fundamentalism and female power*. New Brunswick, NJ: Rutgers University Press.

Brasher, B. E. 2001: *Give Me That Online Religion*. San Francisco: Jossey-Bass.

Bromley, D. G. and Shupe, A. D. 1980: The Tnevnoc Cult. *Sociological Analysis*, 40 (4), 361–6.

Bromley, D. G. and Shupe, A. D. 1981: *Strange Gods: the great American cult scare*. Boston: Beacon Press.

Brown, C. G. 2001: *The Death of Christian Britain: understanding secularisation 1800–2000*. London and New York: Routledge.

Bruce, S. 1986: *God Save Ulster: the religion and politics of Paisleyism*. Oxford: Clarendon Press.

Bruce, S. (ed.) 1992: *Religion and Modernization: sociologists and historians debate the secularization thesis*. Oxford: Clarendon Press.

Bruce, S. 1995: *Religion in Modern Britain*. Oxford: Oxford University Press.

Bruce, S. 1996: *Religion in the Modern World: from cathedrals to cults*. Oxford: Oxford University Press.

Bruce, S. 2000: *Fundamentalism*. Cambridge: Polity.

Bruce, S. 2002: *God is Dead: secularization in the West*. Oxford: Blackwell.

Bruce, S. 2003: *Politics and Religion*. Cambridge: Polity.

Brusco, E. E. 1995: *The Reformation of Machismo: Evangelical conversion and gender in Colombia*. Austin: University of Texas Press.

Cahill, D., Bouma, G., Dellal, H. and Leahy, M. 2004: *Religion, Cultural Diversity and Safeguarding Australia*. <www.amf.net.au/PDF/religion-CulturalDiversity/Main_Report.pdf>

Campbell, C. 1972: The cult, the cultic milieu and secularization. In M. Hill (ed.), *A Sociological Yearbook of Religion in Britain*, vol. 5. London: SCM, 119–36.

Campbell, C. 1999: The Easternisation of the West. In B. R. Wilson and J. Cresswell (eds), *New Religious Movements: challenge and response*. London and New York: Routledge, 35–48.

Caporale, R. and Grumelli, A. (eds) 1971: *The Culture of Unbelief*. Berkeley: University of California Press.

Carey, S. 1987: The Indianization of the Hare Krishna movement. In R. Burghart (ed.), *Hinduism in Great Britain*. London: Tavistock, 81–99.

Chadwick, O. 1975: *The Secularization of the European Mind in the Nineteenth Century*. Cambridge: Cambridge University Press.

Chaves, M. 1997: *Ordaining Women: culture and conflict in religious organizations*. Cambridge, Mass.: Harvard University Press.

Chaves, M. 2004: *Congregations in America*. Cambridge, Mass.: Harvard University Press.

Chaves, M. and Gorski, P. S. 2001: Religious pluralism and religious participation. *Annual Review of Sociology*, 27, 261–81.

Chidester, D. n.d.: *Scientology: a religion in South Africa*. Los Angeles: Freedom Publishing.

Christiano, K. J., Swatos, W. H. Jr and Kivisto, P. 2002: *Sociology of Religion: contemporary developments*. New York: Alta Mira Press.

Chryssides, G. 1998: *The Elements of Unitarianism*. Shaftesbury: Element.

Coleman, S. 2000: *The Globalisation of Charismatic Christianity: spreading the gospel of prosperity*. Cambridge: Cambridge University Press.

Corbridge, S. and Harriss, J. 2000: *Reinventing India: liberalization, Hindu nationalism and popular democracy*. Cambridge: Polity.

Davidman, L. 1991: *Tradition in a Rootless World: women turn to Orthodox Judaism*. Berkeley: University of California Press.

Davie, G. 1994: *Religion in Britain since 1945: believing without belonging*. Oxford: Blackwell.

Davie, G. 2001: The persistence of institutional religion in modern Europe. In L. Woodhead (ed.), *Peter Berger and the Study of Religion*. London: Routledge, 101–11.

Davie, G. 2002: Praying alone? Church-going in Britain and social capital. *Journal of Contemporary Religion*, 17 (3), 329–34.

Davies, C. 1996: Coffee, tea and the ultra-Protestant and Jewish nature of the boundaries of Mormonism. In D. J. Davies (ed.), *Mormon Identities in Transition*. London: Cassell, 35–45.

Davies, D. J. 2003: *An Introduction to Mormonism*. Cambridge: Cambridge University Press.

Dawkins, R. 2006: *The God Delusion*. London: Bantam Press.

Dawson, L. L. and Cowan, D. E. (eds) 2004: *Religion Online: finding faith on the Internet*. New York and London: Routledge.

Dawson, L. L. and Hennebry, J. 2004: New religions and the Internet: recruiting in a new public space. In L. L. Dawson and D. E. Cowan (eds), *Religion Online: finding faith on the Internet*. New York and London: Routledge, 151–73.

Delanty, G. 2003: *Community*. London and New York: Routledge.

Demerath, N. J. III 2003: Civil society and civil religion as mutually dependent. In M. Dillon (ed.), *Handbook of the Sociology of Religion*. Cambridge: Cambridge University Press, 348–58.

Dillon, M. 1999: *Catholic Identity: balancing reason, faith, and power*. Cambridge: Cambridge University Press.

Durkheim, E. 1915: *The Elementary Forms of the Religious Life*, trans. Joseph Ward Swain. London: Allen & Unwin.

Ebaugh, H. R. and Chafetz, J. S. (eds) 2000: *Religion and the New Immigrants: continuities and adaptations in immigrant congregations*. Walnut Creek, Calif.: Alta Mira Press.

Edgell, P., Gerteis, J. and Hartmann, D. 2006: Atheists as 'other': moral boundaries and cultural membership in American society. *American Sociological Review*, 71 (2), 211–23.

Elliott, A. and Lemert, C. 2006: *The New Individualism: the emotional costs of globalization*. London and New York: Routledge.

Ellul, J. 1989: *What I Believe*, trans. Geoffrey W. Bromiley. Grand Rapids, Mich.: William B. Eerdmans Publishing Company.

Embry, J. L. 1994: *Black Saints in a White Church: contemporary African American Mormons*. Salt Lake City: Signature Books.

Evans-Pritchard, E. E. 1965: *Theories of Primitive Religion*. Oxford: Clarendon Press.

Faludi, S. 2000: *Stiffed: the betrayal of modern man*. London: Vintage.

Festinger, L., Riecken, H. W. and Schachter, S. 1956: *When Prophecy Fails*. Minneapolis: University of Minnesota Press.

Feuerbach, L. 1989/1841: *The Essence of Christianity*, trans. George Eliot. Amherst, New York: Prometheus.

Finke, R. 1997: The consequences of religious competition: supply-side explanations for religious change. In L. A. Young (ed.), *Rational Choice Theory and Religion: summary and assessment*. New York: Routledge, 46–65.

Finke, R. and Stark, R. 1992: *The Churching of America 1776–1990: winners and losers in our religious economy*. New Brunswick, NJ: Rutgers University Press.

Flanagan, K. 2001: The return of theology: sociology's distant relative. In R. K. Fenn (ed.), *The Blackwell Companion to Sociology of Religion*. Oxford: Blackwell, 432–44.

Flanagan, K. and Jupp, P. C. (eds) 1996: *Postmodernity, Sociology and Religion*. London: Routledge.

Flory, R. W. and Miller, D. E. (eds) 2000: *GenX Religion*. New York and London: Routledge.

Frykholm, A. J. 2004: *Rapture Culture: left behind in evangelical America*. New York: Oxford University Press.

Geertz, C. 1968: Religion as a cultural system. In M. Banton (ed.), *Anthropological Approaches to the Study of Religion*. London: Tavistock, 1–46.

Gellner, E. 1992: *Postmodernism, Reason and Religion*. London: Routledge.

Giddens, A. 1991: *Modernity and Self-Identity: self and society in the late modern age*. Cambridge: Polity.

Gouldner, A. W. 1955: Metaphysical pathos and the theory of bureaucracy. *American Political Science Review*, 49, 496–507.

Grunberger, R. 1991: *A Social History of the Third Reich*. Harmondsworth: Penguin.

Habermas, J. 1973: *Legitimation Crisis*, trans. Thomas McCarthy. Boston: Beacon Press.

Habermas, J. 1987: *The Theory of Communicative Action*, vol. 2: *The Critique of Functionalist Reason*, trans. Thomas McCarthy. Cambridge: Polity.

Habermas, J. 2002: To seek to salvage an unconditional meaning without God is a futile undertaking: reflections on a remark by Max Horkheimer. In J. Habermas (ed.), *Religion and Rationality: essays on reason, God, and modernity*. Cambridge: Polity, 95–109.

Habermas, J. 2006: Religion in the Public Sphere. *European Journal of Philosophy*, 14 (1), 1–25.

Hadden, J. K. and Shupe, A. D. 1987: Televangelism in America. *Social Compass*, 34 (1), 61–75.

Hadden, J. K. and Shupe, A. D. 1988: *Televangelism: power and politics on God's frontier*. New York: Henry Holt.

Hall, D. E. (ed.) 1994: *Muscular Christianity: embodying the Victorian age*. Cambridge: Cambridge University Press.

Hall, J. R. and Schuyler, P. 1997: The mystical apocalypse of the Solar Temple. In T. Robbins and S. J. Palmer (eds), *Millennium, Messiahs, and Mayhem: contemporary apocalyptic movements*. New York: Routledge, 285–311.

Halliday, F. 1999: 'Islamophobia' reconsidered. *Ethnic and Racial Studies*, 22 (5), 892–902.

Hamilton, M. B. 1995: *The Sociology of Religion: theoretical and comparative perspectives*. London: Routledge.

Hamilton, R. F. and Form, W. H. 2003: Categorical usages and complex realities: race, ethnicity, and religion in the United States. *Social Forces*, 81 (3), 693–714.

Hartmann, D., Zhang, X. and Windschadt, W. 2005: One (multicultural) Nation under God? The changing meanings and uses of the term 'Judeo-Christian' in the American media. *Journal of Media and Religion*, 4 (4), 207–34.

Hay, D. 1987: *Exploring Inner Space: scientists and religious experience*. London: Mowbray.

Heelas, P. 1994: The limits of consumption and the post-modern 'religion' of the New Age. In R. Keat, N. Whiteley and N. Abercrombie (eds), *The Authority of the Consumer*. London: Routledge, 102–15.

Heelas, P. 1996: *The New Age Movement: the celebration of self and the sacralization of modernity*. Oxford: Blackwell.

Heelas, P. and Woodhead, L. 2005: *The Spiritual Revolution: why religion is giving way to spirituality*. Oxford: Blackwell.

Heeren, J., Lindsey, D. B. and Mason, M. 1984: The Mormon concept of Mother in Heaven: a sociological account of its origins and development. *Journal for the Scientific Study of Religion*, 23 (4), 396–411.

Heilman, S. C. and Friedman, M. 1991: Religious fundamentalism and religious Jews: the case of the haredim. In M. E. Marty and R. S. Appleby (eds), *Fundamentalism Observed*. Chicago: University of Chicago Press, 197–264.

Helland, C. 2000: Online-religion/religion-online and virtual communitas. In J. K. Hadden and D. E. Cowan (eds), *Religion on the Internet: research prospects and promises*. New York: JAI, 205–223.

Herberg, W. 1983/1955: *Protestant – Catholic – Jew: an essay in American religious sociology*. Chicago: University of Chicago Press.

Hervieu-Léger, D. 2000: *Religion as a Chain of Memory*, trans. Simon Lee. New Brunswick, NJ: Rutgers University Press.

Hervieu-Léger, D. 2001: *La Religion en miettes ou la question des sectes*. Paris: Calmann-Lévy.

Hill, M. 1973: *A Sociology of Religion*. London: Heinemann.

Hoover, S. M., Clark, L. S. and Rainie, L. 2004: *Faith Online*. Washington, DC: Pew Internet and American Life Project. <www.pewInternet.org>

Horkheimer, M. 1995: *Critical Theory: selected essays*, trans. Matthew J. O'Connell et al. New York: Continuum.

Hornsby-Smith, M. P. 1987: *Roman Catholics in England: studies in social structure since the Second World War*. Cambridge: Cambridge University Press.

Hornsby-Smith, M. P. 1992: Recent transformations in English Catholicism: evidence of secularization? In S. Bruce (ed.), *Religion and Modernization: sociologists and historians debate the secularization thesis*. Oxford: Clarendon Press, 118–44.

Hornsby-Smith, M. P. 2004: The changing identity of Catholics in England. In S. Coleman and P. Collins (eds), *Religious Identity and Change: perspectives on global transformations*. Aldershot: Ashgate, 42–56.

Huntington, S. P. 2002: *The Clash of Civilizations and the Remaking of World Order*. New York: Simon & Schuster.

Huntington, S. P. 2004: *Who Are We? America's Great Debate*. New York: Simon & Schuster.

Iannaccone, L. R. 1997: Rational choice: framework for the scientific study of religion. In L. A. Young (ed.), *Rational Choice Theory and Religion: summary and assessment*. New York: Routledge, 25–45.

Introvigne, M. 2005: A symbolic universe: information terrorism and new religions in cyberspace. In M. T. Højsgaard and M. Warburg (eds), *Religion and Cyberspace*. London and New York: Routledge, 102–17.

Introvigne, M. and Mayer, J.-F. 2002: Occult Masters and the Temple of Doom: the fiery end of the Solar Temple. In D. G. Bromley and J. G. Melton (eds), *Cults, Religion and Violence*. Cambridge: Cambridge University Press, 170–88.

Introvigne, M. and Stark, R. 2005: Religious competition and revival in Italy: exploring European exceptionalism. *Interdisciplinary Journal of Research on Religion* 1 (1). <www.bepress.com/ijrr/vol1/iss1/art5>

Jarman, N. 1997: *Material Conflicts: parades and visual displays in Northern Ireland*. Oxford: Berg.

Johnson, D. P. 1979: Dilemmas of charismatic leadership: the case of the People's Temple. *Sociological Analysis*, 40 (4), 315–23.

Juergensmeyer, M. 2003: *Terror in the Mind of God: the global rise of religious violence*, 3rd edn. Berkeley: University of California Press.

Jung, C. G. 1961: *Modern Man in Search of a Soul*. London: Routledge & Kegan Paul.

Karner, C. 2006: *The Thought World of Hindu Nationalism: analyzing a political ideology*. New York: Edward Mellen Press.

Karner, C. and Aldridge, A. 2004: Theorizing religion in a globalizing world. *International Journal of Politics, Culture and Society*, 18 (1/2), 5–32.

Kelly, L. 2003: Bosnian refugees in Britain: questioning community. *Sociology*, 37 (1), 35–49.

Kennedy, R. J. R. 1944: Single or triple melting-pot? Intermarriage trends in New Haven, 1870–1940. *American Journal of Sociology*, 49 (4), 331–9.

Kepel, G. 1994: *The Revenge of God: the resurgence of Islam, Christianity and Judaism in the Modern World*, trans. Susan Milner. Cambridge: Polity.

Kepel, G. 1997: *Allah in the West: Islamic movements in America and Europe*, trans. Susan Milner. Cambridge: Polity.

Kepel, G. 2002: *Jihad: the trail of political Islam*, trans. Anthony F. Roberts. Cambridge, Mass.: Harvard University Press.

Kershaw, I. 1989: *The 'Hitler Myth': image and reality in the Third Reich*. Oxford: Oxford University Press.

Kim, A. E. 1993: The absence of pan-Canadian civil religion: plurality, duality, and conflict in symbols of Canadian culture. *Sociology of Religion*, 54 (3), 257–75.

Kivisto, P. (ed.) 2005: *Incorporating Diversity: rethinking assimilation in a multicultural age*. Boulder, Colo.: Paradigm Publishers.

Kivisto, P. and Rundblad, G. 2000: Overview: multicultural America in the post-civil rights era. In P. Kivisto and G. Rundblad (eds), *Multiculturalism in the United States: current issues, contemporary voices*. Thousand Oaks, Calif.: Pine Forge Press, pp. xxi–xlvi.

Knott, K. 1998: *Hinduism: a very short introduction*. Oxford: Oxford University Press.

Kosmin, B. A., Mayer, E. and Keysar, A. 2001: *American Religious Identification Survey*. New York: City University of New York.

Kunin, S. D. 2003: *Religion: the modern theories*. Edinburgh: Edinburgh University Press.

Lane, C. 1981: *The Rites of Rulers: ritual in industrial society – the Soviet case.* Cambridge: Cambridge University Press.

Lanternari, V. 1963: *The Religions of the Oppressed: a study of modern messianic cults*, trans. Lisa Sergio. New York: Alfred A. Knopf.

Lawson, R. 1997: The Apocalyptic fringe groups of Seventh-day Adventism. In T. Robbins and S. J. Palmer (eds), *Millennium, Messiahs, and Mayhem: contemporary apocalyptic movements.* New York: Routledge, 207–28.

Leach, E. R. 1969: Virgin Birth. In E. Leach (ed.), *Genesis as Myth and Other Essays.* London: Cape, 85–112.

Leach, E. R. 1982: *Social Anthropology.* London: Fontana.

Lenski, G. 1963: *The Religious Factor.* New York: Doubleday.

Lifton, R. J. 1961: *Thought Reform and the Psychology of Totalism: a study of 'brainwashing' in China.* New York: Norton.

Lockhart, W. H. 2000: 'We Are One Life,' but not of one gender ideology: unity, ambiguity, and the Promise Keepers. *Sociology of Religion*, 61 (1), 73–92.

Luckmann, T. 1967: *The Invisible Religion: the problem of religion in modern society.* London: Collier-Macmillan.

Lukes, S. 1973a: *Emile Durkheim: his life and work.* London: Allen Lane.

Lukes, S. 1973b: *Individualism.* Oxford: Blackwell.

Lukes, S. 1975: Political ritual and social integration. *Sociology*, 9 (2), 289–308.

MacEoin, D. 1997: Baha'ism. In J. R. Hinnells (ed.), *A New Handbook of Living Religions.* Harmondsworth: Penguin, 618–43.

Marler, P. L. and Hadaway, C. K. 2002: 'Being religious' or 'being spiritual' in America: a zero-sum proposition? *Journal for the Scientific Study of Religion*, 41 (2), 289–300.

Marshall, G. 1980: *Presbyteries and Profits: Calvinism and the development of capitalism in Scotland, 1560–1707.* Oxford: Clarendon Press.

Marshall, G. 1982: *In Search of the Spirit of Capitalism: an essay on Max Weber's Protestant Ethic thesis.* London: Hutchinson.

Martin, D. A. 1965: Towards eliminating the concept of secularization. In J. Gould (ed.), *The Penguin Survey of the Social Sciences, 1965.* Harmondsworth: Penguin, 169–82.

Martin, D. A. 1978: *A General Theory of Secularization.* Oxford: Blackwell.

Martin, D. A. 1990: *Tongues of Fire: the explosion of Protestantism in Latin America.* Oxford: Blackwell.

Martin, D. 2002: *Pentecostalism: the world their parish.* Oxford: Blackwell.

Marx, K. and Engels, F. 1957: *On Religion.* Moscow: Foreign Languages Publishing House.

Mason, D. 2000: *Race and Ethnicity in Modern Britain.* Oxford: Oxford University Press.

Mayer, J.-F. 2000: Religious movements and the Internet: the new frontiers of cult controversies. In J. K. Hadden and D. E. Cowan (eds), *Religion on the Internet: research prospects and promises.* New York: JAI, 249–76.

McGrath, A. E. 2004: *The Twilight of Atheism: the rise and fall of disbelief in the modern world.* Westminster, Md.: Doubleday.

McGuire, M. B. 1992: *Religion: the social context*. Belmont, Calif.: Wadsworth.

McGuire, M. B. 2003: Contested meanings and definitional boundaries: historicizing the sociology of religion. In A. L. Greil and D. G. Bromley (eds), *Defining Religion: investigating the boundaries between the sacred and the secular*. London: JAI, 127–38.

McLellan, D. 1973: *Karl Marx: his life and thought*. London: Macmillan.

McLellan, D. 1987: *Marxism and Religion: a description and assessment of the Marxist critique of Christianity*. London: Macmillan.

McMullen, M. 2000: *The Baha'i: the religious construction of a global identity*. New Brunswick, NJ: Rutgers University Press.

McSweeney, B. 1980: *Roman Catholicism: the search for relevance*. Oxford: Blackwell.

Melton, J. G. 1992: *Encyclopedic Handbook of Cults in America*. New York: Garland Publishing.

Melton, J. G. and Bromley, D. G. 2002: Challenging misconceptions about the new religions–violence connection. In D. G. Bromley and J. G. Melton (eds), *Cults, Religion and Violence*. Cambridge: Cambridge University Press, 42–56.

Miller, D. 1998: *A Theory of Shopping*. Cambridge: Polity.

Miller, D. E. 1997: *Reinventing American Protestantism: Christianity in the new millennium*. Berkeley: University of California Press.

Mittelberg, D. and Waters, M. C. 1992: The process of ethnogenesis among Haitian and Israeli immigrants in the United States. *Ethnic and Racial Studies*, 15 (3), 412–35.

Modood, T. 1997: 'Difference', cultural racism and anti-racism. In P. Werbner and T. Modood (eds), *Debating Cultural Hybridity*. London: Zed Books, 154–72.

Mullins, M. 1997: Aum Shinrikyō as an apocalyptic movement. In T. Robbins and S. J. Palmer (eds), *Millennium, Messiahs, and Mayhem: contemporary apocalyptic movements*. New York: Routledge, 313–24.

Nesbitt, E. 2004: 'I'm a Gujarati Lohana and a Vaishnav as well': religious identity formation among young Coventrian Punjabis and Gujaratis. In S. Coleman and P. Collins (eds), *Religious Identity and Change: perspectives on global transformations*. Aldershot: Ashgate, 174–90.

Niebuhr, H. R. 1957/1929: *The Social Sources of Denominationalism*. New York: Meridian.

Nisbet, R. A. 1967: *The Sociological Tradition*. London: Heinemann.

O'Dea, T. F. 1957: *The Mormons*. Chicago: University of Chicago Press.

O'Dea, T. F. 1966: *The Sociology of Religion*. Englewood Cliffs, NJ: Prentice-Hall.

O'Toole, R. 1996: Religion in Canada: its development and contemporary situation. *Social Compass*, 43 (1), 119–43.

Outhwaite, W. 1994: *Habermas: a critical introduction*. Cambridge: Polity.

Parkin, F. 1982: *Max Weber*. Chichester: Ellis Horwood; London: Tavistock.

Parkin, F. 1992: *Durkheim*. Oxford: Oxford University Press.

Parsons, T. 1954: The theoretical development of the sociology of religion. In T. Parsons, *Essays in Sociological Theory*, rev. edn. New York: Free Press, 197–211.

Parsons, T. 1960: Some comments on the pattern of religious organization in the United States. In T. Parsons, *Structure and Process in Modern Societies*. New York: Free Press, 295–321.

Parsons, T. 1967: Christianity and modern industrial society. In T. Parsons, *Sociological Theory and Modern Society*. New York: Free Press, 385–421.

Parsons, T. 1977: *The Evolution of Societies*. Englewood Cliffs, NJ: Prentice-Hall.

Parsons, T. 1991: *The Social System*. London: Routledge.

Partridge, C. (ed.) 2003: *UFO Religions*. London and New York: Routledge.

Peach, C. 1980: Which triple melting pot? A re-examination of ethnic intermarriage in New Haven, 1900–1950. *Ethnic and Racial Studies*, 3 (1), 1–16.

Penton, M. J. 1985: *Apocalypse Delayed: the story of Jehovah's Witnesses*. Toronto: University of Toronto Press.

Popper, K. R. 1963: *Conjectures and Refutations: the growth of scientific knowledge*. London: Routledge & Kegan Paul.

Punshon, J. 1984: *Portrait in Grey: a short history of the Quakers*. London: Quaker Home Service.

Putney, C. 2001: *Muscular Christianity: manhood and sports in Protestant America, 1880–1920*. Cambridge, Mass.: Harvard University Press.

Reader, I. 2002: Dramatic confrontations: Aum Shinrikyō against the world. In D. G. Bromley and J. G. Melton (eds), *Cults, Religion and Violence*. Cambridge: Cambridge University Press, 189–208.

Richardson, J. T. and Introvigne, M. 2001: 'Brainwashing' theories in European parliamentary and administrative reports on 'cults' and 'sects'. *Journal for the Scientific Study of Religion*, 40 (2), 143–68.

Rieff, P. 1965: *Freud: the mind of the moralist*. London: Methuen.

Ritzer, G. 1996: *The McDonaldization of Society: an investigation into the changing character of contemporary social life*. London: Sage.

Ritzer, G. 2004: *The Globalization of Nothing*. London: Sage.

Robbins, T. 1988: *Cults, Converts and Charisma: the sociology of new religious movements*. London: New York.

Robbins, T. and Anthony, D. (eds) 1990: *In Gods We Trust*. New Brunswick, NJ: Transaction Publishers.

Robbins, T. and Palmer, S. J. 1997: Patterns of contemporary apocalypticism in North America. In T. Robbins and S. J. Palmer (eds), *Millennium, Messiahs, and Mayhem: contemporary apocalyptic movements*. New York: Routledge, 1–27.

Robbins, T., Anthony, D., Doucas, M. and Curtis, T. 1976: The last civil religion: Reverend Moon and the Unification Church. *Sociological Analysis*, 37, 111–26.

Robertson, R. 1970: *The Sociological Interpretation of Religion*. Oxford: Blackwell.

Robertson, R. 1991: The central significance of 'religion' in social theory: Parsons as an epical theorist. In R. Robertson and B. S. Turner (eds), *Talcott Parsons: theorist of modernity.* London: Sage, 1–21.

Robertson, R. 1993: Community, society, globality, and the category of religion. In E. Barker, J. A. Beckford and K. Dobbelaere (eds), *Secularization, Rationalism and Sectarianism: essays in honour of Bryan R. Wilson.* Oxford: Clarendon Press, 1–17.

Roof, W. C. 1999: *Spiritual Marketplace: baby boomers and the remaking of American religion.* Princeton, NJ: Princeton University Press.

Ruane, J. and Todd, J. 1996: *The Dynamics of Conflict in Northern Ireland: power, conflict and emancipation.* Cambridge: Cambridge University Press.

Ruether, R. R. 1979: *Mary – the Feminine Face of the Church.* London: SCM.

Runnymede Trust 1997: *Islamophobia: a challenge for us all.* London: Runnymede Trust.

Ruthven, M. 1997: *Islam: a very short introduction.* Oxford: Oxford University Press.

Ruthven, M. 2004: *Fundamentalism: the search for meaning.* Oxford: Oxford University Press.

Said, E. W. 2001: The clash of ignorance. *The Nation*, 22 October.

Saks, M. 1998: Beyond the frontiers of science? Religious aspects of alternative medicine. In J. R. Hinnells and R. Porter (eds), *Religion, Health and Suffering.* London: Routledge, 381–98.

Saler, B. 1993: *Conceptualizing Religion: immanent anthropologists, transcendent natives, and unbounded categories.* Leiden: Brill.

Sargant, W. 1957: *Battle for the Mind.* London: Heinemann.

Scharf, B. R. 1970: *The Sociological Study of Religion.* London: Hutchinson.

Scott, A. 1990: *Ideology and the New Social Movements.* London: Unwin Hyman.

Sharot, S. 1992: Religious fundamentalism: neo-traditionalism in modern societies. In B. R. Wilson (ed.), *Religion: contemporary issues.* London: Bellew, 24–45.

Shils, E. 1965: Charisma, order, and status. *American Sociological Review*, 30 (2), 199–213.

Shils, E. and Young, M. 1953: The meaning of the Coronation. *The Sociological Review*, 1 (2), 63–82.

Shupe, A. D., Stacey, W. A. and Darnell, S. E. (eds) 2000: *Bad Pastors: clergy misconduct in modern America.* New York: New York University Press.

Silk, M. 1984: Notes on the Judeo-Christian tradition in America. *American Quarterly*, 36 (1), 65–85.

Simmel, G. 1997: *Essays on Religion*, trans. Horst Jürgen Helle. New Haven: Yale University Press.

Smith, P. 1987: *The Babi and Baha'i Religions: from messianic Shi'ism to a world religion.* Cambridge: Cambridge University Press.

Smith, T. 2002: Religious diversity in America: the emergence of Muslims, Buddhists, Hindus, and others. *Journal for the Scientific Study of Religion*, 41 (3), 577–85.

Spiro, M. E. 1966: Religion: problems of definition and explanation. In M. Banton (ed.), *Anthropological Approaches to the Study of Religion.* London: Tavistock, 85–126.

Stark, R. 1990: Modernization, secularization, and Mormon success. In T. Robbins and D. Anthony (eds), *In Gods We Trust.* New Brunswick, NJ: Transaction Publishers, 201–18.

Stark, R. 1998: The basis of Mormon success: a theoretical application. In J. T. Duke (ed.), *Latter-day Saint Social Life: social research on the LDS Church and its members.* Provo, Utah: Brigham Young University, 29–70.

Stark, R. and Bainbridge, W. S. 1985: *The Future of Religion: secularization, revival and cult formation.* Berkeley: University of California Press.

Stark, R. and Bainbridge, W. S. 1996: *A Theory of Religion.* New Brunswick, NJ: Rutgers University Press.

Stark, R. and Iannaccone, L. R. 1997: Why the Jehovah's Witnesses grow so rapidly: a theoretical application. *Journal of Contemporary Religion,* 12 (2), 133–57.

Steigmann-Gall, R. 2003: *The Holy Reich: Nazi conceptions of Christianity, 1919–1945.* Cambridge: Cambridge University Press.

Stiglitz, J. 2002: *Globalization and its Discontents.* London: Penguin.

Sutcliffe, S. J. 2003: *Children of the New Age: a history of spiritual practices.* London and New York: Routledge.

Taylor, C. 1991: *The Ethics of Authenticity.* Cambridge, Mass.: Harvard University Press.

Thomas, E. R. 2006: Keeping identity at a distance: explaining France's new legal restrictions on the Islamic headscarf. *Ethnic and Racial Studies,* 29 (2), 237–59.

Thompson, K. 1976: *Auguste Comte: the foundation of sociology.* London: Nelson.

Thumma, S. L. 1998: Exploring the megachurch phenomena: their characteristics and cultural context. <http://hartsem.edu/bookshelf/thumma_article2.html>

Tocqueville, A. de 1945 [1835, 1840]: *Democracy in America,* trans. Henry Reeve. New York: Alfred A. Knopf.

Trinh, S. and Hall, J. R. 2000: The violent path of Aum Shinrikyō. In J. R. Hall (ed.), *Apocalypse Observed: religious movements and violence in North America, Europe and Japan.* London and New York: Routledge, 76–110.

Troeltsch, E. 1931: *The Social Teaching of the Christian Churches,* trans. Olive Wyon, 2 vols. London: Allen & Unwin.

Turner, B. S. 1974: *Weber and Islam: a critical study.* London: Routledge & Kegan Paul.

Turner, B. S. 1991: *Religion and Social Theory.* London: Sage.

Turner, V. W. 1995: *The Ritual Process: structure and anti-structure.* New York: Aldine de Gruyter.

Verba, S. 1965: The Kennedy assassination and the nature of political commitment. In B. S. Greenberg and E. B. Parker (eds), *The Kennedy*

Assassination and the American Public: social communication in crisis. Stanford, Calif.: Stanford University Press, 348–60.

Vertovec, S. 2005: Opinion: super-diversity revealed. <www.compas.ox.ac.uk/publications/releases/Superdiversity%20article.pdf>

Voas, D. and Crockett, A. 2005: Religion in Britain: neither believing nor belonging. *Sociology*, 39 (1), 11–28.

Voas, D., Crockett, A. and Olson, D. V. A. 2002: Religious pluralism and participation: why previous research is wrong. *American Sociological Review*, 67 (2), 212–30.

Wach, J. 1944: *The Sociology of Religion*. Chicago: University of Chicago Press.

Wallis, R. (ed.) 1975: *Sectarianism: analyses of religious and non-religious sects.* London: Peter Owen.

Wallis, R. 1976: *The Road to Total Freedom: a sociological analysis of Scientology*. London: Heinemann.

Wallis, R. 1984: *The Elementary Forms of the New Religious Life*. London: Routledge & Kegan Paul.

Wallis, R. and Bruce, S. 1984: The Stark–Bainbridge theory of religion: a critical analysis and counter proposals. *Sociological Analysis*, 45 (1), 11–27.

Wallis, R. and Bruce, S. 1992: Secularization: the orthodox model. In S. Bruce (ed.), *Religion and Modernization: sociologists and historians debate the secularization thesis*. Oxford: Clarendon Press, 8–30.

Walter, T. and Davie, G. 1998: The religiosity of women in the modern West. *British Journal of Sociology*, 49 (4), 640–60.

Warner, M. 1978: *Alone of All Her Sex: the myth and cult of the Virgin Mary*. London: Quartet.

Warner, R. S. 1993: Work in progress toward a new paradigm for the sociological study of religion in the United States. *American Journal of Sociology*, 98 (5), 1044–93.

Warner, R. S. and Wittner, J. G. (eds) 1998: *Gatherings in Diaspora: religious communities and the new immigration*. Philadelphia: Temple University Press.

Warner, W. L. 1959: *The Living and the Dead: a study of the symbolic life of Americans*. Chicago and New Haven: Yale University Press.

Warner, W. L. 1962: *American Life: dream and reality*. Chicago: University of Chicago Press.

Watson, H. 1994: Women and the veil: personal responses to global process. In A. S. Ahmed and H. Donnan (eds), *Islam, Globalization and Postmodernity*. London: Routledge, 141–59.

Weber, M. 1948: Politics as a vocation. In H. H. Gerth, and C. Wright Mills, (eds and trans.), *From Max Weber: essays in sociology*. London: Routledge and Kegan Paul, 77–128.

Weber, M. 1952: *Ancient Judaism*, trans. Hans H. Gerth and Don Martindale. New York: Free Press.

Weber, M. 1965: *The Sociology of Religion*, trans. Ephraim Fischoff. London: Methuen.

Weber, M. 2001/1920–1: *The Protestant Ethic and the Spirit of Capitalism*, trans. Talcott Parsons. London and New York: Routledge.

Wessinger, C. 1997: Millennialism with and without the mayhem. In T. Robbins and S. J. Palmer (eds), *Millennium, Messiahs, and Mayhem: contemporary apocalyptic movements*. New York: Routledge, 47–59.

Whelehan, I. 1995: *Modern Feminist Thought: from the second wave to 'post-feminism'*. Edinburgh: Edinburgh University Press.

Wilcox, M. 2002: When Sheila's a lesbian: religious individualism among lesbian, gay, bisexual, and transgender Christians. *Sociology of Religion*, 63 (4), 497–513.

Willaime, J.-P. 1995: *Sociologie des Religions*. Paris: Presses Universitaires de France.

Willaime, J.-P. 2004: The cultural turn in the sociology of religion in France. *Sociology of Religion*, 65 (4), 373–89.

Williams, R. H. 2000: Introduction: Promise Keepers: a comment on religion and social movements. *Sociology of Religion*, 61 (1), 1–10.

Wilson, B. R. 1966: *Religion in Secular Society: a sociological comment*. London: Watts.

Wilson, B. R. 1970: *Religious Sects: a sociological study*. London: Weidenfeld & Nicolson.

Wilson, B. R. 1975: *The Noble Savages: the primitive origins of charisma and its contemporary survival*. Berkeley: University of California Press.

Wilson, B. R. 1976: *Contemporary Transformations of Religion*. Oxford: Clarendon Press.

Wilson, B. R. 1981: Time, generations, and sectarianism. In B. R. Wilson (ed.), *The Social Impact of New Religious Movements*. New York: Rose of Sharon Press, 217–34.

Wilson B. R. 1982: *Religion in Sociological Perspective*. Oxford: Oxford University Press.

Wilson, B. R. 1992: Reflections on a many sided controversy. In S. Bruce (ed.), *Religion and Modernization: sociologists and historians debate the secularization thesis*. Oxford: Clarendon Press, 195–210.

Wilson, B. R. 2001: Salvation, secularization, and de-moralization. In R. K. Fenn (ed.), *The Blackwell Companion to Sociology of Religion*. Oxford: Blackwell, 39–51.

Wilson, B. R. and Dobbelaere, K. 1994: *A Time to Chant: the Soka Gakkai Buddhists in Britain*. Oxford: Clarendon Press.

Wittgenstein, L. 1958: *Philosophical Investigations*, trans. G. E. M. Anscombe, 2nd edn. Oxford: Blackwell.

Woodhead, L. and Heelas, P. 2000: *Religion in Modern Times: an interpretive anthology*. Oxford: Blackwell.

Wuthnow, R. 1988: *The Restructuring of American Religion: society and faith since World War II*. Princeton, NJ: Princeton University Press.

Wuthnow, R. 1996: *Sharing the Journey: support groups and America's new quest for community*. New York: Free Press.

Wuthnow, R. 1998: *After Heaven: spirituality in America since the 1950s.* Princeton, NJ: Princeton University Press.

Wuthnow, R. 2005: *America and the Challenges of Religious Diversity.* Princeton, NJ: Princeton University Press.

Yinger, J. M. 1970: *The Scientific Study of Religion.* London: Routledge.

Yip, A. K. T. 2000: Leaving the church to keep my faith: the lived experiences of non-heterosexual Christians. In L. J. Francis and Y. J. Katz (eds), *Joining and Leaving Religion: research perspectives.* Leominster: Gracewing, 129–45.

Yip, A. K. T. 2005: Queering religious texts: an exploration of British non-heterosexual Christians' and Muslims' strategy of constructing sexuality-affirming hermeneutics. *Sociology* 39, (1), 47–65.

Yip, A. K. T. 2007: Religion and the politics of spirituality/sexuality: reflections on researching British lesbian, gay, and bisexual Christians and Muslims. *Sociology of Religion*, forthcoming.

Young, M. and Willmott, P. 1957: *Family and Kinship in East London.* London: Routledge & Kegan Paul.

Zeitlin, I. M. 1984: *Ancient Judaism: biblical criticism from Max Weber to the present.* Cambridge: Polity.

Index